In Memory of My Beloved
Mother, Yetta Rubin
and
Sister, Corrine Ruth Harris

Practice-Oriented Study Guide

Research Methods for Social Work

SIXTH EDITION

Allen Rubin
University of Texas at Austin

Earl R. Babbie
Chapman University

Prepared by

Allen Rubin

Australia • Brazil • Canada • Mexico • Singapore • Spain • United Kingdom • United States

Printed in the United States of America

1 2 3 4 5 6 7 10 09 08 07

Printer: Thomson West

ISBN-13: 978-0-495-10079-9
ISBN-10: 0-495-10079-X

Cover Credit: Andy Bishop/Alamy

Thomson Higher Education
10 Davis Drive
Belmont, CA 94002-3098
USA

For more information about our products, contact us at:
Thomson Learning Academic Resource Center
1-800-423-0563

For permission to use material from this text or product, submit a request online at **http://www.thomsonrights.com.**
Any additional questions about permissions can be submitted by email to **thomsonrights@thomson.com.**

Contents

PREFACE

This *Study Guide* is designed for use in conjunction with the sixth edition of *Research Methods for Social Work,* by Allen Rubin and Earl Babbie. Its purpose is to enhance your comprehension of the material in the text, with a major focus on applying that material to problems that you may be likely to encounter in your social work practice.

Each chapter corresponds to the chapter of the same number in the Rubin and Babbie text, and will begin with the major objectives of that chapter from the standpoint of the main points that a practitioner should know in applying the material to practice. You may want to examine the objectives before reading the chapter, not only to prepare you to better understand the chapter, but also to see its relevance to practice. Knowing in advance how research methods material can be applied to practice may make the material more relevant and interesting to you, and therefore easier to learn. The same could be said for the chapter summary that follows the objectives. The summary will also focus on practice applications. In addition to reading the summary before you read the chapter of the text, you may want to reread it afterward, to improve your grasp of the material.

After you have read the chapter and reread the summary and feel you have a reasonable grasp of the content, you will be ready to answer the review questions that follow the summary. These questions test your knowledge of the material and ability to apply it to social work practice. After you write down your answers to the review questions, you may check their accuracy by examining the correct answers in the Answers to Review Questions at the end of this *Study Guide*. You may want to reexamine the Rubin and Babbie text to improve your understanding of the material relevant to those questions you answered incorrectly. Going through this process may improve your performance on exams, and perhaps your performance as a practitioner as well.

After completing the review questions, you will encounter several brief exercises that give you an opportunity to practice applying the text material for that chapter. In preparing to work on each exercise, it may be helpful to reread the portion of the text chapter that pertains to the concepts you need to understand in order to complete the exercise. You may want to ask your instructor for guidance on which exercises to do and which will be discussed in class.

After the exercises you will find several discussion questions. These discussion questions may not have a specific "correct" answer, but by writing out your answers, in your own words, you may be better prepared for class discussions of these issues and may better understand these issues, particularly in regard to social work practice applications.

Finally, at the end of each chapter you will find a crossword puzzle. The crossword puzzle will contain important terms from the corresponding chapter in the text. It will also contain many other words that are not connected to the text material. As you answer the latter words, the letters that get filled in the puzzle will help you figure out the correct terms from the text. The clues for the terms from the text are in capital letters. The answers to each crossword puzzle can be found in the Answers to Crossword Puzzles section at the end of the book. I hope that working on the crossword puzzles will be a fun way to cement your memorization and understanding of key research concepts.

In addition to the questions and exercises in this *Study Guide*, you also may benefit from working on the review questions and exercises that appear at the end of each chapter of the main text. Included there you will find some Web Site Exercises designed to give you experience in finding and using resources on the internet.

Good luck with your research course. I hope you enjoy it and find it highly relevant to social work practice. If you have any comments on the helpfulness of this *Study Guide*, or suggestions for improving it, I would be delighted to hear from you.

CHAPTER 1

Why Study Research?

OBJECTIVES

1. Identify three reasons why it is important for social work practitioners to understand research methodology and utilize research in their practice.

2. Explain why it can be said that social work research seeks to accomplish the same humanistic goals as social work practice.

3. Discuss why social work research can be called a compassionate, problem solving endeavor.

4. Identify examples of how agreement reality and experiential reality can agree or disagree in a social work agency.

5. Provide an example of how a social worker may encounter tradition as a basis for practice knowledge, and discuss the advantages and disadvantages of relying on tradition as a guide to practice.

6. Provide an example of how a social worker may encounter authority as a basis for practice knowledge, and consider the advantages and disadvantages of relying on authority as a guide to practice.

7. Describe the findings of reviews of social work effectiveness.

8. Explain why it is important to be able to critique research quality.

9. Describe the features of the scientific method and how to apply them in social work practice.

10. Provide examples of how the following errors in personal inquiry can occur in social work practice: inaccurate observation, overgeneralization, selective observation, ex post facto hypothesizing, illogical reasoning, ego involvement in understanding, and premature closure of inquiry.

11. Explain why it is important to test social work "practice wisdom" that is generally accepted but not previously tested.

PRACTICE-RELEVANT SUMMARY

Social work practitioners, like everyone else, must deal with two realities in their pursuit of truth. One is agreement reality. When you start working in a social work agency, you will find that many or all of the agency staff agree that certain things are true. Often they are correct in their shared beliefs; sometimes they are wrong. The other reality is experiential reality, which pertains to things you will learn as a result of your direct experience. It is possible that your experiential reality as a practitioner may lead you to question the agreement reality you encounter, or that the agreement reality shared by others may lead you to question the reality you have experienced.

For example, if you read research about how effective (or ineffective) certain social work interventions are with certain types of social work clients, you may find evidence that a particular intervention favored by the staff in your agency is not the most effective way to provide services. Perhaps an alternative intervention has been found to be more effective. Thus, you may begin to question the agency's agreement reality about how best to provide services. Likewise, if your own observations suggest that your clients do not seem to be benefiting from the agency's favored intervention approach, these observations (your experiential reality) may lead you to question the agency's agreement reality about how best to provide services. If you express your emerging skepticism to your agency colleagues, however, they may be so insistent that their agreement reality is correct, and that you just don't get it -- or that you just need more time to see the light -- that your confidence in your own observations (your experiential reality) may be eroded.

If you take a scientific approach to your social work practice, your pursuit of truth will not be limited to only one reality. Instead, you will want two criteria to be met. What you do as a practitioner should be guided by both logic and experience. The experience you rely on may be your own or it may be reported by others in the professional literature. The main point here is that you will have an open mind and not just rely solely on what others tell you is true or what your own experiences lead you to believe as a sufficient guide to your practice.

Early in your practice, you will understandably rely heavily on two important sources of knowledge to guide your practice: tradition and authority. Relying on tradition involves conforming to an agency's traditionally preferred ways of doing things. Relying on authority means considering the reputed expertise of the source of the information in deciding whether to be guided by that information. Tradition and authority are double-edged swords in the search for practice knowledge. They provide inexperienced practitioners with a starting point, but they are sometimes wrong. Relying on them too heavily can impede your openness to finding flaws in the transmitted practice wisdom and, consequently, to finding better ways to practice. The need to go beyond tradition and authority (and agreement reality) in guiding your practice is supported by our profession's research literature on the effectiveness of social work practice. Studies have questioned the effectiveness of various social work interventions that have come into vogue at different points in our profession's history, including today. These studies have shown that we cannot assume that whatever a well-trained social worker does will be effective. Some things are effective; some aren't. Some things work only with certain types of clients, problems or settings. Alternative interventions may work better with different types of clients, problems or settings.

To date social work practice still contains interventions and procedures that have not yet received adequate testing. Not all studies that test our interventions and procedures, however, are of equal quality. Some are excellent; some are weak. Practitioners need to understand the fundamentals of research methodology so they can discriminate between strong studies that can and should guide their practice from weak studies whose findings are suspect. An understanding of research methodology can also help practitioners collaborate with researchers and foster an agency environment conducive to carrying out good research on how best to help agency clients. This understanding is further useful when confronting studies that attack the social work profession and social welfare enterprise. Social workers are responsible to the people they serve (including the public) to have enough knowledge of research fundamentals to be able to accurately critique such studies and make people aware of any serious flaws in them. In short, the main reason that social work practitioners should understand and utilize research is compassion for their clients. It is because we care about helping clients that we seek scientific evidence about how best to do so. It is because we care about helping clients that we need to understand research methods well enough to be guided by strong studies and not to be guided by studies that are so limited scientifically that they may recommend things that are not in the best interests of our clients.

When we do not take a scientific approach to practice, we become more vulnerable to committing common errors in casual, personal inquiry. These errors include inaccurate observation, overgeneralization, selective observation, ex post facto hypothesizing, illogical reasoning, ego involvement in understanding, and premature closure of inquiry. Inaccurate observation occurs when we are too casual in our observations, not making deliberate attempts to reduce errors. Overgeneralization occurs when our generalizations are based on an insufficient number of observations. Selective observation occurs when we look for things that match our predilections and ignore things that don't match them. Ex post facto hypothesizing occurs when we go fishing for reasons to explain away discrepancies between observations and beliefs. We also may use illogical reasoning to explain away inconsistencies between observations and beliefs, such as when we say that the exception proves the rule. Ego involvement can lead to error when we resist accepting observations that make us look less desirable. The premature closure of inquiry occurs when we rule out certain lines of inquiry that might produce findings that we would find undesirable. We can guard against making the above errors by taking a scientific approach to social work practice.

REVIEW QUESTIONS

1. Social work practitioners make decisions based on:

   a. Tradition
   b. Authority
   c. Agreement reality
   d. Their experience
   e. All of the above

2. A social work practitioner disregards the findings of research studies indicating that Intervention A is ineffective with her agency's clientele and that Intervention B is more effective. Instead, she uses Intervention A because her supervisor recommends it and all the other practitioners in the agency have been using it for years. This is an example of:

   a. Tradition
   b. Authority
   c. Experiential reality
   d. The scientific method
   e. All of the above
   f. Only a and b

3. A social worker attends a workshop on culturally competent practice, where he is told that frail elderly Asian Americans are more likely to be well cared for by their extended families than are their white counterparts. Therefore, when he is shortly thereafter assigned to provide services to a frail elderly Korean woman, he assumes that her extended family is caring for her adequately. This is an example of:

   a. Evidence-based practice
   b. Relying on authority
   c. Overgeneralization
   d. All of the above
   e. Only b and c

4. The above social worker later learns that the client was not cared for adequately by her extended family, and therefore concludes that what he was told at the workshop was wrong. This is an example of:

   a. Evidence-based practice
   b. Logical reasoning
   c. Overgeneralization
   d. Only a and b

5. A social work practitioner has attended several costly continuing education workshops that have given her advanced expertise and a great reputation in delivering a new intervention. Five equally rigorous studies that evaluate the effectiveness of the intervention are published. Four conclude it is worthless; one concludes it is effective. The social worker dismisses the four studies indicating the intervention is worthless as poor research without even reading them carefully and concludes that the study supporting the intervention is the only decent study. This is an example of:

   a. Evidence-based practice
   b. Selective observation
   c. Ego involvement
   d. Overgeneralization
   e. Both b and c are correct

6. Social work research seeks to:

   a. Produce knowledge for knowledge's sake
   b. Test psychological and sociological theories
   c. Provide practical knowledge to solve problems social workers confront in their practice
   d. All of the above

7. Reviews of experimental research on social work practice effectiveness have found that:

   a. Social work practice is sometimes ineffective
   b. It is safe to assume that interventions that are effective will be equally effective with all types of clients
   c. Social workers who are well trained in practice skills will be effective
   d. All of the above
   e. Only b and c are true

8. Understanding the fundamentals of research methodology helps practitioners to:

   a. Discriminate scientifically strong studies that should guide practice from scientifically weak studies with suspect findings.
   b. Foster an agency environment that supports the carrying out of scientifically strong studies that are useful to practitioners.
   c. Point out the flaws in weak studies that attack the social work profession or the social welfare enterprise.
   d. Evaluate and improve the quality of the data they routinely collect as part of their daily practice.
   e. All of the above.

9. The social workers in a child guidance center decide that the best way to measure whether their services are effectively reducing depression in children is by administering the Children's Depression Inventory to their clients before and after treatment. They do so, but then find that the inventory is indicating no reduction in depression. Rather than wonder about whether their services are really effective, they conclude that the Children's Depression Inventory is not a good instrument for measuring reductions in depression among children. This is an example of:

   a. Ex post facto hypothesizing
   b. Selective observation
   c. Evidence-based practice
   d. Overgeneralization

10. It is the policy of a child guidance center to provide non-directive play therapy to all of its younger clients, regardless of diagnosis. One of its staff members, a social worker, questions whether a cognitive-behavioral intervention approach might be more effective with conduct disordered children and therefore proposes to review the research literature to see if the scientific evidence supports her notion. Her supervisor, however, nixes her proposal because: 1) Every well trained, clinically sophisticated child therapist knows that play therapy is the treatment of choice; and 2) The center has won national acclaim for its reputation for providing expert play therapy services. This is an example of:

    a. Premature closure of inquiry
    b. Ego involvement
    c. Good, savvy supervision
    d. Scientific supervision
    e. a and b only are correct
    f. c and d only are correct

11. Your esteemed practice mentor, who has been selected by NASW as social worker of the year and who is president of a clinical social work society, tells you that based on her 25 years of experience and practice wisdom a particular intervention is best for your client. If you take a scientific approach to social work practice you should consider her wisdom on this matter:

    a. Provisional
    b. Subject to refutation
    c. In need of supportive evidence based on comprehensive, systematic, objective observations
    d. All of the above
    e. None of the abov

12. An esteemed researcher, who has been selected by NASW as social work researcher of the year and who is president of a social work research society, completes a scientifically strong study indicating that a particular intervention is the most effective for clients like yours. If you take a scientific approach to social work practice you should consider her study's conclusions on this matter:

    a. Provisional
    b. Subject to refutation
    c. In need of replication
    d. All of the above
    e. None of the above

EXERCISE 1.1

Interview a social work practitioner or a social work student who has been doing their field placement for while. Ask them about the services, interventions or practice techniques that they most strongly believe in. Ask them how they came to develop this strong belief. What do they base it on? Research? Observations? Other? If observations, were the observations conducted in an objective and systematic manner? Explore how open they are to question and refutation about this belief. What would it take, if anything, to change their mind? Take notes on their comments, and discuss your notes in class. Discuss in class the degree to which interviewees seem to be guided by the scientific method in their stance about their beliefs.

EXERCISE 1.2

In social work practice we continually must make quick decisions based on limited information. Consequently, we must learn to accept the fact that we occasionally will make errors, or at least think of better ways of handling a situation after it is too late. Sometimes we make the right decision for the wrong reasons; sometimes we make wrong decisions that nonetheless seemed logical and justifiable at the time. Recall a decision you have made or observed in your practice experience (or field practicum) that was flawed because it was based exclusively on tradition or authority or because it reflected one of the following errors of human inquiry: inaccurate observation, overgeneralization, selective observation, or ego involvement in understanding. (If you have had insufficient social work experience to come up with an example from your own practice, recall a flawed decision from your other life experiences.)

1. Describe the decision.
2. Explain how it reflected one of the problems listed above and described in Chapter 1.
3. Discuss how a scientific approach may have improved the decision.

EXERCISE 1.3

Conduct a brief interview with several social work practitioners. Ask them about whether or how often they examine research studies to guide them in decisions about which interventions to employ or which services to provide. If they rarely or never utilize such studies, ask them to explain their reasons. If they do utilize such studies to guide their practice, ask them to comment on their experiences in utilizing the research, the benefits of doing so, and any problems they've encountered. Take notes on their answers, and bring your notes to discuss in class.

DISCUSSION QUESTIONS

1. Suppose you are a child therapist in a child guidance center, where you provide play therapy. You learn of one play therapy approach that is nondirective and another that is directive. Discuss how you would utilize tradition and authority in deciding which approach to use. Discuss the problems in relying exclusively on tradition and authority as your guide.

2. Suppose you have invested a great deal of time and money to attend workshops to obtain special, advanced expertise in a promising new intervention approach that none of your colleagues is trained to provide. Suppose you decide to learn for yourself, through your experiential reality in providing the intervention, whether it seems to be more effective than alternative approaches in helping clients. Discuss the errors in personal inquiry to which you would be vulnerable. Discuss some ways that a scientific inquiry about the effectiveness of the intervention would help safeguard against those errors.

CROSSWORD PUZZLE

ACROSS

2 ______ Omega Sorority
5 Large vehicle
9 Undergraduate degree
11 YOU CAN KNOW THINGS THROUGH DIRECT ______
14 Simon ______
15 Either ______
16 Farm animal
17 Waiter's reward
18 ______ as a pin
19 Uncomfortable bed
20 Alone
21 University email address ending
22 Name for 16 across
24 What's the ______?
25 Command to Fido
26 A RISKY SOURCE OF KNOWING
30 ______ a girl!
32 Pair
33 Sixth sense
35 Abbreviation for an American minority group
37 Undergraduate subject concentration
39 Give it a ______
40 OBSERVATION IS NOT SCIENTIFIC

DOWN

1 UNSCIENTIFIC TYPE OF HYPOTHESIZING
2 Quotes
3 Swiss Alps girl in a children's story
4 Data entered into a computer
5 IN SCIENCE, ALL KNOWLEDGE IS CONSIDERED ______
6 Born in the ______
7 ______ me if you can
8 Bluegrass state abbreviated
9 Something to study for an exam
10 Superficially artistic
12 Mounds
13 Freudian term for self, or type of trip
19 Tales from the ______
20 Spades or clubs
22 Part of a marina
23 Periods to settle ties (abbreviated)
27 School in Madison (abbreviated)
28 ______ Thumb
29 SCIENTISTS ATTEMPT TO BE IN THE SEARCH FOR EVIDENCE
31 Kubrick's demon computer in "2001"
34 EX-POST FACTO ______
35 German denial
36 Phone company acronym
38 Each

ACROSS

44 A class that may make you sweat
46 Use this when calculating circumferences
47 Evergreen tree
48 ONE REASON TO USE RESEARCH
49 Ice cream ______
50 I think, therefore I ______
51 Cute Spielberg alien
52 Day's opposite
54 Not in
55 Buy
57 Amino ______
59 ______ boy!
60 Old fashioned music store purchase
61 SOCIAL WORKERS NEED TO USE ________ AND BE VIGILANT IN LOOKING FOR FLAWED REASONING
64 SCIENTIFIC PRACTITIONERS SEARCH FOR ______
67 Slang for like
68 Relatives
70 ______ Kneivel
71 Freudian term
72 RESEARCHERS WILL SOMETIMES ______ PREVIOUS STUDIES
73 Recedes
75 Proposed feminist legislation that was not enacted (abbreviated)
76 From ______ (the gamut)
77 Co-author of a research text
81 Mr. ______ (talking horse)
82 AN IMPORTANT PART OF THE SCIENTIFIC METHOD
89 Toiled very hard
93 Birthstone
95 Stopped living
96 Holiday drink
97 Diet food
98 ALL KNOWLEDGE IS SUBJECT TO ______
100 Assess or appraise
101 Chess pieces
102 Shade provider

DOWN

40 See ______ run!
41 Letter before gee
42 ANOTHER RISKY SOURCE OF KNOWLEDGE
43 ______ tu, Brute?
45 Hawaiian necklace
49 Eros
53 Ad ______ committee
54 Golden ______
55 Result of ankle sprain
56 I'm ______ my wit's end
58 Deep sea ______
62 Alias
63 Dieter's beer
65 Society teen
66 Where Napoleon was exiled
69 Revenge of the ______
74 Stigma
77 Opponent
78 ______ and board
79 Name tag info (abbreviated)
80 Bag of bread
83 Sad
84 Dutch cheese
85 ______ of passage
86 Blood tube
87 Much ______ about nothing
88 Seep
89 Direction from Minneapolis to Chicago
90 Wash
91 Pie ______ mode
92 Repeat of 21 across
93 Miner's find
94 Repeat of 44 across
99 Christian bible (abbreviated)

CHAPTER 2

Evidence- Based Practice

OBJECTIVES

1. Define and describe the nature of evidence-based practice.
2. Contrast evidence-based practice with practice based on authority or tradition.
3. Identify the historical underpinnings of evidence-based practice.
4. Identify the steps involved in being an evidence-based practitioner.
5. Formulate an evidence-based practice question.
6. Identify two kinds of evidence-based practice questions.
7. Describe the steps taken in a thorough search for evidence.
8. Contrast top-down and bottom-up searches of evidence and the advantages and disadvantages of each.
9. Discuss why the evaluation phase is important as the last phase of the evidence-based practice process.
10. Discuss five controversies in evidence-based practice.

PRACTICE-RELEVANT SUMMARY

A new model of social work practice based primarily on the scientific method is called *evidence-based practice*. With precedents as old as the profession itself, evidence-based practice is a process in which practitioners make practice decisions in light of the best research evidence available. Rather than rigidly constrict practitioner options, the model encourages practitioners to integrate scientific evidence with their practice expertise and knowledge of the idiosyncratic circumstances bearing on specific practice decisions. It also involves evaluating the outcomes of their decisions. Although evidence-based practice is most commonly discussed in regard to decisions about what interventions to provide clients, it also applies to decisions about how best to assess the practice problems and decisions practitioners make at other levels of practice – such as decisions about social policies, communities, and so on.

Unlike forms of practice based on authority, evidence-based practice involves critical thinking, questioning, recognizing unfounded beliefs and assumptions, thinking independently as to the logic and evidence supporting what others may convey as practice wisdom, and using the best scientific evidence available in deciding how to intervene with individuals, families, groups, or communities. Evidence-based practitioners need to track down evidence as an ongoing part of their practice. They need to know how to find relevant studies and to understand research designs and methods so that they can critically appraise the validity of the studies they find. They need to base the actions they take on the best evidence they find and to use research methods to evaluate whether the evidence-based actions they take result in the outcomes they seek to achieve.

When you engage in evidence-based practice the evidence you find sometimes will be difficult to apply. Sometimes it will be inconclusive. Sometimes it will indicate what actions *not* to take. Sometimes it will imply an intervention the client does not want. Being supported by the best evidence does not mean that an intervention will be effective with your client.

The first step in the evidence-based practice process involves formulating a question to answer a specific practice decision. The question might be open-ended, asking about the gamut of interventions that have been studies. Or it might be narrower, asking about one or two interventions specified in advance.

The second step involves searching for the evidence. Busy practitioners will probably want to conduct online searches. Two major search strategies involve a bottom-up versus a top-down approach. Using the bottom-up strategy, you would search the literature looking for any and all sources that provide evidence pertaining to the practice question you formulated. You would then read and critically appraise the quality of the evidence in each source, judge whether it is applicable to your unique practice decision, and ultimately choose a course of action based on what you deem to be the best applicable evidence available. Using the top-down strategy, instead of starting from scratch to find and appraise all the relevant studies yourself, you will rely on the results of evidence-based searches that others have done. Although the top-down approach will be less time-consuming for very busy practitioners, its disadvantage is that the experts who conducted the reviews are fallible and sometimes even biased. Two good sources for finding reviews using the top-down approach are at the websites of the Cochrane Collaboration and the Campbell Collaboration.

The third step in the evidence-based practice process involves critically appraising the quality of the evidence found. Two of the main questions commonly asked in appraising the quality of the evidence reported in practice effectiveness studies are: (1) Was treatment outcome measured in a reliable, valid, and unbiased manner? (2) Was the research design strong enough to indicate conclusively whether the intervention or something else most plausibly explains the variations in client outcome? Different evidence-based practice hierarchies have been developed that can help guide appraisals of evidence. At the top of those evidentiary hierarchies are sources reporting or reviewing studies with the strongest designs in regard to the above two questions about the quality of evidence.

The fourth step in the evidence-based practice process involves determining which evidence-based intervention is most appropriate for your particular client(s). Interventions supported by the best evidence are not necessarily effective with every client or situation. Strong studies providing valid evidence that an intervention is effective typically find that the intervention is *more likely* to be effective than some alternative, not that it is effective with every case. The intervention supported by the strongest studies might involve procedures that conflict with the values of certain cultures or individual clients. You might have to use your clinical expertise, your knowledge of the client, client feedback, and your cultural competence in making a judgment call.

The fifth step in the evidence-based practice process involves applying the chosen intervention. You might first have to obtain training in it. You might also have to arrange for supervision. If you are unable to obtain sufficient training or supervision, you should try to refer the client to other practitioners who have the requisite training and experience in the intervention.

The sixth step in the evidence-based practice process involves evaluating whether the chosen intervention appears to be effective for your particular client or practice situation. This step is important because supporting the effectiveness of interventions typically do not find that the tested interventions are guaranteed to work with every client or situation.

Various objections have been expressed about evidence-based practice. The objections often involve misconceptions about evidence-based practice. Perhaps the most valid and important concern expressed involves real-world obstacles to implementing evidence-based practice in everyday practice settings. These obstacles involve lack of agency support, not enough time, lack of access to Internet databases, and insufficient resources to obtain training and supervision.

REVIEW QUESTIONS

1. Evidence-based practitioners will:

   a. **NOT** question the practice wisdom of supervisors and experts
   b. Scientifically evaluate their own practice effectiveness
   c. Assume that if practice evaluations are valid, they will hear about them
   d. Read only studies about what works, not about what doesn't work

2. Evidence-based practitioners will make practice decisions based on:

   a. Their practice expertise
   b. Client characteristics
   c. Client values
   d. The best available evidence
   e. All of the above

3. Critical thinking means:

   a. Being too negative
   b. Relying on practice wisdom
   c. Recognizing unfounded beliefs and assumptions
   d. Having a crisis mentality

4. The best scientific evidence might:

   a. Be inconclusive
   b. Hard to find
   c. Indicate what *not* to do
   d. All of the above

5. An evidence-based practice question:

   a. Never should specify an intervention in advance
   b. Always should specify an intervention in advance
   c. Never should be altered during the search for evidence
   d. None of the above

6. Which of the following statements is true about searching for evidence?

   a. It is always safe to rely exclusively on the reviews of experts.
   b. The prime advantage of the top-down approach is its feasibility.
   c. The prime advantage of the bottom-up approach is its feasibility.
   d. The top-down and bottom-up approaches are mutually exclusive.

7. A useful Internet site for an online search for evidence is:

   a. The Cochrane Collaboration
   b. The Campbell Collaboration
   c. Google Scholar
   d. All of the above

8. Studies supplying the best evidence about practice effectiveness will:

   a. Measure outcome in an unbiased manner
   b. Not bother with ruling out plausible alternative explanations
   c. Rely heavily on anecdotal case reports
   d. All of the above

9. Interventions supported by the strongest studies with the best evidence:

   a. Will **NOT** involve procedures that conflict with client values
   b. Will **NOT** involve procedures that conflict with certain cultures
   c. Will typically find that the intervention is more *likely* to be effective than some alternative,
   d. **NOT** that it is effective with every case
   e. a and b above, only are true

10. Which of the following statements is/are true about applying the intervention supported by the best research evidence?

    a. Because it is the most effective, you should apply it even if you have not been trained in it.
    b. Because it is the most effective, you should apply it even if you are unable to obtain supervision in it.
    c. Formulate, in collaboration with the client, treatment goals that can be measured in evaluating whether the selected intervention really helps the client
    d. All of the above

11. Evidence-based practice:

    a. Is perceived by some as **NOT** allowing practitioners needed flexibility in responding to unique client attributes and circumstances
    b. Is perceived by some as denigrating professional expertise
    c. Is perceived by some as being merely a cost-cutting tool
    d. All of the above
    e. None of the above

EXERCISE 2.1

Interview two social work practitioners and ask them about their views about evidence-based practice. Make sure you cover the following questions:

1. Have they heard of it?
2. How do they define it?
3. How do they view the controversies and misconceptions about it discussed in this chapter?
4. Do they engage in it? If yes, how often? If not or rarely, why not more often?

Take notes on their comments, and discuss your notes in class.

EXERCISE 2.2

Find two more social work practitioners who engage in evidence-based practice at least on some occasions or who wish they could. This time, focus your interview on the real world obstacles they face in implementing evidence-based practice in their everyday practice. How do they intend, or how have they attempted, to cope with those obstacles? Take notes on their comments, and discuss your notes in class.

EXERCISE 2.3

Your client, Sal, is a 16-year-old male whose family moved from Puerto Rico to New York City three years ago. He has recently gotten into trouble for truancy, vandalism, underage drinking, and beating up other boys at school. He has been diagnosed with a conduct disorder. Formulate an evidence-based practice question to guide your selection of an intervention for Sal. Conduct a bottom-up search for the intervention with the best evidence. Write a brief summary of several of the interventions you find and the type of research designs that supported them. Compare your summary with the summaries of your classmates.

EXERCISE 2.4

Select two of the interventions you found in Exercise 2.3. Formulate an evidence-based practice question that specifies those two interventions in advance. Conduct a top-down search to see which of the two interventions is supported by the best evidence. Write a brief summary of what you find. Compare your summary with the summaries of your classmates.

DISCUSSION QUESTIONS

1. Suppose your search finds an intervention whose effectiveness is supported by the best evidence for clients with problems like your client's problems, but you find no studies that involved clients whose ethnicity matches your client's ethnicity. Discuss how you would nevertheless continue to apply the evidence-based practice process to your client.

2. The evidence-based practice process includes the use of professional expertise, instead of necessarily implementing in a mechanical, cookbook fashion the intervention with the best evidence. Re-examining some of the flaws in unscientific sources of social work practice knowledge discussed in Chapter 1 (such as selective observation and ego involvement in understanding) discuss how some of those flaws can distort the evidence-based practice process.

CROSSWORD PUZZLE

1	2	3	4	■	5	6	7		8	9	10	11
12				■	13			■	14			
15			■	16				17			■	
18			19		■	20			■	21	22	
23					24	■		■	25			
	■	26				■	27					
■	28	■	■	29		30		■	31			■
32		33	34		■	35		36		■	37	38
39					■	40				41		
42				■	■	43						
44		■	45	46	47	■	48				■	■
	■	■	49					■	50		51	52
53	54	55			■	■	56	57		■	58	
59				■	60	61	■	62		63		
64		■	65						■	66		

ACROSS

1 EVIDENCE-BASED PRACTICE IS A PROCESS IN WHICH PRACTITIONERS MAKE PRACTICE DECISIONS IN LIGHT OF THE _____ RESEARCH EVIDENCE AVAILABLE
5 WITH 7 DOWN: A SOURCE OF REVIEWS OF RESEARCH ON THE EFFECTS OF HEALTH CARE INTERVENTIONS
12 Butter substitute
13 Yoko _____
14 River in France and Belgium
15 New Deal power production project (abbreviated)
16 First names of 2006 French Open winner, a lead character in a French romantic comedy, and others
18 Four rubber road trip necessities
20 Monogram of *Treasure Island* author
21 Vehicle for 64 Across
23 A grouch and an award
25 Love in Spain
27 Slang for 12 Down
29 Art _____ (style of Chrysler Building spire)
31 He beat AES twice in the 1950s
32 Entrance halls with skylights
35 ___ Major or Minor
37 State for lovers (abbreviated)
39 Achy anagram for Spain
40 Marks something with different colored spots or patches
42 Two cups
43 Oglers
44 TLC provider
45 Forerunner of EBP
48 Nickname of early morning radio and MSNBC talk show host
49 John, Paul, George, and ______
50 Who's hand did 50 Across want to hold?
53 Cake topper or hockey penalty
56 Angelina Pitt ____ Jolie
58 Continent below NA and CA
59 WITH 35 DOWN: USEFUL PLACE TO SEARCH FOR EVIDENCE
60 Chevy maker
62 Freudian interest
64 Occupant of 22 Across
65 REPLICATED TYPES OF EXPERIMENTS: RANDOMIZED CLINICAL ________
66 No ____, ands or buts

DOWN

1 ______- UP SEARCH FOR EVIDENCE
2 He left the building wearing blue suede shoes
3 VERB IN STEP 2 OF THE EVIDENCE-BASED PRACTICE PROCESS
4 Preposition that is a homophone for a number
5 Follower of a dot in many Website addresses
6 Unique person
7 SEE 5 ACROSS
8 White alternative
9 Taken as a given
10 Region containing ME, MA, RI, and VT
11 Wild throws, fumbles or typos
16 _______ a beet
17 Clinton said it depends on how this word is defined
19 ___ de cologne
22 Bob wanted Jacob to stay ____ young
24 Direction from Cleveland to Pittsburgh
25 On a wing ___________
28 Stigma
30 Cows chew these
32 CRITICALLY _____ THE RELEVANT STUDIES YOU FIND
33 ___ Tin Tin
34 SEE 59 ACROSS
36 Unwanted mass email
38 Fool
41 Jay of late night
46 ___ man on campus
47 Alphabetical sequence
51 Its academy is in Colorado Springs (abbreviated)
52 They beat the Titans in the Super Bowl
54 op. ____.
55 Not him or her
57 Burns and Sullivan
60 WWII soldier
61 Pa's soul mate**63**And on his farm he had a pig,

CHAPTER 3

Philosophy and Theory in Science and Research

OBJECTIVES

1. Contrast the terms: ideology, paradigm and theory.

2. Provide examples to illustrate how paradigms and theory can influence social work research and practice.

3. Distinguish contemporary positivism from the original form of positivism.

4. Distinguish contemporary positivism from postmodernism.

5. Compare and contrast contemporary positivism, interpretivism, and critical social science.

6. Distinguish ideographic and nomothetic models of understanding human behavior, and give an example of how researchers using each model would attempt to develop social work practice knowledge.

7. Provide examples to illustrate how four different social work practice models could influence the way a social work research question is posed or studied.

8. Illustrate how inductive and deductive logic are used in scientifically oriented social work practice.

9. Give an example of a hypothesis relevant to social work practice, identify its independent and dependent variables, and list the attributes of those variables.

10. Contrast and distinguish qualitative methods of social work inquiry from quantitative methods, and provide an example of how each can provide useful information in answering a practice problem that social workers may encounter.

PRACTICE-RELEVANT SUMMARY

Not all social work practitioners and researchers share the same philosophical assumptions or value the scientific method. Some, for example, are *ideologues*, who prefer ideology to science. An *ideology* is a closed system of beliefs and values that shapes the way those who believe in it understand the world and behave. Its assumptions are fixed and strong, not open to questioning. Ideologues "know' they are right and don't want to be confused with facts.

Other social workers might question certain aspects of the scientific method. Some even doubt whether an objective external reality exists, arguing instead that there are only multiple subjective realities. The different philosophical stances one can take about the nature of reality and how to observe it are called paradigms. *Paradigms* are fundamental models or schemes that organize our view of the world. Some extreme forms of the postmodernist or social constructivist paradigms deny the existence of an objective external reality and say it is unknowable. In contrast, researchers guided by contemporary *positivist paradigms* emphasize objectivity, precision, and generalizability in their inquiries. Researchers guided by the *interpretivist paradigm* are less concerned with precision and generalizability and more interested in probing deeper into the subjective meanings of human experience. *Critical social science paradigm* researchers use a variety of methods employed by researchers following other paradigms, but they are distinguished by their rejection of scientific neutrality and objectivity and their mission to interpret findings through the filter of their empowerment and advocacy aims.

A theory is a systematic set of interrelated statements intended to explain some aspect of social life or enrich our sense of how people conduct and find meaning in their daily lives. Social work practice and research may be closely linked to theory. Linking research to theory does not necessarily mean that social workers conducting research should be emphasizing the building or testing of social scientific theories. It just means that theory can be used in some way to enhance the research. Nevertheless, some researchers can carry out useful studies without having a particular theory in mind. Many studies evaluating the effectiveness of a service or intervention, for example, are carried out without aiming to test or build a particular theory, and their findings can have significant value in building our profession's knowledge base about how best to help people.

Linkage to theory can come in two forms: inductive and deductive. Using the *deductive model,* we move from the general to the particular. We start with a general theory as our guide, next develop hypotheses based on the theory, and then make observations of operationalized indicators to test that hypothesis. Using the *inductive model,* we move from the particular to the general. We begin with a set of observations, look for patterns in those observations, and attempt to generate hypotheses and theory based on the patterns we observe.

In actual practice, deduction and induction alternate. We may inductively generate hypotheses and then deductively test them, or we may deductively test hypotheses and then inductively seek to better understand our results by conducting a new set of observations.

The basic building blocks of theories are called *concepts.* Concepts are abstract elements representing classes of phenomena. To research a specific concept, we must select its operationalized indicators—that is, we must specify how the concept will be observed. The operationalized indicators of concepts are called *variables.* In constructing theories, we look for relationships among concepts, and in research we look for relationships among variables. When we specify expected relationships among variables, we are formulating *hypotheses*. These hypotheses can be tested to see if they are supported empirically. If they are empirically supported, then the theory is supported. But a disorganized pile of concepts, observations, and relationships do not make up a theory. The theory's components must be connected to each other logically and must coalesce to help explain related phenomena.

Variables that cause or explain something are called *independent variables,* and variables that are explained by or are the effects of the independent variable are called *dependent variables*. Variables are logical groupings of attributes. *Attributes* are characteristics. Gender, for example, is a variable composed of the attributes male and female.

Social work practice and research are guided by *practice models*. Practice models help us to organize our views about social work practice and may synthesize existing theories. The list of practice models is diverse, and the models tend not to be mutually exclusive. Some models expand over time, and the distinctions between the models can become increasingly blurred. The way research questions are posed or studied will be influenced by the practice model guiding the investigator.

There are two models for attempting to study and understand the causes of human behavior. The *idiographic model* aims at explanation by seeking to understand everything about a particular case, using as many causative factors as possible. The *nomothetic model* tries to generalize to populations in probabilistic terms about the most important causative factors for a general phenomenon studied across a large number of cases.

Differences in philosophical assumptions can lead to differences over preferred research methods. Two overarching types of research methods are quantitative methods and qualitative methods. *Quantitative methods* emphasize the need to be precise, to verify hypotheses, to determine causality, and to come up with findings that can be analyzed statistically and generalized. *Qualitative methods* are less likely to involve numbers and are less concerned with precision, generalization, or testing out what really causes what. Instead, qualitative methods try to tap deeper, subjective meanings and generate tentative new insights or new hypotheses. Although some have argued about these two research approaches in ways that imply they are in competition with one another and are inherently incompatible, many others view them as playing an equally important and complementary role in building social work knowledge. Some of the best research studies have combined qualitative and quantitative methods.

Regardless of which research approach is used, researchers would like to believe that their findings are true and are not just a reflection of their own subjective biases. However, objectivity is not easy to achieve. Some would argue that no research is free of biases. Researchers want their findings to be important, and this desire can predispose them toward unintentionally interpreting their findings in distorted ways. When you conduct or read research studies, one of your chief concerns should be whether the way the research is conducted provides safeguards to prevent the researcher's biases from influencing the nature of the data gathered and how they are interpreted. Much of this book is about how you can provide those safeguards or determine whether others have done so.

REVIEW QUESTIONS

1. A paradigm is a:

   a. Frame of reference for interpreting the world
   b. Theory
   c. Law
   d. Concept

2. If we postulate that witnessing parental violence increases the likelihood of behavioral problems in children, then:

   a. Whether a child witnesses parental violence is the independent variable.
   b. Whether a child develops behavioral problems is the dependent variable.
   c. Both a and b are correct.
   d. Neither a nor b is correct.

3. Which of the following statements is ***not*** true regarding objectivity and subjectivity in scientific inquiry?

   a. Both quantitative and qualitative methods seek to attain objectivity.
   b. Researchers have no vested interests in finding certain results.
   c. We can assume objectivity has been achieved when different observers, with different vested interests, agree.
   d. None of the above; all are true.

4. Which of the following is ***not*** true about quantitative and qualitative methods?

   a. Quantitative methods emphasize precision and generalizable statistical findings.
   b. Qualitative methods emphasize deeper meanings, using observations not easily reduced to numbers.
   c. The two methods are incompatible and cannot be combined in the same study.
   d. Which type of method to emphasize depends on the conditions and purposes of the inquiry.
   e. None of the above; all are true.

5. A study of a particular homeless family that seeks to understand everything about that particular family and all the causes for its homelessness would exemplify:

   a. The idiographic model
   b. The nomothetic model
   c. Postmodernism
   d. Probabilistic reasoning

6. A study of a large number of homeless families that seeks to generalize about the most important factors causing homelessness across the entire population would exemplify:

   a. The idiographic model
   b. The nomothetic model
   c. Postmodernism
   d. Subjective inquiry

7. A researcher who hangs out with a small group of homeless people to develop an in-depth subjective understanding of their lives is being guided by what paradigm?

   a. Positivism
   b. Postpositivism
   c. Interpretivism
   d. Critical theory paradigm

8. A researcher who may use any variety of methods but who seeks to interpret findings not in a neutral manner, but through the filter of their empowerment or advocacy aims, is being guided by what paradigm?

   a. Positivism
   b. Postpositivism
   c. Interpretivism
   d. Critical theory paradigm

9. Which of the following is the *best* example of a hypothesis that might be held by a social worker providing a support group to caregivers of relatives with AIDS?

   a. Compassionate family members should care for their relative with AIDS.
   b. The caregivers will feel a considerable degree of stigma.
   c. Many caregivers will be in denial.
   d. Participation in the support group will reduce caregivers' levels of depression.

10. Which of the following approaches to scientific inquiry can be used commonly by a social work practitioner?

    a. Deductive reasoning
    b. Inductive reasoning
    c. Both inductive and deductive reasoning
    d. Reductionistic reasoning

11. A practitioner notices on three successive occasions when her client—a teenage girl in joint custody—has visited her father for the weekend, she seems more depressed and anxious. The practitioner then wonders whether there is something about the father's behavior, or the father-daughter relationship, that is contributing to the depression and anxiety. This is an example of:

    a. Inductive reasoning
    b. Deductive reasoning
    c. Both inductive and deductive reasoning
    d. Reductionistic reasoning

12. According to Rubin and Babbie, which of the following statements about practice models for social work practice is ***NOT*** true?

    a. They tend to be based on the synthesis of existing theories.
    b. They are mutually exclusive; they do not overlap.
    c. They get reinterpreted over time, in a manner that may broaden them but blur their distinctions.
    d. They can influence how we choose to research social work problems.

13. The prediction or observation that abused children are more likely than nonabused children to become perpetrators of abuse is an example of:

    a. Probabilistic reasoning
    b. A relationship
    c. Independent and dependent variables
    d. All of the above

14 .A social work supervisor, trained in and oriented to psychoanalysis, notices that her supervisee has a high rate of premature terminations. She recommends that he attend more continuing education workshops on object relations theory and decides to measure whether his treatment completion rate increases after he attends the workshops. This is an example of:

    a. Primarily inductive reasoning
    b. Primarily deductive reasoning
    c. Both inductive and deductive reasoning equally
    d. The functionalist practice model

15 —17: Suppose we predict that social service consumers in urban regions are more likely to prematurely terminate services than consumers in rural regions, while the latter are more likely to complete services.

15. In the above example, "urban region" would be:

    a. An attribute
    b. A variable
    c. A relationship

16. In the above example, "region" would be:

    a. An attribute
    b. A variable
    c. A relationship

17. In the above example, "service completers" would be:

    a. An attribute
    b. A variable
    c. A relationship

EXERCISE 3.1

Along with several classmates, interview a social professor who is known to have done some research. Ask them about the nature of the research they have done. What were the research questions? What paradigms were followed? Why? How did the paradigm influence the design of the studies and the interpretation of findings? Take notes and discuss your notes in class.

EXERCISE 3.2

Three researchers seek to conduct studies on the impact of welfare reform on the young children of mothers on welfare who must obtain employment. One researcher adheres to a positivist paradigm. Another adheres to an interpretivist paradigm. The third adheres to a critical social science paradigm. Contrast the ways in which each would conduct their studies, in light of their paradigms.

EXERCISE 3.3

Select a problem of concern to social work practitioners. Describe how it would be studied differently depending on whether the idiographic or nomothetic model of understanding guides the inquiry.

EXERCISE 3.4

1. Suppose two social workers are co-therapists providing play therapy with a group of preschoolers with conduct disorders. One relies on a behaviorist practice model rooted in learning theory and the principles of operant conditioning. The other relies on a developmental practice model, rooted in notions of providing a nondirective atmosphere where children can work on developmental tasks. Give examples of how each practice model might influence the practitioners to look for different indicators of the quality of the therapeutic process.

2. Suppose you wanted to evaluate the effectiveness of the above play therapy group. Give examples of how the outcome indicators of effectiveness that you choose to examine may differ depending on whether you were guided by a psychosocial practice model versus a behaviorist practice model.

EXERCISE 3.5

In the deductive model of science, the scientist begins with an interest in some aspect of reality, develops a hypothesis based on theory, and tests it through careful, objective observation of specific indicators. Illustrate how social work practitioners providing direct services or working at the macro level go through an analogous process.

EXERCISE 3.6

Specify two possible relationships relevant to social work practice. Identify the independent and dependent variable in each hypothesis, and describe the attributes of each variable.

DISCUSSION QUESTIONS

1. If you were to conduct social work research, do you think you would be most influenced by the positivist, interpretivist, or critical theory paradigm? Why?

2. Discuss, using a specific illustration, how a social work practitioner can use both inductive and deductive logic in working with a particular case, community, or organization.

3. Identify a particular practice model with which you closely identify. Discuss how that practice model might help and hinder your practice decisions and your effectiveness as a social work practitioner.

4. Discuss how the practice model you explored in question 3 could influence the kinds of research questions you might choose to investigate.

CROSSWORD PUZZLE

ACROSS

1 PARADIGM EMPHASIZING OBJECTIVITY
8 Morning hours
10 Signal for help
12 "______ apple a day...."
13 "Just say ______"
14 Burial structure
15 Computer command for completed term paper
16 ______ or not, here I come
17 PREMODERNISTS, MODERNISTS, AND POSTMODERNISTS DEAL WITH DETERMINING WHAT'S REALLY ______.
18 Penny, nickel, dime, or quarter
19 Moon, planet, or ball
20 Cheer
22 Use sunscreen if you want this
23 If you don't study for your research exam, you may be in ______ doo doo.
24 MALE AND FEMALE ARE ______ OF GENDER
26 First woman
28 No pain, no ______
30 Hammer or wrench
31 Not down
33 TYPE OF VARIABLE THAT IS EXPLAINED
35 Golfer's aim
36 Days after Xmas event
37 Tied
38 J. ______ (pop singer's nickname)
39 SYSTEM OF RELATIONSHIPS EXPLAINING THINGS
41 ______ look back
42 ______ Cool J. (Rap singer)
43 Thou ______ not steal
46 METHOD OF INQUIRY SEEKING BROAD GENERALIZATIONS
48 Internet site for auctions
49 Donald ______
51 Get ______ of
53 365 days (usually)
54 PRACTICE ______ (Guidelines for social workers)
55 ______ SOCIAL SCIENCE (paradigm emphasizing using research for social change)
56 A philosophy that rejects the concept of free will and instead views all behaviors as being determined by causes.
60 TYPE OF LOGIC THAT STARTS WITH OBSERVATIONS
62 Something withdrawn from income
64 Up and about
66 METHOD OF INQUIRY (focused on explaining a single case fully)
67 ______ITATIVE INQUIRY (emphasizes objectivity)

DOWN

1 WORLD VIEWS
2 "We're number ______!"
3 TYPE OF VARIABLE THAT EXPLAINS ANOTHER VARIABLE
4 Plaything
5 A SET OF ATTRIBUTES
6 Onset
7 Rear teeth
8 ______ Onassis
9 After dinner ______
10 Mick Jagger is one
11 ATTRIBUTE OF MUCH QUALITATIVE INQUIRY
15 PARADIGM QUESTIONING KNOWABILITY OF OBJECTIVE REALITY
21 Hello casually
25 City in Montana
27 ______ITATIVE INQUIRY
29 A CHERISHED SET OF BELIEFS THAT MAY HINDER OBJECTIVITY
32 TYPE OF KNOWLEDGE PURSUED IN DETERMINISTIC SOCIAL SCIENCE
34 Strong
40 Shade tree or nightmarish street
41 TYPE OF LOGIC THAT STARTS WITH A HYPOTHESIS AND THEN CONDUCTS OBSERVATIONS
44 Present
45 Boys
47 Cardiologist's concern
50 ______ abuse and neglect
52 Indonesian Island
56 Wanted ______ or alive!
57 Lion's sound
58 Snack
59 Harm
61 Canned fish
63 Man's best friend
64 King kong
65 Tiny ______

CHAPTER 4

The Ethics and Politics of Social Work Research

OBJECTIVES

1. Illustrate the ethical issues involved in the norm of voluntary participation and informed consent, including an example of a hypothetical study in which some practitioners or researchers might reasonably argue that violation of that norm is justified.

2. Illustrate through an example how a noble social worker might conduct a study that unintentionally violates the ethical norm of no harm to participants.

3. Define and distinguish between the ethical norms of anonymity and confidentiality in social work research.

4. Provide two examples of how a social work research study might violate the ethical norm regarding deceiving subjects. One example should be clearly unjustified, and one should be arguable.

5. Describe and illustrate how a social work researcher could unjustifiably violate ethical norms in analysis and reporting.

6. Describe and illustrate the ethical dilemma regarding the right to receive services versus the responsibility to evaluate service effectiveness.

7. Discuss the ethical obligations of social work practitioners to support research in the field.

8. Identify codes in the NASW Code of Ethics relating to how practitioners violate practice ethics if they refuse to participate in, contribute to, or utilize social work research.

9. Identify which ethical principles were involved in the examples of ethical controversies presented in Chapter 4, and discuss the dilemmas debated in each.

10. Describe the function of institutional review boards.

11. Illustrate how a social work research study could be biased or insensitive regarding gender or culture, and identify steps that can be taken to try to avoid that bias or insensitivity.

12. Identify two ways in which ethical concerns regarding research can be distinguished from political concerns.

13. Illustrate how values and ideology can influence the research process.

14. Discuss why some believe that social work research is never really value-free, and describe contrasting perspectives of what researchers should therefore do in light of the influence of values.

15. Illustrate how the influence of ideological priorities on social work research can stifle debate and ultimately hinder desired social change.

PRACTICE-RELEVENT SUMMARY

Social work research, like social work practice, is guided by codes of ethics. Some of the codes for research parallel codes for practice, and some of the codes for practice bear on the practitioner's responsibilities vis-à-vis research. For example, just as practitioners are guided by the principle of client self-determination, researchers should honor the principle of voluntary participation and informed consent by participants. At the same time, just as some practitioners might argue that in some cases the principle of self-determination needs to be violated (such as when clients intend to seriously harm themselves or others), some researchers might argue that in some cases the principle of voluntary participation and informed consent needs to be violated (such as when the study is investigating improper and harmful treatment of clients in institutions).

Another ethical principle—one practitioners and researchers can easily agree on—is that participants (or clients) should not be harmed by the research (or intervention). And yet sometimes the harm can be subtle or hard to anticipate, such as when survey respondents are asked about disturbing, unpopular, or demeaning behaviors, characteristics, or attitudes.

One ethical code that research clearly shares with practice is the protection of the subject's (client's) identity. Confidentiality means that the researcher or practitioner knows who said or did what but promises not to reveal their identity. In some research studies it is possible to go a step further, by assuring anonymity. Anonymity prevents even the researcher from identifying a given response with a given respondent. Sometimes it is possible to assure anonymity to research participants, and sometimes it is not. Confidentiality, however, should always be protected. The only exception to this dictum occurs when we learn that a client or subject is being abused or is at imminent risk of seriously harming themselves or others. Subjects need to be informed of this possibility as part of the informed consent process before they agree to participate in a study.

Deceiving subjects about the researcher's identity or research purposes is another important ethical concern, one that frequently poses a dilemma. Although it is often useful and even necessary to identify one's research purposes, sometimes the nature of the study requires that these purposes be concealed. In some studies it may be possible to justify using deception on the grounds that there is no other way to do the study and in light of the study's humanitarian value. In other studies this justification may not be convincing. If the use of deception is justified, subjects should be debriefed after the study. Also, as with all ethical guidelines, no study should be conducted without the approval of a human subjects committee that confirms the researcher's belief that the benefits of a study outweigh its risks.

Ethical concerns exist even after a study is completed and its findings are about to be reported. Researchers are obliged to inform readers of the study's technical shortcomings as well as its negative findings. They are also obliged not to portray accidental findings as if they resulted from a carefully preplanned analysis. Perhaps the most practice-relevant ethical dilemma has to do with the right to receive services versus the responsibility to evaluate service effectiveness. Does our professional responsibility to ensure that the services we provide have been scientifically tested for beneficial or harmful effects justify withholding services from some clients so as to compare experimentally the outcomes for those who receive services and those who don't? This dilemma is easiest to resolve when alternative services can be compared (rather than denying service to one group), when limited resources require placing clients on waiting lists, or when withholding services from clients experiencing a serious crisis would endanger them.

Several studies in social work and allied fields have gained notoriety in connection to ethical issues. In the famous Tuskegee syphilis study, a social worker exposed ethical violations involving the deception and harming of poor African American men suffering from syphilis, who were told they would receive free treatment for the disease when in fact the researchers had no intention of treating it. Instead, they were merely studying the progress of the disease. Stanley Milgram's social psychological laboratory studies of obedience to authority have been criticized for causing psychological suffering among participants who were duped into thinking they were obeying orders to seriously hurt people. Laud Humphreys's study of homosexual acts between strangers meeting in public restrooms was criticized on several grounds, including invasion of privacy and deceiving subjects into thinking he was only a voyeur-participant. A social worker, William Epstein, almost had his professional membership revoked when he duped editors and reviewers of professional journals with a bogus article that he submitted to test for editor bias in favor of publishing studies whose findings supported social work effectiveness over studies whose findings questioned social work effectiveness. A Texas experiment on the effectiveness of a federal pilot program to wean people from the welfare rolls had to abandon the use of a control group when critics argued that all welfare recipients should have been informed of the study and been given the opportunity to receive the pilot program's medical and child care benefits.

Researchers can try to ensure that their studies are ethical by obtaining the consent of an independent panel of professionals, called an *Institutional Review Board (IRB)*. IRB reviews are mandatory for research in agencies receiving federal money. IRB panelists review research proposals involving human subjects and rule on their ethics.

Feminist and minority scholars have expressed ethical concerns about studies that are biased or insensitive regarding gender and culture, arguing that such studies can harm women and minorities by offending them, by not pursuing findings that bear on their needs or ways to help them, and by inappropriately generalizing to them. Numerous guidelines have been offered to try to avoid cultural and gender bias and insensitivity in one's research.

There is a fine line between ethical and political issues in social work research. Ethical issues tend to deal more with research methods employed; political issues tend to deal more with how research will be used or its costs. Two common political objections that social workers are likely to encounter regarding proposed research in agencies include the fear that negative findings will hurt agency funding and the fear of bad publicity or lost revenues connected to withholding services in order to establish a control group.

Another source of objections to certain lines of research inquiry is ideologically rooted. Traditionally, scientifically oriented professionals have maintained that one's values, politics, or ideology should not influence one's research. Instead, researchers should strive to maximize objectivity. Recently, however, these notions have come under attack by some scholars who argue that social research is never entirely value-free. Although social work has a long tradition of using research as a tool to achieve ends prescribed by social work values, there is controversy within the profession over whether our values or ideological aims and beliefs should ever take priority over seeking the truth in our research. Research on women or minorities is commonly associated with this controversy, particularly when a study produces, or is apt to produce, findings that may provoke hostility from colleagues who fear that those findings will impede their political or ideological aims.

REVIEW QUESTIONS

1. A social work professor conducts a study to see if students become more tolerant in their attitudes about gay and lesbian issues during the semester. The professor distributes questionnaires, then leaves the room, assuring students that completing the questionnaire is voluntary and that they may return it anonymously via campus mail. Most students do not respond; those who do are the ones most deeply committed to issues of gay and lesbian rights. This illustrates:

    a. Adhering to the guideline of voluntary participation
    b. The conflict between the ethical concern for voluntary participation and the scientific goal of generalizability
    c. Ethical concern with the protection of identity
    d. All of the above
    e. Only a and b

2. Bill and Sarah, two agency social workers, mail client satisfaction questionnaires to agency clientele, requesting their anonymous responses about what they do and do not like about the services they are receiving. Bill and Sarah enter code numbers on each return envelope so they will know who returned the questionnaire and will thus be able to identify clients who did not respond to the survey, for the purposes of follow-up mailings. What ethical principle(s) are Bill and Sarah violating?

    a. Confidentiality
    b. Anonymity
    c. Deceiving subjects
    d. All of the above
    e. Only a and b
    f. Only b and c

3. According to the NASW Code of Ethics, social workers can violate their professional ethical responsibilities vis-à-vis research:

    a. When they refuse to participate in research studies that can develop knowledge for professional practice
    b. When they refuse to utilize research studies that contain new knowledge for professional practice
    c. When they do not keep current with emerging knowledge relevant to social work
    d. All of the above
    e. None of the above; practitioners can violate ethical responsibilities regarding research only when they conduct research that violates ethical guidelines

4. The controversy surrounding the Epstein study of a bogus article dealt primarily with what ethical principles?

    a. Analysis and reporting
    b. Anonymity and confidentiality
    c. Deceiving subjects and not obtaining their informed consent to participate
    d. Right to receive services versus responsibility to evaluate services

5. Which of the following ethical issues is most relevant to the Texas welfare study in which benefits were withheld from 800 Texans?

    a. Anonymity and confidentiality
    b. Right to receive services versus responsibility to evaluate services
    c. Deceiving subjects
    d. Analysis and reporting

6. Institutional Review Boards:

    a. Must approve the ethics of all federally funded research in the United States involving human subjects
    b. Vary in the amount and format of material they require
    c. Exempt some studies from a full review
    d. All of the above

7. Which of the following is ***NOT*** a political objection to a proposed study?

    a. Its results might endanger agency funding.
    b. Its procedures would be unpopular among agency staff.
    c. It might harm participants.
    d. Its results might impede the desired aims of an ideological movement.

8. Which of the following is ***NOT*** a guideline to avoid cultural bias and insensitivity in research involving minorities?

    a. Immerse yourself in the culture before finalizing your research design.
    b. Involve minority scholars and representatives of minority group in designing the research.
    c. Use the best instruments you can find from studies not involving minorities, and if those studies found the instruments to be scientifically rigorous, do not change them.
    d. Use minority, and perhaps bilingual, interviewers to interview minority respondents.
    e. Avoid an exclusive focus on the deficits of minorities.
    f. None of the above; all are recommended guidelines for research on minorities.

9. Which of the following is a recommended guideline to avoid gender bias and insensitivity in research?

   a. Assume that if a measurement instrument can be used successfully with one gender, it will be valid for the other gender.
   b. Generalize findings from one gender to the other; assume no differences.
   c. Look for ways in which the findings are the same for men and women; do not look for differences.
   d. All of the above.
   e. None of the above.

10. Which of the following statements is true about research politics and ideology?

   a. All scholars believe that research can be, and ought to be, value-free.
   b. Social work has a long tradition of using research to attain desired ends.
   c. All feminists agree that research should not be done if its results could hinder desired political aims of feminists.
   d. Politically rooted taboos against certain lines of inquiry never do a disservice to the people they seek to protect.
   e. Science is untouched by politics.
   f. All of the above.
   g. None of the above.

EXERCISE 4.1

Listed below are several research situations, like some of those noted in the chapter, that you may encounter in your professional practice. Rank order them according to how seriously they violate either the ethical guidelines discussed in this chapter or the social work profession's code of ethics.

a. While parents await their children in the waiting room of a Child Guidance Center, the center's social work staff instructs them to complete a questionnaire on child-rearing attitudes. The staff will use the findings of this study to prepare a proposal for funding for a parent education program.

b. A community organizer decides to observe, interview folks at, and write about a demonstration against police brutality that is expected to be a lawful. The demonstration unexpectedly becomes violent, and property is destroyed. Law enforcement officials show up and demand that the organizer identify people observed breaking the law. Rather than risk arrest as an accomplice after the fact, the organizer complies.

c. Social workers in a battered women's program conduct an evaluation of the effectiveness of the services provided by the program, hoping to bring visibility and resources to the program by publishing the findings. The findings, however, unexpectedly indicate the services are not effective. In light of these findings the social workers decide they must not have conducted a proper study of the services that they are convinced are effective, and they decide not to let anyone know about the study.

d. Two social work students with the same field placement in a public child welfare agency decide to do a research class team project involving interviews with abusive parents. They obtain a list of parents reported to their agency for abuse and then contact them with the explanation that they have been selected at random from the general population to take a sampling about child-rearing attitudes. They say this so as to not make the parents defensive in the interviews.

e. Two other social work students decide to do their class research project by observing the nocturnal activities at a shelter for the homeless. The shelter has a limited number of beds and cannot accommodate everyone seeking housing. The two students show up and wait in line early enough to get beds and then watch and record the goings on at night while they pretend to be asleep.

f. A new intervention is advertised as an extremely effective, powerful brief therapy for posttraumatic stress disorder among victims of sexual assault. Although sufficient resources exist to provide this treatment to all clients at a rape crisis center, the decision is made to provide it to only half the clients, so its effects can be compared to the effects of the center's routine services.

g. An in-service training director in a family service agency interviews social work staff about their training needs. To test whether they may be trying to look good by saying they know more than they really know, the director asks if they have sufficient understanding about a fictitious intervention modality.

EXERCISE 4.2

1. For each of the above rankings, explain the reason for your rankings and identify the one or two ethical issues most relevant to the situation.

2. Which situations would you consider minor ethical violations? Which would you consider major ethical violations? Why?

EXERCISE 4.3

List each of the major ethical guidelines emphasized in Chapter 3. Beside each briefly describe the purpose of a hypothetical research study that would be valuable to carry out but that would violate that guideline.

EXERCISE 4.4

Referring to Figure 3-1, prepare an informed consent form for the Buckingham study on Living with the Dying, which is described in Chapter 3 of the text.

EXERCISE 4.5

Your agency wants you to conduct a study of recent immigrants to assess their need for services. What steps would you take before implementing any study in order to minimize cultural bias and insensitivity?

EXERCISE 4.6

Make up and describe two hypothetical studies: one in which it would be justified to delay the provision of services to some clients in order to evaluate the services, and one in which that delay would not be justified.

DISCUSSION QUESTIONS

1. Examine the NASW Code of Ethics. Discuss your views on how strongly and clearly the code implies that social work practitioners are unethical if they refuse to participate in social work practice research or if they fail to utilize practice research to guide their practice.

2. Answer the questions raised in the text at the end of the discussion of Epstein's "Bogus Article to Test Journal Bias" asking you what you think about the controversy surrounding that illustration.

3. Answer the questions raised in the text at the end of the discussion of "Welfare Study Withholds Benefits from 800 Texans" asking you what you think about the controversy surrounding that illustration.

4. Discuss why bias and insensitivity regarding gender and culture are considered to be ethical violations. Identify at least five guidelines to avoid gender bias or insensitivity and at least five guidelines to avoid cultural bias or insensitivity.

5. Discuss your view of the ethics and politics of *The Bell Curve*. Were its authors unethical in conducting or reporting the study the way they did? Why or why not? Include in your discussion the issue of political correctness and its implications for scientific inquiry and for finding new ways to improve social welfare.

CROSSWORD PUZZLE

ACROSS

1 SITE OF UNETHICAL SYPHILIS STUDY THAT STARTED IN 1932
7 Not them
9 RESEARCHERS HAVE AN ETHICAL OBLIGATION TO CONDUCT AN HONEST ______ OF THEIR DATA EVEN IF IT YIELDS NEGATIVE FINDINGS
16 Key ______ pie
17 DUPING OR MISLEADING (SUBJECTS) – AN ETHICAL TABOO
19 Baseball pitchers want this statistic to be low
20 Useful
21 Freud's self
22 Baseball sluggers want this statistic to be high
23 ______ TO RECEIVE 13 DOWN
27 SOME MIGHT ARGUE THAT THIS MIGHT JUSTIFY A MEANS
28 Atop
29 PARTICIPATION IN RESEARCH SHOULD BE ______
34 Greek letter involved in calculating circumferences
35 Unusual
36 RESEARCH SHOULD DO ______ ______ TO PARTICIPANTS (TWO WORDS)
37 ______ Antony (Italian spelling for Roman who asked to borrow ears)
38 I did it ______ way
40 ORGANIZATION WITH A CODE OF ETHICS

DOWN

1 A STUDY OF TRADE HERE CAUSED ETHICAL TROUBLE
2 Strike heavily
3 ______ and kin
4 Sends forth
5 Set like jelly
6 Phys. ______ (exercise class)
7 Educational institute in Boulder
8 A TYPE OF BIAS THAT MIGHT BE UNETHICAL
9 ______ Maria
10 River in Africa
11 SOMETHING GUARANTEED WHEN THE RESEARCHER CANNOT LINK A GIVEN RESPONSE WITH A RESPONDENT
12 Tee shirt size between md and xlg
13 CLIENTS HAVE A RIGHT TO RECEIVE THESE, BUT THE RESPONSIBILITY TO EVALUATE THEM MAY POSE AN ETHICAL DILEMMA
14 ACRONYM FOR A HUMAN SUBJECTS REVIEW COMMITTEE
15 Popeye the ______ man
18 Former spouse
24 ______ 500 (Memorial day auto race in Midwest city)
25 INFORMED ______
26 Say what?
30 Lay ______ (hide)
31 Short snooze

ACROSS

42 American ______
43 ______ the land of the free ....
45 Mimic
47 In ______ ______ (stuck: two words)
49 I am ______ (or ______ I am)
51 A PROMISE NOT TO DIVULGE A PERSON'S RESPONSES PUBLICLY
55 Big Sur is here (abbrev.)
56 Prefix meaning inverse
57 Lyric poem
58 Pretended
60 Mistake
63 ______ ATROCITIES IN MEDICAL EXPERIMENTATION DURING THE HOLOCAUST
65 ______ said, she said
66 Dutch cheese
68 ______ Corleone (Marlon Brando's academy award role)
70 ______ HARM TO PARTICIPANTS
71 ______ OF ETHICS
73 ______ PRIORITIES CAN RESTRICT INQUIRY OUT OF FEAR THAT CERTAIN TRUTHS MIGHT BE MISUSED TO HARM A CAUSE
76 THESE SHOULD BE OUTWEIGHED BY BENEFITS WHEN TRYING TO RESOLVE ETHICAL DILEMMAS
78 Fictional girl of the Alps
79 Goldi______
82 Not she
83 Kid's card game
84 Hawaiian necklace
86 DO THIS WITH BENEFITS AND COSTS
88 Smack
89 ______ Cola
90 We took a ______ (lost big time)
92 Mediocre letter grade
93 Fugue composer
94 YOU HAVE AN ETHICAL OBLIGATION TO BE DOING THIS WITH YOUR NEGATIVE FINDINGS AND STUDY LIMITATIONS
95 SOMETHING THAT SHOULD OUTWEIGH THE COSTS
97 Narrow inlet of the sea between steep cliffs
98 Research assistant's abbreviated title
100 SCIENTIFIC MAGAZINE THAT ONCE RECEIVED A BOGUS ARTICLE
103 Loss of soil
107 A farewell to ______
108 ______ Gore
109 INSENSITIVITY ABOUT THIS MIGHT BE CONSIDERED UNETHICAL
110 Possessive form of thou

DOWN

32 Test
33 ______ Beauty
34 In favor of
39 ______ CONSENT
40 Famous consumer advocate
41 Huge simian
44 RESEARCH ON THIS CAN BE POLITICALLY, IDEOLOGICALLY, OR ETHICALLY CONTROVERSIAL
46 Hello
48 Educational institute in Knoxville or Austin (abbrev.)
50 Created
51 Abbreviation for someone who objected to Vietnam military service on moral or religious grounds
52 A 1960'S STUDY THAT CAUSED AN ETHICAL CONTROVERSY OBSERVED HUMAN ______
53 Wedding vow words
54 Graduate ______ of social work
59 Kennedy, Turner, and Koppel
61 Appliance that broadcast FDR's fireside chats
62 Wharf
64 Where to find 41 down
67 A FINE LINE CAN BE FOUND BETWEEN ETHICAL AND ______ ISSUES IN SOCIAL WORK RESEARCH
68 Cutting into small cubes
69 YOU MIGHT JOIN THIS ORGANIZATION AFTER YOU EARN YOUR SOCIAL WORK DEGREE
71 M divided by V
72 69 DOWN HAS A CODE OF THESE
74 Houston football player of yore
75 You ______ girl!
77 Third son of Adam
78 Step on it!
80 Kitchen gadget
81 Quaker pronoun related to 110 across
85 Devour
87 SYNONYM OF 8 DOWN (A TYPE OF BIAS)
88 The cat in the ______
90 WAS IT ETHICAL WHEN EPSTEIN SUBMITTED HIS ______ ARTICLE TO TEST JOURNAL BIAS?
91 ______ the beginning .....
93 GENDER OR CULTURAL ______
95 Water transport
96 To and ______
97 Get a shot every fall to avoid getting this disease
99 No matter which
100 Between soph and sr
101 Meditation word
102 Apache or Navajo (abbrev.)
104 In ______ to .... (memo phase)
105 Neuter pronoun
106 Exclamation of surprise or desire

CHAPTER 5

Culturally Competent Research

OBJECTIVES

1. Identify and describe the distinguishing attributes of culturally competent research.

2. Describe the ways in which culturally insensitive research can harm the research process, the people that the research is about, and the validity of research findings.

3. Describe how to formulate a research problem in a culturally competent manner.

4. Describe how cultural competence can enhance sampling and the recruitment and retention of research participants.

5. Describe how cultural competence can enhance measurement and how the lack of cultural competence can hinder measurement.

6. Describe and explain the extra steps that are needed to ensure that measurement procedures validated with one culture are reliable and valid with a different culture.

7. Distinguish between three different levels of measurement equivalence, and explain culturally competent procedures for attaining measurement equivalence.

8. Describe how the lack of cultural competence can hinder the analysis and interpretation of data.

9. Discuss the role of assessing acculturation and the immigration experience in culturally competent research.

PRACTICE-RELEVANT SUMMARY

You may have already learned how important cultural competence is in social work practice (especially if this is not your first semester as a social work student). Cultural competence is also very important in social work research. Cultural competence can help researchers obtain and provide information that is relevant and valid for minority and oppressed populations and thus can improve practice and policy with those populations.

In research, the term *cultural competence* means being aware of and appropriately responding to the ways in which cultural factors and cultural differences should influence what we investigate, how we investigate, and how we interpret our findings. Culturally insensitive research can produce misleading results, can offend minority respondents, and can poison the climate for future research among minority and oppressed populations.

Culturally competent research studies will strive include a sufficient and representative sample of participants from minority and oppressed populations. Studies that do not include adequate representation from specific minority and oppressed populations in their samples are not generalizable to those populations. For example, different cultural groups utilize services differently, have different expectations of services, and interpret and react differently to the problems for which they seek services. Successfully recruiting and retaining minority participants in research requires special culturally sensitive knowledge and efforts, such as being responsive to the concerns of minority communities in the way research problems are formulated. Insensitivity to those concerns can lead not only to problems in recruitment and retention of participants, but also to findings that are not relevant to the needs perceived by members of those communities.

Culturally competent research will use measurement procedures that have been shown to be reliable and valid for the minority and oppressed populations participating in the research. Cultural competence also can affect how data are analyzed and interpreted. Culturally competent researchers will compare the various minority groups to each other. Different minority groups differ from the majority group in different ways. Because minority groups are more likely to be poor than majority populations, culturally competent researchers will include *socioeconomic factors* in their analyses when they are studying other ways in which minority and majority populations differ. Culturally competent researchers will also consider the *immigration experience* and *acculturation* as factors to include in their research as they study differences between minority and majority populations. Sensitivity to these factors will also alert researchers to study differences within a particular minority group. *Acculturation* is the process in which a group or individual changes after coming into contact with a majority culture, taking on the language, values, attitudes, and lifestyle preferences of the majority culture.

Before beginning any investigation you should be well read in the literature on the culture of and minority or oppressed populations that you seek to study. This should include readings that describe the culture and its values as well as research studies dealing with issues bearing on the participation of its members in research. Additional early steps in seeking to improve your cultural competence might include using participant observation methods to immerse yourself in the culture of interest and enhance your assessment of your own cultural competence. You should also seek the advice of professional colleagues who are members of the culture or who have a great deal of experience in working with its members. Your colleagues can help you not only to learn more about the culture, but also to formulate research questions that are responsive to the needs and perspectives of its members. So too can the input of community members and their leaders. In fact, representatives of minority cultures that your study will focus on should be included in the formulation of your research questions and in all subsequent stages of the research. This will not only help you formulate research questions that are responsive to minority group concerns, it also can help you prevent or deal with culturally related problems that might arise in later stages of the research design and implementation – problems that you might not otherwise have anticipated. Likewise, it can foster a sense of community commitment to the research and more receptivity to future studies. Using focus groups might help, too, by identifying how community representatives view issues relevant to your study.

Recommended culturally competent approaches for overcoming barriers to the recruitment and retention of participants from minority and oppressed populations include obtaining endorsement from community leaders, assuring community confidentiality, employing local community members as research staff, providing adequate compensation for participation, alleviating transportation and childcare barriers, choosing sensitive and accessible settings, using and training culturally competent interviewers, using bilingual staff, understanding cultural factors influencing participation, using anonymous enrollment with stigmatized populations, using special sampling techniques, learning where to look, connecting with and nurturing referral sources, using frequent and individualized contacts and personal touches, using anchor points, and using tracking methods. Tracking methods include *phone tracking, mail tracking, agency tracking,* and *field tracking*. Regardless of which tracking method used, your persistence may be the most important factor in obtaining satisfactory retention rates.

There are three main threats to culturally competent measurement: 1) the use of interviewers whose personal characteristics or interviewing styles offend or intimidate minority respondents or in other ways make them reluctant to divulge relevant and valid information; 2) using of language, either in self- or interviewer-administered instruments, that minority respondents do not understand; and 3) cultural bias. Four steps for avoiding language problems include: 1) using bilingual interviewers; 2) translating measures into the language of the respondents; 3) back-translation; and 4) pretesting the measures to see if they are understood as intended. *Back-translation* begins with a bilingual person translating the instrument and its instructions to a target language. Then another bilingual person translates from the target language back to the original language (not seeing the original version of the instrument). Then the original instrument is compared to the back-translated version, and items with discrepancies are modified further.

The forgoing steps, however, won't guarantee that a measurement instrument that appeared to be valid when tested with one culture will be valid when used with members of another culture. When we modify such instruments, we should assess whether the modified instrument used with the minority culture is really equivalent to the version validated with the dominant culture. We need to do the same when a measure is validated in one country, but then applied in another country. The term *measurement equivalence* means that a measurement procedure developed in one culture will have the same value and meaning when administered to people in another culture. Three types of measurement equivalence that tend to be of greatest concern are: linguistic equivalence, conceptual equivalence and metric equivalence. *Linguistic equivalence* is attained when an instrument has been translated and back-translated successfully. *Conceptual equivalence* means that instruments and observed behaviors have the same meanings across cultures. *Metric equivalence* means that scores on a measure are comparable across cultures. Procedures that can be used to assess measurement equivalence include: assessing whether an instrument has the same factors (or dimensions) in each culture, assessing whether scores on the instrument are correlated with measures of acculturation or other factors that are thought to differ between the two cultures of concern, and testing its validity separately in the different cultures in which you plan to use it.

REVIEW QUESTIONS

1. An African American researcher wants to study factors influencing whether Native American adolescents living on a particular reservation and who abuse substances will participate in a substance abuse treatment program. Which of the following would be part of a culturally competent approach to her study?

   a. Read about the tribe's culture and its values before seeking approval from the Tribal Council.
   b. Read studies about the use of substance abuse services by Native American adolescents before seeking approval from the Tribal Council.
   c. Read about the tribe's history before seeking approval from the Tribal Council.
   d. All of the above.
   e. None of the above.

2. A Latino researcher wants to study factors influencing caregiver burden among Korean Americans. Which of the following would be part of a culturally competent approach to his study?

   a. He can maintain his belief in the superiority of his own Latino culture as long as he also learns about the Korean American culture.
   b. He should be aware of ethnocentrism, but not try to avoid it.
   c. He should try to avoid ethnocentrism.
   d. All of the above.
   e. None of the above.
   f. a and b, only, are true.

3. A researcher finds that frail elderly Korean Americans are more likely to be well cared for by their extended families than are their white counterparts. Which of the following would be a culturally competent implication to report?

    a. Asian Americans are more likely to care for their frail elderly relatives than are their white counterparts.
    b. Korean American children are more likely to care for their disabled parents than are children in the general population.
    c. Frail elderly Korean Americans from affluent families are less likely to need nursing home care than their white counterparts.
    d. All of the above.
    e. None of the above

4. Social work doctoral students who are USA citizens living in three different United States cities want to conduct dissertation research on factors affecting social service utilization among undocumented immigrants from Mexico. One of the students is Mexican American. One is African American. One is Asian American. Which of them do/does **NOT** need to improve their cultural sensitivity?

    a. The Mexican American student.
    b. The African American student.
    c. The Asian American student.
    d. All of the above. (None of them needs to improve their cultural sensitivity.)
    e. None of the above. (All of them need to improve their cultural sensitivity.)

5. Which of the following would be a culturally competent way to recruit research participants in a study of the effectiveness of a child abuse prevention program in three communities – one whose residents are predominantly African American, one whose residents are predominantly Mexican American, and one whose residents are predominantly Chinese American?

    a. Use the same recruitment approach in each community.
    b. Use the same strategy for locating prospective participants in each community.
    c. Obtain endorsement for the study from esteemed community leaders in each community.
    d. All of the above.
    e. None of the above.

6. Employing local community members as research staff will **NOT**:

    a. reassure participants as to confidentiality
    b. help in locating recruiting prospective participants
    c. help in explaining informed consent forms
    d. provide more jobs to the community

7. Reimbursement to poor folks for participating in research:

   a. should be as large as possible
   b. should be large enough to provide an incentive but not so large that it becomes coercive
   c. should always be in the form of money
   d. All of the above
   e. Only a and c are true

8. Matching interviewer and interviewee ethnicity will:

   a. ensure interviewer cultural competence
   b. always be more important than prior interviewing training and experience in interviewing members of the target population
   c. always increase the likelihood that stigmatized populations will agree to be interviewed
   d. All of the above
   e. None of the above

9. Using bilingual interviewers will:

   a. facilitate translation equivalence
   b. ensure conceptual equivalence
   c. ensure metric equivalence
   d. All of the above

10. Using anonymous enrollment with stigmatized populations will:

    a. help prospective participants feel safe participating in the study
    b. enhance conceptual equivalence
    c. require probability sampling procedures
    d. be possible only in qualitative studies
    e. All of the above.

11. Trying to locate and engage members of hidden and stigmatized populations in a research study can be enhanced by:

    a. using snowball sampling procedures
    b. using judgmental sampling procedures
    c. using anonymous enrollment procedures
    d. All of the above
    e. None of the above

12. When using tracking methods to retaining the participation of homeless individuals in your study, you should:

    a. make phone calls to anchor points
    b. make reminder contacts a week or two in advance of an interview
    c. ask service providers or other community agencies whether they have been in recent contact with participants whom you are unable to locate
    d. All of the above
    e. None of the above

13. A scale developed in English in the United States is translated and then successfully back-translated into Spanish. Therefore we can feel very confident about the scale's:

    a. linguistic equivalence
    b. conceptual equivalence
    c. metric equivalence
    d. All of the above

EXERCISE 5.1

Suppose you conduct an experiment in Los Angeles to evaluate the effectiveness of a social work intervention that attempts to prevent referrals for child abuse. Of the 40 clients randomly assigned to each group, 10 are white, 10 are African American, 10 are Mexican American, 5 are Asian American and 5 are Native American. The referral rate in your experimental group is 25 percent, as compared to 50 percent in your control group. Discuss how you would analyze and interpret your results in a culturally competent manner. For example, what generalizations would you make? Would you want to do any further analyses of the data, and if so, what?

EXERCISE 5.2

What if in the above experiment you randomly assigned 20 clients to each group, 15 who are white, 2 who are African American, 1 who is Mexican American, 1 who is Asian American and 1 who is Native American. None of the participants in your experimental group get referred for child abuse, as compared to 50 percent in your control group. Discuss how you would analyze and interpret your results in a culturally competent manner. For example, what generalizations would you make? What would you recommend for future research?

EXERCISE 5.3

An existing scale written in English has been found to have excellent reliability and validity in the United States. You would like to use it in a study of recently immigrated Latinos living in Miami. But first you want to develop a Spanish version of the scale and then test its measurement equivalence. Describe the steps you would take to accomplish that.

DISCUSSION QUESTIONS

1. You invite Native American students at your university to participate in a study to see if an instrument is valid for Native Americans. Your classmate, who you did not think is Native American, volunteers to participate, telling you that her great grandmother was a Cherokee. Would you include her in your study? Why or why not?

2. Do you think you are ethnocentric? Why or why not? Suppose you visit a country where women must always be veiled and are stoned severely if their ankles are showing or they are not wearing a veil. Moreover, they are not allowed to vote. If they are caught in adultery, they are put to death in a painful manner. How would you feel about all that? Does your answer affect whether or not you think you are ethnocentric and how you feel about your possible ethnocentrism or lack thereof?

CROSSWORD PUZZLE

ACROSS

1 ______COUNCIL: GROUP THAT MAY HAVE TO ENDORSE RESEARCH INVOLVING NATIVE AMERICANS
5 ______POINTS: PIECES OF INFORMATION TO HELP FIND TRANSIENT RESEARCH PARTICIPANTS
10 "The King______ ______" (2 words)
11 Ark builder
12 ______TRACKING (YOU'LL NEED STAMPS)
13 SOME MINORITY RESEARCH PARTICIPANTS MIGHT NOT BE ______ IN THE MAJORITY LANGUAGE
16 ______RR (transportation for many NYC commuters)
17 Early Brit
19 ______errors (cognitive mistakes)
23 Ready______ not
24 "The bells are ______ for me and my gal......."
25 Gap

DOWN

1 Scottish cap
2 Genetic material
3 Amin
4 ______ INTERVIEWERS WILL BE NEEDED WITH SOME MINORITY PARTICIPANTS
6 Direction from Tulane to Bryn Mawr
7 ANOTHER TYPE OF MEASUREMENT EQUIVALENCE
8 Abhor
9 ______ my god!
13 General Motor's headquarters city in Michigan
14 ANOTHER TYPE OF MEASUREMENT EQUIVALENCE
15 CULTURALLY INSENSITIVE RESEARCH MIGHT FOCUS TOO LITTLE ON THE ______ OF MINORITIES
18 Two syllable prefix for motive or motion

ACROSS

27 CHANGE PROCESS AFTER ENTERING A MAJORITY CULTURE
28 _____ a loss for words
29 Bolt's mate 30 Slays
33 Lengthy tale
34 _____ the hop (early rock song)
35 _____ were a rich man (2 words)
36 Eye _____
38 TYPE OF MEASUREMENT EQUIVALENCE
40 Generation _____
42 Impersonator
45 Common college degree (abbrev.)
46 Gainsay
47 A CULTURALLY SENSITIVE INSTRUMENT SHOULD HAVE MEASUREMENT _____
51 Wildebeast
52 Deceased comedian's last name or deceased clarinetist's first name
53 Elevator Inventor
55 Undergrad degree or slang term for nonsense
56 USE ANONYMOUS ENROLLMENT WITH _____ POPULATIONS
62 Cease
63 _____ spores
64 Signal for help or steel wool soap pad
65 Jab

DOWN

19 FIELD _____ INVOLVES TALKING WITH PEOPLE ON THE STREETS ABOUT WHERE TO FIND RESEARCH PARTICIPANTS WHOM YOU HAVE NOT BEEN ABLE TO LOCATE USING OTHER METHODS
20 Short for hiccup
21 Big business abbreviation
22 Scottish men's wear
25 Ratted on
26 Small island
31 "_____ I Loved You " (song from Carousel)
32 Lacking rigidity
34 _____ if! (valley girl expression)
37 _____ TRACKING INVOLVES ASKING SERVICE PROVIDERS ABOUT LOCATING RESEARCH PARTICIPANTS
39 YOU'LL NEED TO _____ SOME RESEARCH STAFF TO HELP THEM BECOME CULTURALLY COMPETENT
41 Representatives
42 Capital of Yemen
43 William or Sean
44 Where to find Salinger's catcher
45 Private urban educ. institute in Mass. (abbrev.)
48 Stops
49 Source of "Mamma Mia" music
50 For fear that
51 Monopoly starting point
54 Rests on one's buttocks
57 Sticky stuff
58 AWOL hunters
59 Mischievous one
60 Where to find a gorilla in the Bronx
61 A large deer
62 ETO commander in WWII who later chose RMN

CHAPTER 6

Problem Formulation

OBJECTIVES

1. Identify examples of how social work researchers and practitioners follow the same problem-solving process.

2. List each phase of the research process, and explain how phases are interrelated and can loop back to earlier phases.

3. Develop a research question that would be highly relevant to social work practice.

4. Identify some major obstacles to the feasibility of studying the foregoing research question.

5. Provide an example of an exploratory research topic of value to social work practice, and discuss how the exploratory results might lead to a descriptive or explanatory study.

6. Provide a hypothetical example of a valuable descriptive study and explain how its findings might set the stage for an explanatory or exploratory study.

7. Provide an example of a useful explanatory study and explain how its findings might loop back to the need for more exploratory study.

8. Provide an example of a practice-relevant cross-sectional study, a practice-relevant trend study, a practice-relevant panel study, and a practice-relevant cohort study.

9. Give examples of how a particular research topic could be studied using individuals, groups, or social artifacts as the units of analysis.

10. Provide a hypothetical example of the ecological fallacy in a hypothetical social work research study.

PRACTICE-RELEVANT SUMMARY

Social work researchers and practitioners follow essentially the same problem-solving process. Both begin by formulating a problem. Next they generate, explore, and select alternative strategies for solving the problem. The chosen approach is then implemented and evaluated, and the findings are disseminated. In both practice and research these phases are contingent on one another. Problems encountered at any phase may require looping back to earlier phases and rethinking one's approach. Even the successful completion of the entire process implies the likelihood of looping back, since one's findings are likely to stimulate new ideas about problems or solutions one would like to study.

In selecting research topics, the impetus should come from the information needs confronting practitioners, administrators, and policymakers attempting to solve practical problems in social welfare, service delivery, or practice. Thus, social work research has an "applied" emphasis, rather than just seeking knowledge for its own sake or solely to satisfy the researcher's idiosyncratic curiosity. The answers to your research questions should be highly relevant to others concerned about social welfare or social work practice.

An important early step in the problem formulation phase involves considering feasibility obstacles to one's research ideas. Common feasibility obstacles include fiscal costs, time constraints, ethical problems, and difficulty obtaining required cooperation from participants and agency administrators and practitioners. Another important early step is the literature review. Although the literature summary in a research proposal may be concise, the researcher should be thoroughly grounded in the literature, which often can ensure that the research questions chosen for study adequately address the burning issues in the field and build on the work of others. Common places to find relevant literature include abstracts, bibliographies, guides, and indexes. Computerized searches may be helpful; another possibility is scanning the tables of contents of recent periodicals.

Research can be for the purpose of exploration, description, and/or explanation. Exploratory studies typically use flexible research methods and are less concerned with producing generalizable facts than with providing a tentative familiarity with a topic and stimulating new ideas that can be tested out later. Descriptive studies emphasize accuracy, precision, and generalizable data. Explanatory studies also value accuracy, precision, and generalizability, but go beyond merely attempting to describe a population's characteristics; they seek to test out hypotheses. The same study can have more than one of these purposes, and the distinction between these purposes in some studies can be fuzzy.

Research studies can be conducted at one point in time or over a longer period. When they focus on point in time, they are cross-sectional studies. Because they observe things at only one time point, cross-sectional studies are limited in attempting to understand causal processes over time. Longitudinal studies, on the other hand, conduct their observations over an extended period and therefore can describe processes occurring over time. Three types of longitudinal studies are trend studies, cohort studies, and panel studies. *Trend studies* observe changes within the same population over time. *Cohort studies* examine how subpopulations change over time. *Panel studies* are like trend and cohort studies, but instead of gathering data from a new set of people each time, they return to gather data from the same individuals each time.

Not all social work research studies gather data from individuals, however. Some gather data on aggregates of people, such as groups or families. Others gather data on social artifacts, such as journal articles, TV commercials, or newspaper editorials. The things that social work researchers seek to observe, describe, and explain—such as individuals, groups, or social artifacts—are called *units of analysis*. Researchers and consumers of research need to be aware of the risk inherent in making assertions about individuals when the units of analysis for the research are groups or other aggregations. The ecological fallacy occurs when mistaken assertions about individuals are made based on the characteristics that describe an aggregation. For example, if antiabortion graffiti is more likely to appear in low-income neighborhoods that have many abortion clinics, it would be wrong to assert that low-income individuals are more likely to produce antiabortion graffiti.

REVIEW QUESTIONS

1. Which of the following statements about social work research and practice is true?

   a. Practice is practical; research is academic and impractical.
   b. They follow different problem-solving processes.
   c. Only in practice do you have the flexibility to loop back to earlier phases of the process.
   d. All of the above.
   e. None of the above.

2. A good basis for selecting a social work research topic would be:

   a. Information needed to guide a decision about what services to provide
   b. A lack of awareness of the characteristics and needs of a new target population
   c. Whether social workers are implementing an intervention in the intended fashion
   d. Reasons prospective clients don't use services
   e. All of the above
   f. None of the above

3. What would you recommend to a colleague who asked for your advice about the following research question she was considering for a research proposal: Does alcohol abuse influence work performance?

    a. Consider and/or show why the answer is not a foregone conclusion.
    b. Be more specific about both variables in the research question.
    c. Make sure you can get access to observable data.
    d. All of the above.
    e. None of the above.

4. Suppose you are preparing a research proposal to interview family members of persons living with AIDS. Which of the following statements is ***NOT*** true?

    a. It would be fairly easy to underestimate the fiscal costs of the study.
    b. It is reasonable to anticipate that agencies working with the target population would be eager to support and cooperate with your study.
    c. The time constraints of the study easily could turn out to be much worse than anticipated.
    d. Ethical concerns could impede the study's feasibility.
    e. None of the above; they are all true.
    f. All of the above; none is true.

5. Which of the following statements is/are true about the literature review process during problem formulation?

    a. References to studies appear in guides to the literature (like abstracts) as soon as the study is published in a journal.
    b. The literature review should usually be conducted after the research question has been sharpened and the research design has been developed.
    c. Good places to start a literature review include abstracts, bibliographies, and library subject guides and computerized search services.
    d. All of the above.
    e. None of the above.

6. If you want to find out the exact proportion of social workers working in each of the various fields of practice (mental health, child welfare, and so on), you would undertake:

    a. A descriptive study
    b. An exploratory study
    c. A trend study
    d. An explanatory study
    e. A cohort study

7. If you want to obtain tentative new insights about the emotional impact on parents of caregiving for their child with AIDS, you would undertake:

   a. A descriptive study
   b. An exploratory study
   c. A trend study
   d. An explanatory study
   e. A cohort study

8. If you want to find out whether the intervention you have designed really reduces depression, you would undertake:

   a. A descriptive study
   b. An exploratory study
   c. A trend study
   d. An explanatory study
   e. A cohort study

9. If you evaluate your support group intervention by comparing the average improvement in depression among the individuals participating in your support group to the average improvement among the individuals participating in a different kind of group, your unit of analysis would be:

   a. Groups
   b. Individuals
   c. Social artifacts
   d. Depression

10. After conducting a study that finds that states with liberal social welfare policies and more liberal voters have higher rates of child abuse than states with conservative social welfare policies and more conservative voters, you conclude that liberals are more likely to abuse children than are conservatives. Which of the following statements is true about this example?

    a. It illustrates the ecological fallacy.
    b. It illustrates reductionism.
    c. It illustrates good deductive reasoning.
    d. Individuals were the unit of analysis.
    e. None of the above.

EXERCISE 6.1

Suppose you are administering a federally funded demonstration project aimed at preserving families in which children are at risk for neglect or abuse because one or both parents is abusing alcohol or drugs. Suppose you are required to evaluate the three-year program each year. Suppose that the first-year evaluation finds that instead of having fewer children placed in foster care due to neglect or abuse, the families receiving your services had more children placed in foster care. That is, families that received more home visits from your demonstration program were less likely to be preserved than families receiving much fewer visits from your agency's routine services.

1. Discuss how this finding could loop back to generate a new research process all over again.
2. What would the new research question be?
3. Was the purpose of first study (as indicated above) exploratory, descriptive, or explanatory? Explain. Which of these purposes best applies to your new research question (see the previous question)? Explain.

EXERCISE 6.2

Suppose you administer a very small refugee resettlement agency that struggles each year to procure enough voluntary contributions to survive. Suppose one of your three social workers asks you for release time and some funds to research the following two questions:

1. Is the number of applications for political asylum from countries with large populations larger than the number of such applications from countries with small populations?
2. Is it easier to resettle refugees who had jobs and families in their new country before they arrived than refugees who did not have these?

What criteria regarding topic selection from Chapter 6 would you cite in gently and tactfully denying the staff member's request?

EXERCISE 6.3

Suppose you come up with a research question that strikes you as having great value to your agency and perhaps to social workers in other agencies. Describe the steps you would take to assess thoroughly whether and how to pursue that topic and to formulate your research problem. What issues would you address in this problem formulation process?

EXERCISE 6.4

Suppose you work in a child guidance center where the primary intervention modalities include individual, group, family, and art therapy. Devise a research question, or several questions, illustrating how individuals, groups, and social artifacts could be used as the units of analysis. Explain how each would be used. Be sure that each of the three types of units is illustrated in your answer.

EXERCISE 6.5

Suppose you are interested in studying issues in refugee resettlement. Show how a specific topic in this area would be researched differently for each of the following designs: cross-sectional, trend, cohort, and panel.

EXERCISE 6.6

Suppose you find in one of your studies on refugee resettlement that communities with larger numbers of refugees have higher crime rates. Your research assistant writes a first draft of the research report and concludes that this finding indicates that refugees contribute to a higher crime rate. How would you explain the ecological fallacy the assistant is making?

DISCUSSION QUESTIONS

1. Discuss the steps you would take and the sources you would examine to ensure that your literature review would be thorough.

2. Suppose a social work doctoral student concerned with feminist issues wanted to undertake a doctoral dissertation focusing on the following research question: What role does earlier sexual abuse in their lives play in influencing women's decisions to become topless dancers? Discuss why you think this research question does or does not fall within the boundaries of *social work* research. If you think it does not fall within social work boundaries, discuss how the graduate student could modify the question to fit more clearly within social work boundaries.

3. Some people argue that explanatory studies are more important than exploratory or descriptive studies. Do you agree? Why or why not?

CROSSWORD PUZZLE

ACROSS

1 Polite word in a request
7 Part of a wedding vow
9 Knight's title
12 CIA clandestine operatives
13 THE PURPOSE OF SOME RESEARCH STUDIES IS TO ______ A PHENOMEMON (DEVELOP A ROUGH UNDERSTANDING OF IT)
15 Weird ______ Yankovich
16 Surfer's need
18 (WITH 27 DOWN) PROBLEM CONNECTED WITH GENERALIZING FROM GROUPS TO INDIVIDUALS AS UNITS OF ANALYSIS
21 ______ tag (child's playground game)
22 The empire state (abbrev.)
23 Substitute for a lost item
25 More's opposite
27 Evergreen tree
28 Pull a disabled auto
29 I am, you are, she ______
30 Approximately
32 IF YOU HAVE ENOUGH RESOURCES, YOUR RESEARCH QUESTION MAY BE ______ TO STUDY
33 Initials for an American automobile corporation
34 Not out
35 Short for hello
36 Spare the ______, spoil the child
37 PURPOSE OF STUDIES SEEKING TO ANSWER THE QUESTION "WHY?"
40 Powerful servers in tennis or super test takers
41 Cry of discovery
43 Baby's wail
44 James Bond or Mata Hari
46 ______ Abner
47 Sooner state (abbrev.)
49 Source of artistic inspiration
50 First word in a Shakespeare comedy
55 Second word in a Shakespeare comedy
56 Scottish cap
57 Dan Rather's employer
60 A GOOD SOURCE FOR FINDING AN IMPORTANT RESEARCH TOPIC
63 Bubonic plague carrier
64 French friend
65 TYPE OF LONGITUDINAL STUDY BASED ON SAMPLES DRAWN FROM THE GENERAL POPULATION
67 Popular cola drink
68 Addict's cause of death (abbrev.)
70 Abbreviation for gym class
71 Al Gore, Bob Dole, and George McGovern
73 TYPICAL UNITS OF ANALYSIS
76 ______ way, Jose!
77 The Grapes ______ Wrath
78 Commercial
79 FDR's successor

DOWN

1 TYPE OF LONGITUDINAL STUDY INVOLVING SAME SAMPLE OF PEOPLE EACH TIME
2 Shirt size between Med. and XL (abbrev.)
3 Wide shoe size
4 WITH 31 DOWN: THE PEOPLE OR THINGS SOCIAL RESEARCHERS OBSERVE
5 Town in Normandy, France, near D-Day invasion
6 Spanish for is
7 THE PURPOSE OF SOME RESEARCH STUDIES IS TO ______ PRECISELY THE CHARACTERISTICS OF SOME POPULATION
8 Beast of burden
9 AN IMPORTANT RESEARCH QUESTION SHOULD PASS THE ______ TEST
10 Retirement account or George Gershwin's brother
11 WHAT TO DO WITH 60 ACROSS
14 ______ fiction
17 Adorable alien
19 A GOOD RESEARCH QUESTION SHOULD BE ANSWERABLE IN MORE THAN ______ POSSIBLE WAY
20 Flight Prefix
24 ______ sense
25 Legal document for mortgage lenders
26 Source of financial aid for the disabled (abbrev.)
27 SEE 18 ACROSS
31 SEE 4 DOWN
32 ONE TYPE OF COST TO ANTICIPATE WHEN CONSIDERING A STUDY'S FEASIBILITY
33 SOME UNITS OF ANALYSIS
35 hinder
37 A COMMON PURPOSE OF SOCIAL WORK RESEARCH THAT CAN INVOLVE EXPLORATORY, DESCRIPTIVE OR EXPLANATORY PURPOSES
38 Type of bird or whimsical reason for doing something
39 Region of USA known for lobsters, chowder, and several Ivy League schools (abbrev.)
42 Opposite of her
43 TYPE OF LONGITUDINAL STUDY BASED ON SAMPLES DRAWN FROM MULTIPLE SPECIFIC SUBPOPULATIONS
44 Source of skin cancer
45 Oh come all ______ faithful
48 Attentive
49 Silent performer
51 Alphabetical sequence
53 Robin, to Batman
54 Unwanted target of diet and exercise
57 ______-SECTIONAL STUDIES ARE BASED ON OBSERVATIONS MADE AT ONE POINT IN TIME
58 How to cook a pie
59 Ship's section or type of disciplinarian
61 ______ Henry the Eighth I am
62 Initials of a research text and crossword puzzle author
63 Luke warm
67 Young horse
69 HST's successor
71 ______ Vegas
72 GWB (43) to GHWB (41)
73 ______ I were a rich man (song from Fiddler on the Roof)
74 State where you can find Monticello (abbrev.)
75 Educational institute in Oahu (abbrev.)

CHAPTER 7

Conceptualization and Operationalization

OBJECTIVES

1. Define independent, dependent, and extraneous variables.
2. Provide an example of a properly constructed hypothesis related to social work practice and identify its independent variable and dependent variable.
3. Illustrate how an extraneous variable, when controlled, might explain away a relationship between an independent and dependent variable.
4. Illustrate how the same variable can be independent, dependent, or extraneous, depending on the nature and conceptualization of the study.
5. Provide examples of positive, negative, and curvilinear relationships.
6. Discuss how operational definitions differ from other types of definitions.
7. Provide three examples of abstract social work constructs and how each could be operationally defined using direct observation, self-reports and available records.
8. Discuss the role of existing scales in operationally defining variables, including their advantages and disadvantages.
9. Identify four issues to be considered in choosing the most appropriate existing scale as an operational definition for a particular variable in a particular study.
10. Provide an example of how the choice of how to operationally define a variable can influence the findings of a study related to social work practice.
11. Explain why some researchers believe that we can measure anything that exists, and illustrate how in attempting to measure things that exist, they often measure things that don't really exist in the real world.
12. Define mediating and moderating variables and discuss how they differ.
13. Define and illustrate reification.

PRACTICE-RELEVANT SUMMARY

If you've had experience in social work practice settings, you probably have observed that the terms emphasized in this chapter—terms like *operational definitions, extraneous variables,* and so forth—are not commonly used by social work practitioners. And yet those terms are highly applicable to the daily practices of social workers.

Consider, for example, the material on conceptual explication discussed at the beginning of the chapter. In the assessment phase of direct practice, we deal with presenting problems that we investigate clinically. We seek to understand why a particular target problem is occurring. What is causing it? What seems to have been helpful to the client system in the past in dealing with the problem? These questions imply hypotheses, which consist of independent and dependent variables. The postulated, tentative explanation is the *hypothesis*. What we think may explain variation in the target problem is the *independent variable;* the variation in the target problem that we seek to explain is the *dependent variable*.

We even deal with *extraneous variables*. Suppose we are treating a child who has been chronically depressed, and we note that each time his depressive symptoms worsen we provide a brief cognitive-behavioral intervention for several sessions and then the symptoms ameliorate. Suppose we are discussing our independent variable (the nature of our intervention) and dependent variable (degree of depressive symptomatology) with other members of the clinical team, and a colleague notes that the symptoms seem to worsen shortly before school resumes after extended summer and Christmas vacations and then ameliorate after a couple of weeks of classes. In wondering whether the resumption of school is the real cause of the swings in depressive symptomatology, our colleague is postulating this as an extraneous variable. Another colleague might postulate the taking of antidepressant medication as another extraneous variable, noting that the child begins taking the medication at the same times that our intervention takes place and then stops taking it after things get better.

Note that there is nothing inherent in any of these variables that makes them independent, dependent, or extraneous. We can postulate that the closer to school resuming (the independent variable), the more the depressive symptoms (the dependent variable). This would be a positive relationship, because both variables increase together. We can postulate the more consistently the client takes antidepressants (the independent variable), the less the depressive symptoms (the dependent variable). This would be a negative (or inverse) relationship, because as one variable increases the other decreases.

Note also that operational definitions are implicit in this illustration. How would the practitioner, her colleagues, or the client know that depressive symptoms are ameliorating or worsening unless they were able to speak in observable terms about the indicators of depression? Social work practitioners, like social work researchers, have a wide variety of options available for operationally defining concepts. These options come in three broad categories: *self-reports, direct observation,* and the *examination of available records*. In the above illustration, for example, practitioners might observe the client's mood during the interview. They might rely on parent reports of how often the client cries, stays secluded in his room, and so on. They might rely on client self-reports of similar behaviors. Alternatively, they might administer a paper-and-pencil depression scale to the client or examine available school records of classroom attendance, grades and conduct. Or they might even do all of these.

Perhaps the trickiest idea in this chapter is the notion that we can measure concepts like depression on the one hand, yet on the other hand we can point out that abstract concepts like depression don't really exist in the real world. The term *depression* is nothing more than a mental image—a summary device for bringing together observations and experiences that have something in common. Because depression is just a summary word, we cannot measure it directly. But by operationally defining it we can specify the observable components it covers (that is, crying, remaining isolated, and so on) and then directly measure those indicators. In so doing, we indirectly measure the concept of depression.

Many purely qualitative studies do not articulate operational definitions. Rather than restrict their observations to predetermined operational indicators, researchers conducting qualitative studies often prefer to let the meanings of phenomena emerge from their observations.

REVIEW QUESTIONS

1. Which of the following is ***NOT*** an attribute of a good hypothesis?

    a. It should be clear and specific.
    b. It should be a truism.
    c. It should be value-free.
    d. It should be testable.

2. If we test the hypothesis that the well-being of abused children will be better after they are placed with relatives than after they are placed in foster care not with relatives, and we find that this is true only for children above a certain age, then age is what kind of variable?

    a. Independent
    b. Dependent
    c. Control or extraneous
    d. Independent or dependent, depending on whether it is stated at the beginning or end of the hypothesis

3. In the example in question 2 above, level of well-being is what kind of variable?

   a. Independent
   b. Dependent
   c. Control or extraneous
   d. Independent or dependent, depending on whether it is stated at the beginning or end of the hypothesis

4. In the example in question 2 above, where placed (that is, type of placement) is what kind of variable?

   a. Independent
   b. Dependent
   c. Control or extraneous
   d. Independent or dependent, depending on whether it is stated at the beginning or end of the hypothesis

5. In social work studies testing hypotheses involving the variable "marital satisfaction," that variable is:

   a. Always the independent variable
   b. Always the dependent variable
   c. Either independent or dependent, depending on how it is being conceptualized in a particular study
   d. Independent or dependent, depending on whether it is stated at the beginning or end of the hypothesis
   e. Both c and d are true

6. If children who have been in foster care longer also have more behavioral problems, then this is what kind of relationship?

   a. Positive
   b. Negative
   c. Curvilinear
   d. Causal

7. If children who have been in foster care longer have fewer behavioral problems, then this is what kind of relationship?

   a. Positive
   b. Negative
   c. Curvilinear
   d. Causal

8. Suppose children who witness more marital violence express more anxiety than those who witness less violence, but that after a certain extremely high level of violence witnessed they become numb and then express less anxiety than those witnessing moderate levels of violence. This is what kind of relationship?

   a. Positive
   b. Negative
   c. Curvilinear
   d. None of the above

9. Which of the following would ***NOT*** be part of an operational definition of children's well-being?

   a. Degree of unhappiness
   b. Score on a child behavior problem scale
   c. Whether or not in residential care for emotional disorder
   d. School performance records, indicating grades, truancy, or tardiness, for example

10. Which of the following statements is true about the text's argument about measuring anything that exists and about reification?

    a. We can measure indicators of anything that exists.
    b. We can indirectly measure some abstract concepts that don't exist.
    c. It is incorrect to assume that some concepts exist in the real world just because we can measure their indicators.
    d. All of the above.

11. Which of the following statements is true about choosing an existing scale to administer to children as an operational definition of their level of depression before and after treatment?

    a. It should be lengthy; brief scales are too risky.
    b. It should not show changes in scores over time unless the degree of improvement has been substantial.
    c. It should be easy for the children to complete.
    d. It should be reliable and valid.
    e. All of the above are true.
    f. Only c and d are true.

12. A study finds that Intervention A is more effective than Intervention B with African American clients, but the opposite is true for Mexican-American clients. Therefore, ethnicity is what kind of variable?

    a. Independent
    b. Dependent
    c. Moderating
    d. Mediating

EXERCISE 7.1

Select one of the following concepts: level of caregiver burden, quality of life, feminism, culturally sensitive practice.

1. Provide a conceptual, or theoretical, definition of the concept.

2. Specify two different, reasonable ways to operationally define the concept.

EXERCISE 7.2

Consider the following three variables: level of client functioning, quality of worker-client relationship, number of services utilized.

1. Specify a hypothesis involving two of these variables, and explain how the third might operate as an extraneous variable and what could be done to control for it.

2. Specify another hypothesis involving the above variables, but change the independent and dependent variables. Explain how this could be.

EXERCISE 7.3

Consider the variables: (1) duration of caregiving for an elderly parent with Alzheimer's disease, and (2) degree of caregiver burden. Draw a graph depicting a curvilinear relationship between these variables and explain how this could be.

DISCUSSION QUESTIONS

1. Not everyone agrees with the assertion in the textbook that we can measure anything that exists. Some argue that social work practitioners commonly know and deal with things about their clients that they cannot measure. Do you agree? Why or why not?

Using either the concept of feminism or level of caregiver burden, explain what it would mean to reify the concept. Explain how we can measure the concept on the one hand, yet claim it doesn't exist on the other.

CROSSWORD PUZZLE

ACROSS

1 AN EXTANEOUS VARIABLE CAN ALSO BE CALLED A ______ VARIABLE
6 ______ here to eternity
10 This number does not change when squared
11 Failing grade
12 George Washington ______ here
15 Grades before middle school (abbrev.)
18 TYPE OF RELATIONSHIP BETWEEN VARIABLES
22 What appears on the state flag of Texas
23 THE RELATIONSHIP BETWEEN HEIGHT AND WEIGHT IS ______
28 Cute alien
29 Explosive acronym
30 Poetic before
32 Greek letter found on auto tires
34 OPERATIONAL DEFINITIONS SPECIFY HOW TO ______ VARIABLES
37 Barbeque tool or type of antisocial behavior
39 sound
43 EXISTING ______ ARE OFTEN USED AS OPERATIONAL DEFINITIONS
45 Previa, Windstar, or Mazda MPV
46 Exist
47 Table staple
49 EXAMINATION OF ______ RECORDS
53 College entrance exam
54 Direction from New Orleans to Atlanta
55 Full of limes
57 RT's offensive counterpart in football
58 Personnel
59 Desirable sound from a motor or kitten
61 Craze
64 Create anew
68 She loves ______, yeah, yeah, yeah
69 Dorothy's Aunty ______ in Kansas
70 Second musical note
71 A TYPE OF BIAS
74 ______ as a button
75 Stall
78 WHAT YOU CAN DO WITH ANYTHING THAT EXISTS AND SOME CONSTRUCTS THAT DON'T REALLY EXIST

DOWN

1 MENTAL IMAGE
2 ______ a roll
3 Close to
4 Short for regard
5 Lawrence ______ Arabia
6 Escapes
7 WHAT ONE VARIABLE DOES WITH ANOTHER VARIABLE IN A HYPOTHESIS THAT IS SUPPORTED BY EVIDENCE
8 TYPE OF DEFINITION STATED IN OBSERVABLE TERMS
9 1970s TV production company featuring Mary, Rhoda, Ted, and Ed
19 River in France
20 TYPE OF RELATIONSHIP (ALSO CALLED NEGATIVE)
21 Maiden name
24 ______ the waterfront
25 Ceases
26 HYPOTHESES SHOULD BE ______
32 ______ peeve
35 Ballpoint pen company
40 Eggs
41 Way in
42 OPERATIONAL DEFINITIONS SHOULD NOT HAVE GENDER ______
44 Tilts
47 ONE WAY TO OPERATIONALLY DEFINE VARIABLES IS THROUGH ______ REPORTS
50 HYPOTHESES SHOULD BE _____-FREE
51 ONE CATEGORY OF A VARIABLE, SUCH AS MALE OR FEMALE
52 Don't ______ ______ it! (That's very unlikely)
56 Questionable
59 For
60 TLC Provider
62 Major anatomical artery
63 Owed
65 Old pro
66 Flightless bird
67 Swap
71 Magna ______ laude
72 Meadow
73 Player to the left of the LT
76 ______ and behold!
77 Slang for hi, or half of a child's toy

42 OPERATIONAL DEFINITIONS SHOULD NOT HAVE GENDER ______
44 Tilts
47 ONE WAY TO OPERATIONALLY DEFINE VARIABLES IS THROUGH ______ REPORTS
50 HYPOTHESES SHOULD BE _____-FREE
51 ONE CATEGORY OF A VARIABLE, SUCH AS MALE OR FEMALE
52 Don't ______ ______ it! (That's very unlikely)
56 Questionable
59 For
60 TLC Provider
62 Major anatomical artery
63 Owed
65 Old pro

DOWN

66 Flightless bird
67 Swap
71 Magna ______ laude
72 Meadow
73 Player to the left of the LT
76 ______ and behold!
77 Slang for hi, or half of a child's toy

CHAPTER 8

Measurement

OBJECTIVES

1. Define, contrast and give examples of random measurement error and systematic measurement error.

2. Identify two common biases that contribute to systematic measurement error and explain how they operate.

3. Explain the similarities and differences in the ways that written self-reports, interviews, direct behavioral observation and examining available records are vulnerable to measurement errors.

4. Explain the purpose of triangulation and give an example of it.

5. Define reliability.

6. Identify three types of reliability and explain how each could be assessed.

7. Define validity.

8. Identify and define three types of validity.

9. Define instrument sensitivity and discuss why it is important.

10. Explain the difference between criterion and construct validity and give an example of each.

11. Discuss the relationship between reliability and validity.

12. Discuss how reliability and validity are approached in qualitative research in a different manner than in quantitative research.

PRACTICE-RELEVANT SUMMARY

Although social work practitioners and researchers may use different language when they deal with measurement, and although the term *measurement* may be more commonly employed when research is being discussed than during practitioners' daily discourse, measurement is an integral part of social work practice. When practitioners interview clients for the purpose of treatment planning, for example, they are measuring things. They may be measuring the nature and severity of the target problem. They may be measuring other problems and forces that influence the target problem. They may be estimating the extent of motivation, capacity, and opportunity in the client system to alleviate the target problem. They may note that different parts of the client system provide conflicting information, and they may therefore have to make measurement decisions about how to handle these inconsistent measures.

No matter which measurement is being used – direct observation, self-reports or examining available records – the measurement process is extremely vulnerable to errors. Practitioners and researchers alike need to be aware of the potential for these errors to occur and must take steps to deal with them. Although practitioners may use different language than researchers when they notice these measurement problems, they are dealing with essentially the same principles as are discussed in this chapter. For example, if they notice that a person contradicts something he or she said earlier, they will realize that something is amiss in the information being provided, because the information is inconsistent.

When people provide inconsistent information, researchers call the information unreliable. The term *reliability* refers to the degree of consistency in the information. Researchers and practitioners can encounter three major forms of consistency (or inconsistency), or reliability (or unreliability), in their information. One form occurs when informants provide information at one point in time that is consistent (or inconsistent) with information they provided at an earlier point in time. This is called *test-retest reliability*. One problem with this form of reliability is that sometimes the reality being depicted by informants really does change between the two time points at which information is provided. However, researchers may still need to assess this form of reliability, particularly if they are assessing the stability of a measure over time.

Another form of reliability is assessed in connection to whether different pieces of information given at the same point in time, by the same informant, are consistent. This is called *internal consistency reliability*. If a divorced mother tells you, early in an interview, that she wants to keep custody of her son, but later in the interview indicates that perhaps it would be best if he lived with his father, you may note a potential inconsistency between the two statements uttered during the same interview. You would be concerned with the internal consistency reliability of the information. Researchers would be worrying about the same type of reliability if they noted contradictory responses to similar items of the same measurement scale.

A third form of reliability deals with whether different people are consistent in the information they provide. Thus, if a mother portrays a child as well behaved, but the father portrays the child as defiant and disobedient, a practitioner would see inconsistency. Researchers term this form of reliability *interrater reliability*. Researchers are typically concerned with this form of reliability when they are using experts to rate something, such as the quality of an interview or the severity of an emotional problem.

Regardless of which type of reliability we use, the implication of inconsistency is the same: if the information is inconsistent, something is wrong with some part of it. Researchers term this form of measurement error *random error,* because there is nothing occurring in a systematic fashion to consistently produce the same misleading information. Random error commonly occurs when respondents don't understand our questions, are fatigued, or aren't concentrating on what is being said.

Practitioners as well as researchers also recognize that information can be consistent but still be wrong. Thus, the child welfare worker investigating reported child abuse realizes that just because a respondent consistently denies abuse, that doesn't guarantee that the truth is being told. Fear of the consequences of affirming the abuse may lead to a bias that consistently results in erroneous information. Researchers call this type of error (or bias) *systematic error.*

When researchers refer to the degree to which a measurement approach avoids systematic error, they refer to the *validity* of the measure. Measures can be reliable, but not valid. Reliability is a necessary, but not sufficient condition for validity. The two most important types of validity a measure may have are *criterion-related validity* and *construct validity. Criterion-related validity* is assessed by seeing if the measure in question produces information correlated by an independent, external measure of the same construct. Thus, a scale to measure posttraumatic stress disorder (PTSD) would have criterion-relation validity if people undergoing treatment for PTSD score worse on it than people who are not in treatment for PTSD.

There are several subtypes of criterion-related validity. If we validate a measure according to its ability to predict a criterion that will occur in the future, we are dealing with *predictive validity.* If we validate it according to its correspondence to a criterion that is known concurrently, we are dealing with *concurrent validity.* If the criterion we are using involves differentiating between groups that are known to differ in respect to the construct that the instrument intends to measure, we are dealing with *known groups validity.* When selecting an instrument to measure treatment effects, we need to make sure that it is capable of detecting subtle changes over time. This capability is termed the *sensitivity* of an instrument. Knowing that an instrument has known-groups validity by virtue of its ability to differentiate extreme differences between groups does not necessarily mean that it will have adequate sensitivity to detect subtle improvements in one of the groups.

Construct validity is assessed by seeing if the measure in question produces data more consistent with an independent criterion of the same construct than with a criterion of a related construct. Thus, the above PTSD scale would have criterion-related validity but not construct validity, if the difference in scores on it between people undergoing treatment for depression and those not in treatment for depression was greater than the difference between the PTSD criterion groups. In addition to the above form of validity, you may also encounter the terms *face validity* and *content validity. Face validity* refers primarily to whether items in the measure merely appear to be valid indicators of the concept intended to be measured. *Content validity* refers to whether expert judges agree that the measure covers the full range of meanings included within the concept.

Qualitative researchers approach issues of reliability and validity somewhat differently than quantitative researchers. Qualitative inquiry relies less on standardized instruments. Instead, validity is pursued through in-depth observations and interviews with much smaller samples. The idea is not to come up with a particular measure that can be utilized repeatedly in a standardized fashion to quickly measure the same concept across large numbers of people. Instead, the idea is to describe the everyday lives and deep personal meanings of people in such rich detail that readers would understand what was measured and what it meant without having to wonder if a particular instrument has validity or reliability. Qualitative researchers who follow different epistemological paradigms disagree on the nature and extent of the role of assessing the reliability and validity of their work.

REVIEW QUESTIONS

1. Suppose you have a brother and a sister complete a complicated scale to assess the extent of alcohol abuse among their parents. Suppose one's answers indicate a lot of abuse, while the other's answers indicate very little abuse. This would be an example of:

   a. Potential systematic measurement error
   b. Possible unreliability
   c. Possible bias
   d. All of the above

2. The child who denied his parents' truly high level of alcohol abuse (in question 1 above) might be responding in a manner that can be called:

   a. Social desirability bias
   b. Acquiescent response set
   c. Random error
   d. Triangulation

3. If the child responding to the above scale did not understand the complex language in it, his answers would likely contain:

   a. Social desirability bias
   b. Acquiescent response set
   c. Random error
   d. Triangulation
   e. Systematic error

4. In the above scale you find that responses to some items contradict responses to other items. This is an example of:

   a. Poor face validity
   b. Low internal consistency reliability
   c. Low test-retest reliability
   d. Low interrater reliability

5. When we administer the same scale twice to the same people, we are seeking to assess the scale's:

   a. Face validity
   b. Construct validity
   c. Internal consistency reliability
   d. Test-retest reliability
   e. Criterion-related validity

6. You show your scale to your distinguished professor, an internationally renowned expert on the problem being measured, and she enthusiastically agrees that every item on the scale looks excellent.

   a. This supports the scale's face validity.
   b. This does not support the scale's empirical validity.
   c. More testing of the scale's validity is needed.
   d. You can be confident that the scale has criterion-related or construct validity.
   e. All of the above.
   f. a, b, and c are true.

7. You find that people in treatment for low self-esteem have an average score of 20 on your self-esteem scale, indicating much lower self-esteem than people not in treatment, whose average score is 40. Then you administer your self-esteem scale to people in treatment and not in treatment for depression. The average score is 10 for those in treatment for depression and 50 for those not in treatment. You have shown that your scale:

   a. Has criterion-related validity
   b. Lacks construct validity
   c. May be measuring depression more than self-esteem
   d. All of the above

8. Which of the following statements is/are true about how reliability and validity are approached in qualitative studies?

   a. Qualitative inquiry relies less on standardized instruments.
   b. In qualitative inquiry validity is pursued through in-depth observations and interviews.
   c. In qualitative inquiry the idea is to describe the everyday lives and deep personal meanings of people in rich detail.
   d. Qualitative researchers who follow different epistemological paradigms disagree about the role of assessing the reliability and validity of their work.
   e. All of the above.

EXERCISE 8.1

In evaluating the outcome of your family preservation program, you decide to administer lengthy scales to parents, children, and their practitioners in your program and in a comparison program. The scales are designed to assess the well-being of children and the quality of parenting.

1. What are some reasons you might expect to find problems of reliability in the scales?

2. Identify three ways you might assess three different types of reliability regarding the scales.

3. Explain why you would be concerned about the validity of the scales even if you found them reliable. Explain, also, why you might not bother to assess their validity if you found them to be very unreliable.

4. What are some reasons you might expect to find problems of validity in the scales?

5. Identify how you might assess the criterion-related validity of the scales.

EXERCISE 8.2

You are providing a psychoeducational support group intervention to family members caring for a person living with AIDS. You want to measure the degree of stigma the caregivers are experiencing and whether it diminishes after they participate in your group. You can find no suitable measure of stigma, so you design one yourself, consisting of the following four items:

How often do you feel:

Isolated?	___Often	___Rarely	___Never
Ashamed?	___Often	___Rarely	___Never
Hopeless?	___Often	___Rarely	___Never
Like crying?	___Often	___Rarely	___Never

Suppose you assessed the criterion-related validity of your scale and found that individuals entering your group answered "often" much more frequently than individuals who were not caregivers of persons living with AIDS. Suppose, however, that your colleague constructively advised you that although you demonstrated criterion-related validity, that was not enough. In this case, she argued, you need to proceed to assess construct validity.

1. Explain why she may have reached this conclusion. (What is it about your scale and competing constructs that may have led her to suggest this? Can you think of a competing construct she may have in mind?)

2. Following her advice, how would you go about assessing the scale's construct validity?

DISCUSSION QUESTIONS

1. Some clinical social workers believe that existing scales that measure clinical problems (self-esteem, depression, parent-child relationships, and so on) should be used routinely during the assessment and later phases of clinical practice. Some others disagree, relying instead on clinical interviews. What do you think about this?

2. Some social workers are drawn to a field of practice in part because of their own life experiences and previous issues that resemble the problems they encounter in that field. But not all social workers in a particular agency are the same in this respect. They have different life experiences and different issues, and they may be attracted to the type of services provided by their agency for different reasons. Suppose you are working in a child and family service agency where caseloads are heavy and assessments are based exclusively on interviews. You are struck by the frequency with which some (but not all) practitioners attribute a child's or a family's difficulties almost exclusively to the father's or the mother's need to be controlling. What are some sources of systematic and random error in this agency's approach to assessment? How could the agency assess the reliability and validity of its assessment practices?

   Discuss the similarities and differences between qualitative and quantitative inquiry with regard to how issues of reliability and validity are handled.

CROSSWORD PUZZLE

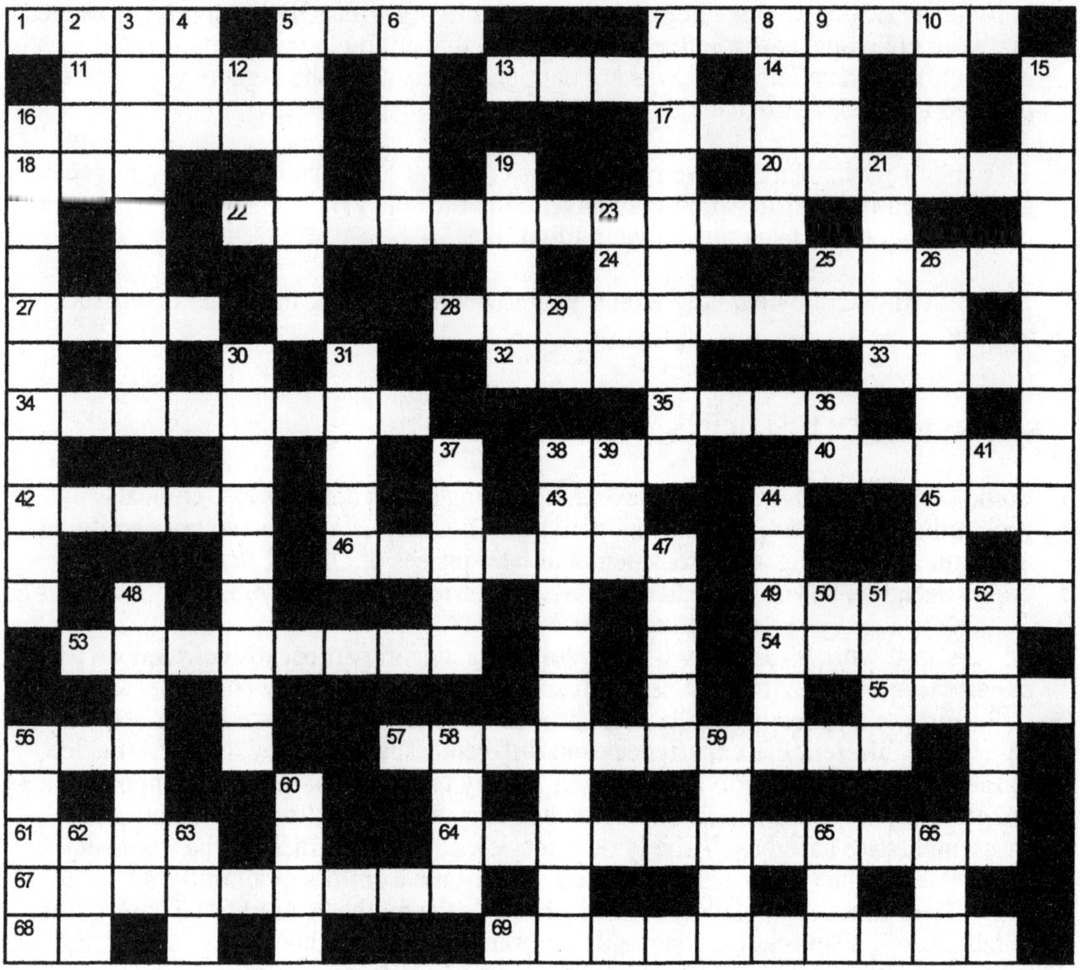

ACROSS

1 LEAST MEANINGFUL TYPE OF VALIDITY
5 Observe
7 TYPE OF VALIDITY REFERRING TO DEGREE TO WHICH A MEASURE COVERS THE RANGE OF MEANINGS WITHIN A CONCEPT
11 Region of Africa
13 LOWEST POSSIBLE COEFFICIENT ALPHA
14 Doctor's command, "Say ______"
16 TYPE OF MEASUREMENT ERROR ASSOCIATED WITH INCONSISTENCY
17 City in Alaska
18 Asner, Poe, Fisher, etc.
20 Goes in
22 ONE TYPE OF CRITERION VALIDITY
24 ______T (I pity the fool who doesn't know this)
25 Not lower
27 Grad
28 TYPE OF RELIABILITY INVOLVING TWO OBSERVERS
32 ______ with the wind
33 Appear
34 ______ CONSISTENCY RELIABILITY
35 New star
38 Mouse chaser
40 Of birds
42 Not active
43 Cry of surprise
45 Spy agency
46 Showing the relative position in a quantitative sequence (adjective for *order*)
49 Van Gogh or Monet
53 A MEASURE THAT REALLY MEASURES WHAT IT INTENDS TO MEASURE HAS THIS
54 Courageous
55 Monthly budget item
56 Tennis segment
57 TYPE OF RELIABILITY REQUIRING TWO ADMINISTRATIONS OF A MEASURE
61 Standard
64 THE ABILITY OF A MEASURE TO DETECT SUBTLE CHANGES OVER TIME
67 PEOPLE OFTEN TEND TO CONVEY A SOCIALLY ______ IMAGE OF THEMSELVES
68 One year ahead of jr.
69 TYPE OF MEASUREMENT ERROR ASSOCIATED WITH BIAS

DOWN

2 Type of educational instit. (abbrev.)
3 TYPE OF VALIDITY THAT RULES OUT ALTERNATIVE CONSTRUCTS
4 Finish
5 "__ ___ is an Island"
6 Toss
7 ANOTHER TYPE OF CRITERION VALIDITY
8 Cites
9 Now's companion
10 River in Egypt
12 What to do on green
15 ONE OF TWO TYPES OF VALIDITY REQUIRED FOR CONSTRUCT VALIDITY
16 CONSISTENCY IN MEASUREMENT
19 Ripening or growing old
21 Kinds
23 Portent
25 Prestigious institute of higher education in Texas, abbreviated
26 A THIRD TYPE OF CRITERION VALIDITY
29 ______ be or not ______ be
30 ______-RELATED VALIDITY (THE DEGREE TO WHICH A MEASURE RELATES WITH SOME EXTERNAL CRITERION
31 Fraction, proportion or quotient
37 Warbucks or longlegs
38 ATTRIBUTE OF RELIABILITY
39 Cry of discovery
41 Spielberg movie
44 TEST RETEST RELIABILITY ASSESSES WHETHER A MEASURE IS ______ OVER TIME
47 Not tight
48 A MULTIDIMENSIONAL SCALE HAS AT LEAST TWO ______
50 Monopoly square (abbreviated)
51 Having a sharp, sour taste
52 One who guards
56 Smoothes woodwork
58 Alleviate
59 *Research Methods for Social Work*
60 TYPE OF SYSTEMATIC MEASUREMENT ERROR: ACQUIESCENT RESPONSE SET ______
62 "…______ the land of the free…."
63 ______ term exam
65 Through
66 ______ANGULATION

CHAPTER 9

Constructing Measurement Instruments

OBJECTIVES

1. Construct items for a questionnaire that include both closed- and open-ended questions.

2. Show how the same variable can be measured with an open- or closed-ended questions.

3. Identify the reasons why it might be better to choose open- or closed-ended questions, and what the trade-offs are in the choice.

4. Develop a questionnaire that is clear and simple to complete and that avoids questions that are double-barreled, overly difficult or complex, irrelevant, biased, or illogically sequenced.

5. Recognize flaws in questionnaires developed by others.

6. Identify alternative questionnaire formats.

7. Write clear instructions for a questionnaire and its different sections.

8. Explain the difference between a questionnaire and a scale.

9. Identify the steps taken in identifying potential items for a scale and the criteria used in deciding which ones to include.

10. Construct a brief, simple scale of a variable.

11. Identify different prominent scaling procedures.

12. Identify procedures for anticipating and preventing cultural bias or cultural insensitivity in scale construction.

13. Discuss the similarities and differences between the construction of quantitative and qualitative measurement instruments.

PRACTICE-RELEVANT SUMMARY

Social workers in various roles and fields of practice early in their careers commonly encounter situations where they must construct measurement instruments. Two common situations in which they must construct measurement instruments are when they need to assess client satisfaction with agency services, and when they have to determine client needs for various services. Typically, they will want or be required to construct instruments that are sound from the standpoint of research methodology, even though their purpose may not be to conduct research in the strictest sense. These, however, are not the only examples.

As practitioners begin the process of instrument construction, an early decision may be whether to ask close- or open-ended questions. Open-ended questions are often simpler to construct, and they give respondents the opportunity to answer in their own words and in the way that is most meaningful for them. The downside of this openness, however, is that you may be overwhelmed by the prospect of attempting to process and analyze the vast range of answers you may get to open-ended questions. Moreover, many of the answers may seem irrelevant or hard to decipher. Closed-ended questions, on the other hand, force respondents to answer according to categories that make sense in terms of your research goals, and they are much easier to process. However, they may miss information that clients could supply if an open-ended format were used. When you use closed-ended questions, make sure that your list of response categories is exhaustive and mutually exclusive.

Regardless of whether open- or closed-ended questions are used, they should be as short as possible. They should ask about things that are relevant to respondents and that respondents are willing to answer and capable of answering They should be worded clearly, in language that respondents understand. Items should not be worded in negative terms. Biasing words or phrases should always be avoided. Also to be avoided are double-barreled questions. These are questions that, sometimes subtly, combine two questions into one, thus leaving the respondent confused about how to answer and the practitioner unsure of what the answer really means.

Questionnaires, or other instruments, should be easy on the eyes and easy to complete. Items should be logically organized. Pages should be uncluttered. It should be clear to respondents where to place their check marks, X's, or other types of response. One option that may simplify responding is the use of contingency questions. These questions are used when some subsequent questions can be answered or skipped depending on how the respondent answers the contingency question. Another simplifying option is to present a matrix format to handle a series of consecutive questions that have the same set of response categories.

It is important to make sure that items are sequenced appropriately. Begin the instrument with items that are easy to answer and interesting. Save the tougher items, or more sensitive ones, for later. Be sensitive to whether and how the answer to one question conceivably might influence an answer to a later question. It is essential that your instrument begin with a clear set of instructions, and that additional instructions appear at the start of each new and different section of the instrument.

Sometimes the instruments you construct will include composite measures in which multiple items are combined to form a quantitative scale. For example, you might include ten items enabling respondents to indicate, on a scale of one to five, how satisfied they are with ten different aspects of service delivery. Then you could sum each client's responses to get an overall satisfaction score for that client. The items you select for your scale should have face validity (as discussed in Chapter 8). Each should represent one important, and different, aspect of the concept you are attempting to measure. In testing out your items, the responses to each item should vary. If everyone, or almost everyone, answers an item the same way, it offers nothing and should be dropped from the scale. Although not everyone should answer a particular item in the same way, the way people answer each item should be related to how they answer other items. This refers to the internal consistency of the scale (as discussed in Chapter 8). Items that do not relate to other items, or that are overly redundant with other items, should be dropped from the scale. Some prominent scaling procedures that you may want to follow in constructing your scale include Likert scaling and semantic differential scales.

In any field, but perhaps especially in social work, it is essential that your instrument be *culturally sensitive*. Steps you can take toward having a culturally sensitive instrument include immersion in the culture of the population to be studied before administering a measure developed on other populations, interviewing knowledgeable informants in the study population about the applicability of the measure, the use of bilingual interviewers, translating and back-translating the measure, and pre-testing.

If you are conducting a qualitative study, your measurement instruments are likely to differ from instruments used in quantitative studies in several key respects. Qualitative instruments are likely to be much less structured, to rely much more heavily on open-ended questions with in-depth probes, and to be administered in an interview format.

REVIEW QUESTIONS

1. When the variable "ethnicity" of parents is classified as White, African American, or Hispanic, the response categories can be called:

   a. Mutually exclusive
   b. Exhaustive
   c. Both of the above
   d. None of the above

2. The questionnaire item "How satisfied were you and your child with our multifamily and play therapy groups?" with response categories on a four-point scale from very satisfied to very dissatisfied, is an example of:

   a. A double-barreled question
   b. An open-ended question
   c. A negative item
   d. A semantic-differential scale

3. A potential shortcoming of closed-ended questions is:

   a. No opportunity to probe for more information
   b. Some important responses may be omitted from the response categories
   c. Some response categories might not be mutually exclusive
   d. All of the above
   e. None of the above

4. A questionnaire item lists possible social service facilities and asks community residents to enter a check mark beside each one they would ***NOT*** want to have located in their community. This is an example of:

   a. A double-barreled question
   b. An open-ended question
   c. A negative item
   d. All of the above

5. Which of the following statements is true about the way you should order items in a self-administered questionnaire?

   a. The order should usually be randomized.
   b. Get the dull items out of the way early; save the interesting ones for later.
   c. Pretesting the questionnaire in different forms can help indicate the best way to order the items.
   d. As long as each item is well constructed, the ordering of items is a minor issue.

6. Which of the following statements is a good guideline for the construction of self-administered questionnaires?

   a. Squeeze as many items as possible on each page to reduce the number of pages.
   b. Provide an introductory statement for each subsection.
   c. Avoid contingency questions; they are too confusing.
   d. All of the above.
   e. None of the above.

7. A Likert scale is developed with half of the items representing positive attitudes about welfare and the other half representing negative attitudes about welfare. Respondent 1 checks "strongly agree" to every item. Respondent 2 checks "strongly disagree" with every item. Respondent 3 checks "agree" with all the positive items and "disagree" with all the negative items. Which of the following statements is true about this example?

   a. Respondent 3 has mixed feelings.
   b. Respondent 1 has the most positive attitude score.
   c. Respondent 3 has the most positive attitude score.
   d. Respondent 2 has the most negative attitude score.
   e. Respondents 1 and 2 have the same attitude score.
   f. Only b and d are true.
   g. Only c and e are true.

8. Which of the following statements is true about the handling of missing data on some items of a scale?

   a. One acceptable option is to exclude from the analysis those few cases with missing data.
   b. It is sometimes acceptable to assign the middle value to cases with missing data.
   c. It might be acceptable to assign the mean (average) value to the missing item.
   d. All of the above.
   e. None of the above.

9. If you are conducting a qualitative study, your measurement instruments are likely to differ from instruments used in quantitative studies in which of the following respects?

   a. Qualitative instruments are likely to be much less structured.
   b. Qualitative instruments are likely to rely much more heavily on close-ended questions.
   c. Qualitative instruments are less likely to be administered in an interview format.
   d. All of the above.
   e. None of the above.

10. Steps you can take toward having a culturally sensitive instrument include:

    a. immersion in the culture of the population to be studied before administering a measure developed on other populations.
    b. interviewing knowledgeable informants in the study population about the applicability of the measure.
    c. using bilingual interviewers.
    d. translating and back-translating the measure.
    e. pretesting.
    f. All of the above.

11. Which of the following statements is true about pretesting questionnaires?

    a. Pretesting is needed only when you suspect an unusually strong possibility of wording errors.
    b. The pretest sample should be large – at least 50 people.
    c. The pretest sample should be should be like the people you intend to include in your study.
    d. All of the above.
    e. None of the above.

EXERCISE 9.1

Develop two versions of a brief questionnaire asking other social work students about their experiences in the social work education program. (For example, is it what they expected? Are they learning what they want? What do they want to do when they graduate? And so on.) Make one version entirely open-ended and the other entirely closed-ended. Administer each to a small group of students (perhaps 10 to 20 of them). Compare the answers you get to the two versions. Identify how the sets of answers differed. What advantages and disadvantages of each approach were illustrated by those answers?

EXERCISE 9.2

Suppose a questionnaire is developed to be administered to fourth- through sixth-grade clients in a Child Guidance Center. What is wrong with each of the following items, if they were on such a questionnaire? (Some items may have more than one thing wrong with them.)

1. Do your folks drink? yes no
2. Do you find your parents authoritarian? yes no
3. Do your mother and father work? yes no
4. How many drinks did your father have last week?____
5. Do you cheat in school? yes no
6. What do you want to do when you grow up? ______________________
7. What would you do if you were working on an assignment in class and the student sitting next to you started teasing you and then hit you after you tried to ignore his teasing?

   Tell the teacher ___
   Hit the student back ___
   Nothing ___
8. When your teacher works as hard as he or she can to make school enjoyable, do you think students should be obedient? yes___ no___
9. Do you agree that your therapist has done his or her job well in the way he or she has worked with you? yes___ no___

EXERCISE 9.3

Suppose you wanted to construct a scale to assess the quality of services delivered to clients. Discuss how you would identify potential items and select them on separate pages, develop two versions of a five-item summated scale to assess the above. Use the Likert scaling for one and the semantic differential for the other.

EXERCISE 9.4

Suppose you developed the following scale to measure the quality of parent-child relationships and got the following response frequencies in a pilot run of the scale with 100 clients. Which items would you drop from the scale? Why?

1. I love my child
   97 Strongly Agree
   3 Agree
   0 Disagree
   0 Strongly Disagree

2. I hate my child
   0 Strongly Agree
   0 Agree
   2 Disagree
   98 Strongly Disagree

3. I often argue with my child
   20 Strongly Agree
   30 Agree
   30 Disagree
   20 Strongly Disagree

4. My child often embarrasses me
   15 Strongly Agree
   25 Agree
   40 Disagree
   20 Strongly Disagree

DISCUSSION QUESTIONS

1. Discuss the steps you would take to ensure cultural sensitivity in constructing an instrument to assess the degree of burden and needs for social services experienced by recent Korean immigrants who are family caregivers of relatives with Alzheimer's disease.

2. Discuss what is wrong with the following questionnaire item, how it would be difficult to answer, and the ways responses might be misleading. In caring for your relative with Alzheimer's disease, do you feel the need for more social support and respite services?

3. Discuss the similarities and differences between the construction of quantitative and qualitative measurement instruments.

CROSSWORD PUZZLE

ACROSS

1 Adam's main squeeze
3 Gyro sandwich ingredient or essayist
7 No no for Jack Sprat
10 Bullmoose party candidate's initials
12 Two pts. (abbrev.)
14 AVOID THIS IN YOUR QUESTIONNAIRE ITEMS AND TERMS
16 Composer of Bolero
18 (WITH 33 DOWN) AVOID THIS IN YOUR INSTRUMENT QUESTIONS AND ITEMS
21 Accumulations
23 Cabinet member who heads this federal agency is supposed to protect the environment (abbrev.)
24 Suffix meaning resident of
25 Pleasant sigh
26 This football player tries to evade the right tackle's blocks (abbrev.)
27 Marina _____ Rey
28 Dorothy and Toto left and returned to this state (abbrev.)
29 Duel provocation
30 Poison _____

DOWN

1 (WITH 19 DOWN) QUESTIONS IN QUALITATIVE MEASURES HAVE THIS QUALITY
2 All men are created _____
4 Aids in a crime
5 Third musical note
6 Sheep sound
8 Abbreviation commonly seen at airports
9 Greek letter
10 Broadcast an event in video
11 Initials of creator of Long John Silver and Friday
13 Severe infectious pulmonary disease initials
15 COMMON TYPE OF COMPOSITE MEASURE
17 BEFORE USING A SCALE FOR THE FIRST TIME IN A STUDY, IT IS ESSENTIAL THAT IT BE_____
19 SEE 1 DOWN
20 A TYPE OF SCALE WITH RESPONSE CATEGORIES RANGING FROM STRONGLY AGREE TO STRONGLY DISAGREE
22 British fellow**32** Opposite of NW

ACROSS

33 ______ if you love Jesus or if the driver ahead of you is asleep at the wheel
34 Go kaput
35 Steady flow
38 Fool or donkey
39 IF YOUR MEASURE WILL BE COMPLETED BY MEMBERS OF DIFFERENT ETHNIC GROUPS, IT SHOULD BE ______ SENSITIVE
40 Asian Festival
41 Matador's foe
42 Administration of TLC
43 Direction from Los Angeles to Las Vegas
45 Direction from Pittsburgh to New York
46 BEFORE USING IT IN YOUR STUDY, YOUR QUESTIONNAIRE SHOULD BE ______
48 Feature of many modern hotel lobbies
49 Locale of The Great Gatsby (abbrev.)
50 ______ hoc committee
51 Smallest state (abbrev.)
52 Lawn clippings that can preserve lawn moisture
53 Craze
55 Two word memo phrase meaning concerning
57 Inexpensive restaurant
58 Prod or quiche ingredient
59 Psychedelic drug
61 Living thing
62 Second musical note
63 What to say when having your tonsils examined
65 Camping vehicle (abbrev.)
66 THESE SHOULD BE IN-DEPTH AND NEUTRAL IN QUALITATIVE MEASURES
68 Parenthetical abbreviation meaning for example
69 MAKE YOUR QUESTIONNAIRE ITEMS ______, SO RESPONDENTS WILL UNDERSTAND YOUR FRAME OF REFERENCE
71 Top
73 Twosome
74 Giant

DOWN

29 A ______ DIFFERENTIAL SCALE USES PAIRED OPPOSITES
31 Beatles hit with Paul McCartney singing solo
32 Town near Omaha Beach
33 SEE 18 ACROSS
35 More certain
36 Prestigious private university in Atlanta
37 Putin's negative reply
39 TYPE OF QUESTION THAT MAY BE ANSWERED OR SKIPPED, DEPENDING ON RESPONSE TO A PREVIOUS QUESTION
41 More weepy
44 AVOID ______ ITEMS WHEN CONSTRUCTING YOUR QUESTIONNAIRE
46 Woman's name that rhymes with unwanted e-mail
47 ______ What?!
50 Breezy indoor quality
53 ______ QUESTIONS CAN BE GROUPED TOGETHER WITH THE SAME SET OF RESPONSE CATEGORIES
54 This can help in catching butterflies or fish
56 Between C and RT in football (abbrev.)
57 There are two of this in nine
59 Dr. Zhivago's love
60 ______ ITEMS ARE BETTER THAN LONG ITEMS
63 Imitated
64 Impressive accomplishment
67 Health club
70 ______ Confidential
72 Nanny has three of this

CHAPTER 10

Causal Inference and Correlational Designs

OBJECTIVES

1. Define the terms *inference* and *causal inference* and their connection to research design in the evaluation of programs and practice.

2. Identify and explain the logic of the three criteria for inferring causality in the evaluation of programs and practice.

3. Recognize threats to internal validity that are and are not controlled in the practice evaluation and other research reports social workers commonly encounter in the professional literature or in agency documents.

4. Distinguish between correlation and causality in the practice information social workers encounter.

5. Identify and define threats to internal validity that are not controlled in correlational evaluations of programs and practice, and explain the logic of why they are not controlled.

6. Identify and explain the advantages and disadvantages of cross-sectional designs in the evaluation of programs and practice.

7. Identify and explain the advantages and disadvantages of case-control designs in the evaluation of programs and practice.

8. Identify and explain the advantages and disadvantages of longitudinal studies in the evaluation of programs and practice.

9. Explain the issue of external validity in evaluations of programs and practice, and distinguish to whom findings can and cannot be generalized in practice evaluation studies.

10. Describe the role and logic of the elaboration model when using correlational designs to evaluate programs and practice.
11. Explain the distinctions between replication, explanation, specification and interpretation in the elaboration model.

12. Illustrate a possible relationship affected by a suppressor, distorter, and antecedent variable in social work practice research.

13. Illustrate a possible spurious relationship in social work practice research.

PRACTICE-RELEVANT SUMMARY

Many social workers, quite early in their careers, find themselves caring quite a bit about a research issue they never anticipated caring about: the design of studies to evaluate practice effectiveness. Often the impetus for their concern is the requirement by funding sources that, in order to obtain funding for a new program or to renew funding for an ongoing program, they must conduct an study to evaluate the effectiveness of the program for which they seek new or renewed funds. To meet this requirement they commonly will seek out the services of a research methodologist who specializes in the evaluation of programs or interventions. If the social workers never learned, or forgot, the material in Chapter 10 (as well as in the next chapter), they probably will be puzzled by the research design expectations of the funding source and will have an uncomfortable relationship with their research consultant.

Some social workers, not well versed in research design, might think it should be sufficient merely to measure how well service recipients are doing after receiving the service. Other social workers, also not well versed in research design, might think it is enough to show that service recipients are better off after receiving services than before, not recognizing the need take into account myriad other factors that could have been operating during the same period to cause the improvement. The same social workers might also mistakenly believe that simply showing that a group that received services is doing better than any old group that did not happen to receive services is enough to prove that the services are effective. This notion overlooks the very real possibility that the two groups were not comparable to begin with and that perhaps the service recipients were just doing better than the others before services were provided.

Social work practitioners may so strongly believe in the value of the services they provide that they see no need to go beyond descriptive designs to be convinced that their services are effective. Funding sources, however, are likely to be more skeptical and to require that the services be evaluated with a design that controls for various threats to the internal validity. Questioning the design's *internal validity* means questioning whether the design adequately depicts whether the evaluated service is really the cause of the service outcome indicator(s) being measured.

To have a reasonably high degree of internal validity, a design should meet three criteria for inferring causality: (1) the cause (service) should precede the effect (outcome indicator being measured) in time; (2) variation in the provision of service should be empirically correlated with variation in outcome; and (3) alternative explanations for the correlation should be ruled out. Designs that do not meet all three criteria can be criticized for failing to control for certain threats to internal validity. One common threat is *history*, which refers to other events that may coincide with the services and that may be the real cause of the desired outcome. Another important threat is *maturation*, or the *passage of time*. Sometimes clients do better as time passes after a traumatic event, regardless of whether they received services during that period. Likewise, sometimes clients improve as they mature developmentally, regardless of the services they may or may not receive. Often the process of pre-testing influences the change that is observed on a posttest. Or perhaps the measures used at posttest were more prone to indicate better functioning than the measures used at pretest. *Statistical regression* can account for improved posttest scores when subjects are selected for treatment based on their extremely undesirable pretest scores. *Selection biases* can result in assigning to the evaluated service those cases that have the best chance to improve, or that are functioning better to begin with, and then comparing them to dissimilar cases with worse prognoses or worse pre-service functioning. Sometimes the *causal time sequence* is unclear, such as when service completers are functioning better than premature terminators. Did the better functioning result from completing the service? Or did it explain why some people were better able to complete services than others?

The best way to control for threats to internal validity, and thus to have a high degree of internal validity, is by using an experimental design to evaluate your program or intervention. (This is not the same as saying that experimental designs are the best designs for any kind of research. Studies that are not attempting to test causality would not use experimental designs but might produce findings of great value.) The cardinal feature of experimental designs is the use of *random assignment* of clients to an experimental group (service recipients) and to a control group (non-recipients), to ensure a high mathematical likelihood that the two groups are comparable on all relevant factors except the receipt of the service being evaluated. In social work practice settings, the non-recipients of the service being tested (that is, those in the control group) need not be denied any type of service. They simply could receive alternative services (usually the agency's routine services), and/or they could be put on a waiting list for the experimental service.

However, experimental designs often are not feasible in the real world of agency practice. Sometimes, therefore, it is necessary to use correlational designs. Three common correlational alternatives to experiments are cross-sectional studies, case-control studies and longitudinal studies. A cross-sectional study examines a phenomenon by taking a cross section of it at one point in time. The case-control design compares groups of cases that have had contrasting outcomes and then collects retrospective data about past differences that might explain the difference in outcomes. Longitudinal studies describe processes occurring over time and thus conduct their observations over an extended period.
Although cross-sectional, case-control, and longitudinal studies don't permit definitive, conclusive inferences about what is really causing what, they can support the plausibility of the notion that a program or intervention is the cause of a particular outcome. Likewise, if they show no relationship between a program or intervention and a particular outcome, then the notion of a causal relationship is less plausible.

However, correlation is not a sufficient basis for inferring causality. Consequently, correlational designs need to be augmented with multivariate statistical procedures that control for the possible influences of extraneous variables. The elaboration model illustrates the logic of that statistical control. For example, if the correlation between intervention and outcome remains essentially unchanged for each category of additional variables introduced in the multivariate analysis, we can say that the original relationship between intervention and outcome has been replicated. If the correlation disappears when additional variables are introduced in the analysis, the original relationship can be explained away as spurious. Sometimes the introduction of additional variables strengthens the original relationship. If so, the additional variables are called *suppressor variables*, because before they were controlled, they were suppressing the true strength of the relationship between intervention and outcome. Sometimes an original relationship might hold for some but not all categories of the additional variable(s) being controlled. The term for this outcome in the elaboration model is *specification*, because controlling for an additional variable *specifies* the conditions under which the original relationship tends to diminish or increase. Sometimes controlling for an additional variable causes an apparent reversal in the relationship between two other variables (from negative to positive or vice versa). When this happens, the additional variable controlled is called a *distorter variable*. Finally, sometimes controlling for an intervening variable helps interpret the mechanism through which the intervention influences outcome. The term for this outcome interpretation in the elaboration model is *interpretation.*

Statistically controlling for extraneous variables, however, does not guarantee that a correlational study will have external validity. In fact, controlling for threats to internal validity by using more strongly controlled experiments won't assure external validity either. *External validity* refers to the extent to which a study's findings can be generalized to settings and individuals beyond the study conditions. The clients participating in a particular study, or the study setting, may be unlike clients and settings elsewhere, and therefore an intervention that worked in the study may not work as well with other clients or in other settings. When you read or report studies it is critical that you pay special heed to the particular characteristics of the study sample and setting and to whom and where the findings can and cannot be generalized.

REVIEW QUESTIONS

1. To evaluate the effectiveness of your case management program aimed at improving school attendance, you compare the changes in school attendance between teens who chose to participate in your program and teens who chose to participate in a program offering a cash incentive for attending school. Attendance increases 50% in your program and 25% in the cash incentive program. You should therefore conclude:

   a. Both programs caused school attendance to increase.
   b. Your case management program caused a greater increase in attendance than did the cash incentive program.
   c. History could account for part of the increase in both programs.
   d. A selection bias could explain the higher increase in your case management program.
   e. Only a and b.
   f. Only c and d.

2. After seeing an adolescent girl and her mother for many family therapy sessions, you realize that the girl's behavior problems are at their worst whenever her mother's moods are at their worst. You should therefore conclude that:

   a. The mother's bad moods are causing the girl's behavior problems.
   b. The girl's behavior problems are causing the mother's bad moods.
   c. The mother's bad moods and the girl's behavior problems are causing each other, in a fashion consistent with social systems theory.
   d. None of the above.

3. An exciting new intervention is developed to alleviate posttraumatic stress symptoms among rape victims. Every practitioner in your rape crisis center tries the new intervention with every new client, and every one of the clients shows remarkable improvement after intervention is completed. You should therefore conclude that:

   a. The intervention has been proven to be effective.
   b. Passage of time, and not the intervention, may have caused the improvement.
   c. History, and not the intervention, may have caused the improvement.
   d. All of the above.
   e. Only b and c.

4. You construct two measures of depression, one to be administered at pretest and one to be administered at posttest. After the pretest, the most depressed clients are assigned to treatment approach A, and the less depressed clients are assigned to treatment approach B. After treatment, the approach A clients show significantly more improvement in level of depression than do the approach B clients. You should therefore conclude that:

   a. The results may be due to statistical regression.
   b. The results may be due to instrumentation effects.
   c. Treatment A is more effective.
   d. Only a and b.

5. Cross-sectional studies control for:

   a. causal time-sequence.
   b. threats to internal validity as well as experiments.
   c. history.
   d. All of the above.
   e. None of the above.

6. Case-control studies control for:

   a. causal time-sequence.
   b. threats to internal validity as well as well most experiments.
   c. history.
   d. All of the above.
   e. None of the above.

7. Suppose a study finds that prisoners who participate in a faith-based program are much less likely to be re-arrested than the non-participants, but that after controlling each prisoner's motivation to change measured before the program began, there is no difference in re-arrest rates between the participants and the non-participants. Which of the following statements is/are true about this result in the elaboration model?

   a. The original relationship was spurious.
   b. It illustrates replication.
   c. It illustrates specification.
   d. It illustrates interpretation.

8. Suppose a study finds that child abuse rates of parents who participate in a child abuse prevention program are somewhat lower than the child abuse rates of parents who do not participate. However, after controlling for whether either parent abuses drugs or alcohol, the child abuse rates for the participants becomes much lower than for the non-participants. Which of the following statements is/are true about this result in the elaboration model?

   a. The original relationship was spurious.
   b. It illustrates replication.
   c. Whether either parent abused substances operated as a suppressor variable.
   d. It illustrates an impossible result in the elaboration model, since there was no correlation to begin with.

EXERCISE 10.1

You work in an agency providing crisis intervention services to runaway adolescents and their families. Your administrator suggests that the program's effectiveness be evaluated by assessing each family immediately after the runaway episode and then assessing each family again after they receive your services. The assessments will measure the quality of the relationship between the runaways and their parents. The administrator knows you read an unforgettable textbook on research methods in your research course and therefore asks for your advice on how people with research expertise are likely to respond to the suggested design, particularly with regard to its validity. What would you say regarding the internal validity of the suggested design? Would you recommend using this design? Identify each threat to internal validity and explain why the suggested design does or does not control for it.

EXERCISE 10.2

Your administrator recognizes the legitimacy of some of your concerns and then suggests a design in which the pre-to-post change among the families receiving your services be compared to the pre-to-post change among referred families who opt not to utilize your services or who choose a different form of service from a different type of agency. Would you agree that this design would have an acceptable degree of internal validity? Why or why not?

EXERCISE 10.3

For reasons of feasibility, a correlational study is the best you can do to evaluate the above program. Which correlational design would you use? Briefly summarize its features. What extraneous variables would be the most critical to control for using the elaboration model? Explain how the elaboration model would control for those extraneous variables.

DISCUSSION QUESTIONS

1. Explain the difference between statistical regression and the passage of time as threats to internal validity.

2. Explain the advantages and disadvantages of cross-sectional, case-control and longitudinal designs.

3. Discuss why and how a study with a high degree of internal validity might not have a high degree of external validity.

4. As a practitioner seeking to utilize published practice evaluations as a guide to your own practice, would you be less likely to be guided by studies with low internal validity or studies with low external validity? Why?

CROSSWORD PUZZLE

ACROSS

1 MEASUREMENT BEFORE INTERVENTION
5 TERM REFERRING TO THE CREDIBILITY OF A STUDY
11 ____-SECTIONAL DESIGN
16 Afraid or shy
18 Words of understanding
19 First letter in Hebrew alphabet
20 Benefit
22 Antique cars
23 Capone and Frankin
25 Droops
27 Regret
28 TYPE OF VALIDITY REGARDING MEETING THE CRITERIA FOR CAUSALITY
30 "You're __"
31 NUMBER OF CRITERIA FOR INFERRING CAUSALITY
33 do __ mi
34 Asian holiday
36 Research assistant's acronym
37 Boxer's goal

DOWN

1 MEASUREMENT AFTER INTERVENTION
2 Adolescent
3 Steady flow of water
4 Set of rows in a stadium
5 Alternative to Mastercard
6 Commercial
7 A VARIABLE THAT, WHEN CONTROLLED, CAUSES AN APPARENT REVERSAL IN AN ORIGINAL RELATIONSHIP BETWEEN TWO OTHER VARIABLES
8 First person singular of be
9 A THREAT TO INTERNAL VALIDITY THAT CAN OCCUR WHEN THE SAME MEASURE IS GIVEN MORE THAN ONCE
10 "______ though I walk through the valley of death"
11 ____- CONTROL STUDY
12 Initials of designer of Polo apparel
13 "___ the land of the free…"
14 A TYPE OF RELATIONSHIP THAT IS EXPLAINED AWAY BY ANOTHER VARIABLE
15 Martin and his son Charlie

ACROSS

38 At home

39 SOMEONE WHOSE SCORE MIGHT STATISTICALLY REGRESS TO HER MEAN

43 Major leaguers

44 No no for vegans

45 Berkeley's pride (abbrev.)

46 "____ Shelter" (Rolling Stones song)

47 Volunteer's state (abbrev.)

48 The chosen ones

50 They are to the left of the RTs

52 Monogram of author of *Robinson Crusoe*

53 _____ Abner

55 Archaic preposition (form of to)

59 San Antonio shrine

59 First American ethnic group (abbrev.)

62 THREAT TO INTERNAL VALIDITY CONNECTED TO TIME PASSAGE

65 Drugs with no active ingredients used in pharmacological research

66 It plays the NL in July

67 Crime committed in an automobile (abbrev.)

68 Direction from Pittsburgh to New York City

69 STATISTICAL THREAT TO INTERNAL VALIDITY

71 Mauna _____ volcano

72 TYPE OF INFERENCE PERMITTED BY INTERNALLY VALID EXPERIMENTS

74 EXTRANEOUS EVENTS THAT POSE A THREAT TO INTERNAL VALIDITY

75 Author of *Portnoy's Complaint*

76 Abbreviation in parentheses meaning "for example"

78 SOMETHING TO AVOID IN GROUP ASSIGNMENT OR MEASUREMENT

80 Alternatives to Macs

82 TYPE OF DESIGN INVOLVING OBSERVATIONS AT MANY TIMES

83 Colorful pond fish

84 METHODOLOGICAL ARRANGEMENTS OF A STUDY

87 Mixture

90 Rich dairy product

91 CASE-____ STUDY

95 Alternatives to butter

96 Pitcher's or quarterback's asset

97 Ping____

98 Justification; players who stop others from scoring

DOWN

17 Clergymen who reside in monasteries

21 Baby cat

24 Be fond of

26 Bride's mate

29 Long arduous journey

32 STRONGEST TYPE OF DESIGN FOR CONTROLLING FOR THREATS TO INTERNAL VALIDITY

35 TYPE OF VALIDITY REFERRING TO GENERALIZING BEYOND STUDY CONDITIONS

40 TYPE OF PROCEDURE USED IN EXPERIMENTS TO ASSIGN CLIENTS TO DIFFERENT TREATMENT GROUP

41 Signal to act

42 Magical, supernatural

49 ___ - mo

51 Spherical representation of our planet

53 Cord used to tie shoe

54 Disorderliness

55 Not capable

56 Gradual reduction

57 Liberal _____ major

58 *Watership* _____

59 Aluminum Company of America acronym

60 __ *Confidential*

63 Object of adoration

64 Symbol for the element nickel

69 English for ole

70 Secret agent

72 "La ______" (Hebrew toast meaning "To life")

73 Prosperous times

75 Speed trap tool

76 Most aloof

77 Con job or undercover police operation

79 Pub order

80 _____ stick

81 Addict

82 The consonants in legume

83 ___ jerk reaction

84 USA capitol

85 Historical period

86 "I'm Henry the Eighth __ ___"

88 ___ Chaney (The man of 1000 faces)

89 Pacino's namesakes

91 Between WY and NM

92 Atop

93 Addict's demise

94 _____ Louvre

CHAPTER 11

Experimental Designs

OBJECTIVES

1. Explain why experimental designs, when designed and implemented properly, have more internal validity than correlational designs for evaluating programs and practice.

2. Design a practice evaluation experiment and a quasi-experiment that would permit causal inferences about practice effectiveness.

3. Describe pre-experimental pilot studies, their uses and their limitations, and when and how to use them.

4. Describe the potential influence of measurement bias in experimental and quasi-experimental practice evaluations.

5. Describe three alternative experimental designs and two alternative quasi-experimental designs and the rationale for using each.

6. Describe the use of waiting lists and alternative, routine services as control conditions, so that clients in control or comparison conditions are not denied services.

7. Describe how diffusion or imitation of treatments, compensatory equalization, compensatory rivalry, or resentful demoralization can affect the validity of an experiment or quasi-experiment.

8. Describe how diffusion or imitation of treatments, compensatory equalization, compensatory rivalry, or resentful demoralization can affect the validity of an experiment or quasi-experiment.

9. Discuss how attrition can affect the validity of an experiment or quasi-experiment and describe steps to minimize attrition.

10. Define and give examples of research reactivity.

11. Compare the advantages and disadvantages of nonequivalent comparison group designs, simple time-series designs, and multiple time-series designs.

12. Explain how nonequivalent comparison group designs are strengthened by using multiple pretests and switching replications.

13. Explain the importance of selecting a comparison group as similar as possible to the experimental group in a nonequivalent comparison groups design.

14. Discuss the ways that practical pitfalls can impede carrying out experiments and quasi-experiments in social work agencies, and describe procedures and qualitative methods that can be used to try to avoid or alleviate them.

PRACTICE-RELEVANT SUMMARY

Measuring change among social service recipients from before to after they receive an intervention – thus using a pre-experimental design with no control group has value on a pilot study basis, but funding sources are likely to require that the effectiveness of services be evaluated with an *experimental design* or a *quasi-experimental* design. The cardinal feature of experimental designs is the use of *random assignment* of clients to an experimental group (service recipients) and to a control group (non-recipients), to ensure a high mathematical likelihood that the two groups are comparable on all relevant factors except the receipt of the service being evaluated. In social work practice settings, the non-recipients of the service being tested (that is, those in the control group) need not be denied any type of service. They simply could receive alternative services (usually the agency's routine services), and/or they could be put on a waiting list for the experimental service. The classical experimental design is the *pretest-posttest control group design,* which compares the two groups according to their improvement from pretest to posttest. A second experimental design, called the *posttest-only control group design,* should be considered when we think that pretest measures might impact treatment effects or bias posttest responses. This design assumes that random assignment ensures pretest equivalence between the two groups, thus permitting the inference that posttest differences reflect the causal impact of the evaluated service. The third experimental design, the *Solomon four-group design,* examines two groups that received pre-testing and post-testing and two groups that received posttests only. This design, rare in social work, permits the ferreting out of effects due to testing and effects due to the tested intervention.

Agency constraints or ethical concerns often may make it impossible to conduct randomized experimental evaluations in social work agencies. Rather than forgo doing any evaluation in such instances, alternative research designs sometimes can be used that have less internal validity than randomized experiments but still provide much more support for causal inferences than do pre-experimental designs. These designs are called *quasi-experimental designs* and are distinguished from "true" experiments primarily because they do not randomly assign subjects to experimental and control groups. When designed well, quasi-experimental designs can provide a substantial degree of internal validity.

One useful and commonly used quasi-experimental design is the *nonequivalent comparison groups design.* It entails finding an existing (comparison) group that appears to be similar to the experimental group and thus can be compared to it. It is essential that you provide data indicating that it appears to be very similar in relevant respects to the experimental group. Both groups are pre-tested and post-tested. Thus, the nonequivalent comparison groups design is like the classical experimental design, except that in lieu of random assignment, data are provided supporting the comparability of the two groups. When you read a report of a study that used a nonequivalent comparison groups design, it is important to remember that if selection biases seem highly plausible in that study then the notion that the groups are really comparable is severely undermined. Unless the researcher can present compelling evidence documenting the comparability of the groups on relevant extraneous variables and on pretest scores, any differences in outcome between the two groups are suspect. How well the researcher documents the comparability of the groups is critical in deciding whether a study using this design is strong enough to guide practice.

If there are doubts about the comparability of the comparison group, the nonequivalent comparison groups design can be strengthened by employing *multiple pretests*. By administering the same pretest at different time points before intervention begins, we can detect whether one group is already engaged in a change process and the other is not. It can also help us detect whether statistical regression is occurring in one group, but not the other. Another way to reduce doubt is by the use of *switching replications*. This entails administering the treatment to the comparison group after the first posttest. If we replicate in that group the improvement made by the experimental group in the first posttest, then we reduce doubt as to whether the improvement at the first posttest was merely a function of a selection bias. If our second posttest results do not replicate the improvement made by the experimental group in the first posttest, then the difference between the groups at the first posttest can be attributed to the lack of comparability between the two groups.

Another commonly used and valuable set of quasi-experimental designs is called *time-series designs*. The main feature of these designs is the conducting of numerous repeated observations before introducing an intervention and conducting numerous additional repeated observations after introducing the intervention. Conducting numerous observations facilitates our ability to infer whether changes reflect treatment effects as opposed to history, maturation or the passage of time, testing effects, or statistical regression.

A particularly feasible time-series design—feasible because it does not require a comparison group—is called the *simple interrupted time-series design*. This design employs multiple pretests and multiple posttests to enable us to ascertain whether maturation or the passage of time or statistical regression is a plausible explanation for any improvement that occurs after the onset of an intervention. To rule out such threats to internal validity, we look for a stable pattern among the pretest scores followed by a stable improvement in the level or slope of the scores soon after the intervention begins. With enough measurement points, this design also helps in judging the plausibility of history as the explanation for any improvement. To further control for history we could use a *multiple time-series design*. This entails finding a comparison group that does not receive the tested intervention and assessing it with the same multiple pretests and posttests administered at the same time as with the group that receives the intervention being evaluated. Thus, the multiple time-series design is stronger than the simple time-series designs because it adds nonequivalent control group design logic to time-series analysis logic. Sometimes our research procedures, and not the intervention we are evaluating, produce the outcomes we seek. The term for this phenomenon is *research reactivity*. An experimental design that attempts to control for two sources of research reactivity is the *placebo control group design*. Clients are randomly assigned to three groups: an experimental group, a control group, and a placebo group. The purpose is to control for *novelty and disruption effects* and *placebo effects* – which occur when the sense of getting special attention or special treatment or the mere power of suggestion can bring about the desired improvement. Placebo group clients receive special attention of some sort other than the tested intervention. Logical arrangements, however, won't ensure that other sources or reactivity or bias are avoided. Random assignment won't prevent measurement bias. No matter how elegant or impressive an experiment or quasi-experiment may be in other respects, if its measurement procedures appear highly vulnerable to bias favoring the experimental group, the value of the study may be egregiously compromised, and its findings may be highly suspect. Neither will random assignment control for sources of research reactivity called *experimental demand characteristics* and *experimenter expectancies*. Research participants can learn what researchers want them to say or do, and then they cooperate with those "demands" or expectations. Bias also can result from *obtrusive observation*, which occurs when the participant is keenly aware of being observed and thus may be predisposed to behave in socially desirable ways.

Likewise, the validity of an experimental or quasi-experimental design can be hindered by something called the *diffusion or imitation of treatment*, such as when practitioners in other units learn about the "special" service being evaluated and try to imitate it. Similar problems not automatically avoided in experimental and quasi-experimental designs include compensatory equalization, compensatory rivalry and resentful demoralization.

Compensatory equalization most typically occurs when staff in a routine service control group seek to compensate for what they perceive as an inequity in treatment by providing enhanced services that go beyond the routine treatment regimen. *Compensatory rivalry* occurs when practitioners or clients in the routine treatment group become more motivated to improve their performance to show they can do as well as their counterparts in the experimental group. The converse of compensatory rivalry is *resentful demoralization*, which occurs when treatment outcome in the control group is hindered as the confidence or motivation of practitioners or clients declines because they know they are not receiving special training or special treatment. To detect whether diffusion or imitation of treatment, compensatory equalization, compensatory rivalry or resentful demoralization are occurring -- and perhaps to intervene to try to minimize these problems -- you can use qualitative methods, such as participant observation of staff meetings and informal conversational interviews with clients and practitioners.

Another problem that logical arrangements won't prevent is *attrition* (also called *experimental mortality*), which occurs when participants prematurely drop out of an experiment or quasi-experiment. Attrition can result in an undesirable sample size, and if many more participants drop out of one group than the other, then the differential dropout rates – and not treatment effects – can explain differences in outcome between the groups. Recommended ways to minimize attrition include reimbursing clients for their participation, avoiding intervention or research procedures that disappoint or frustrate them, and utilizing tracking methods.
No matter how rigorous your experimental or quasi-experimental design may be, in social work practice settings you are likely to encounter practical pitfalls in trying to implement your design. These pitfalls may compromise the fidelity of the intervention being evaluated, contaminate the control condition or the case assignment protocol, or hinder client recruitment and retention.

The term *intervention fidelity* refers to the degree to which the intervention actually delivered to clients was delivered as intended. If the intervention is not implemented properly, then the failure to obtain the desired outcome may have more to do with the failure to implement the intervention properly than with its real effectiveness. *Contamination of the control condition* can occur if control group and experimental group members interact. If this happens, the improvements among the experimental group participants may have a beneficial spillover effect on the control group participants. Consequently, the two groups will not be as different on outcome measures as was predicted, which may lead to the erroneous conclusion that the tested intervention did not make a difference.

Resistance to the case assignment protocol can cause similar problems. Practitioners may resent having to assign cases to treatment conditions on the basis of research requirements rather than on the basis of their own professional judgment about the best service match for each client. If they influence or violate the case assignment protocol, they can seriously undermine the comparability of the treatment and control or comparison groups, and thus wreck a study's internal validity. Client recruitment and retention difficulties can arise when referral agencies are reluctant to refer clients, when those agencies dump "undesirable" clients, clients resent the chance of being assigned to a control condition, clients drop out after being assigned to the control condition, or when agency staff make overly optimistic estimates of the number of clients they'll be able to refer to an evaluation. Evaluators should be prepared to encounter the above pitfalls and should build mechanisms into their studies to prevent, detect, and deal with them. One important suggestion is to engage agency staff members in the design of the research and enlist their support from its inception. Although this may help reduce the likelihood or degree of their resistance to the research, it will not guarantee that their resistance is eliminated. Another is to locate experimental and control conditions in separate buildings or agencies. This may help avoid contaminating the control condition. Intervention fidelity can be promoted by developing a treatment manual. Client recruitment and retention problems might be reduced by planning to recruit clients assertively on an ongoing basis throughout a study, rather than assuming that the initial cohort will be large enough and will remain intact. Client recruitment and retention also might be enhanced by reimbursing clients for their participation.

Conducting a brief pre-experimental *pilot study* before implementing the main study can test the accuracy of agency estimates about the projected number of study participants. It might also detect problems in intervention fidelity, imitation of treatments, resistance to the case assignment protocol, and problems in measurement and data collection.

Qualitative research methods can be useful in anticipating, avoiding, or alleviating practical pitfalls. On-site research staff members can interact formally or informally with agency staff members to identify compliance problems or learn how they are implementing the interventions. They can use videotapes or practitioner activity logs to assess intervention fidelity. They can also identify implementation problems by following along with (shadowing) practitioners in their daily activities. They can participate in in-service trainings or group supervision to identify discrepancies between the intended intervention and what agency trainers or supervisors are proscribing.

REVIEW QUESTIONS

1. Which of the following statements is true about the classical, pretest-posttest control group design?

    a. It controls for all threats to internal validity.
    b. It ensures valid measurement.
    c. It ensures unbiased ratings.
    d. All of the above.
    e. None of the above.

2. To evaluate your psycho-educational group treatment approach for dually diagnosed individuals with chronic mental illness and substance abuse problems, you conduct a randomized experiment comparing clients who managed to attend all your program's group sessions to clients randomly assigned to a control group. Since one-third of the clients assigned to your program did not complete it due to flare-ups in their problems during the course of treatment, you eliminated those clients from your post-testing. You find that almost all those who completed your program improved on the outcome measure, whereas in the control group two-thirds improved and one-third worsened. You should therefore conclude that:

    a. Your program was effective.
    b. Attrition is a plausible explanation for your results.
    c. Maturation or the passage of time is a plausible explanation for your results.
    d. Only a and b.

3. Which of the following statements is true about random assignment to experimental and control groups?

   a. It guarantees that the experimental and control groups will be equivalent in the background characteristics of their clients.
   b. With a large enough sample it offers a high mathematical likelihood of avoiding significant inequivalence between the two groups in the background characteristics of their clients.
   c. It involves careful probability sampling procedures in assigning clients to groups.
   d. Haphazard circumstances can determine who gets assigned to which group.
   e. Both b and c, only, are true.

4. City officials who fund both a child guidance center and a family service agency decide to conduct a randomized experiment to see which facility is more effective and which, therefore, should receive a funding increase or a funding decrease. The child guidance center traditionally has emphasized play therapy with the child and not provided much family therapy. The family service agency has traditionally emphasized family therapy and not provided much play therapy. Administrators and practitioners in both agencies know about each other's approach and about the purpose of the experiment. The experiment, after randomly assigning clients to each of the two agencies and using valid, unbiased pretests and posttests, ends up finding no difference in outcome between the two agencies. Social workers reading about this study therefore should conclude:

   a. The two agencies seem to have approximately equal effects.
   b. It doesn't seem to matter much whether play therapy or family therapy is emphasized with these clients.
   c. The results may be misleading, due to possible diffusion or imitation of treatments.
   d. Only a and b.

5. Which of the following statements is true about the classical experimental design?

   a. Random assignment assures a high likelihood that the study sample is representative of the rest of the target population.
   b. Because of random assignment, the effects observed in the study can be generalized outside of the experimental situation.
   c. In addition to having a high degree of internal validity, it has a high degree of external validity.
   d. All of the above.
   e. None of the above.

6. Random assignment to an experimental and a control group controls for:

   a. diffusion or imitation of treatments.
   b. compensatory equalization.
   c. compensatory rivalry.
   d. All of the above.
   e. None of the above.

7. Random assignment to an experimental and a control group controls for:

   a. novelty and disruption effects.
   b. placebo effects.
   c. experimental demand characteristics.
   d. All of the above.
   e. None of the above.

8. Random assignment to an experimental and a control group controls for:

   a. attrition.
   b. resentful demoralization.
   c. experimenter expectancies.
   d. All of the above.
   e. None of the above

9. Research reactivity occurs when:

   a. the research procedures, and not the intervention, cause a desired outcome.
   b. threats to internal validity are well controlled.
   c. observation is unobtrusive.
   d. All of the above.
   e. None of the above.

10. Which of the following statements is/are true about attrition?

    a. It can result in an undesirable sample size.
    b. It can explain differences in outcome between groups.
    c. Two ways to try to minimize it are by reimbursing clients and utilizing tracking methods.
    d. All of the above.
    e. None of the above.

11. Which of the following statements is/are true about quasi-experimental designs?

    a. They have less internal validity than well-designed experiments.
    b. They are usually more feasible than experiments.
    c. They can have enough internal validity to guide practice.
    d. All of the above.
    e. None of the above.

12. Which of the following statements is/are true about multiple pretests?

    a. They can strengthen the internal validity of a quasi-experimental design.
    b. They usually weaken the internal validity of a non-equivalent comparison group design.
    c. They can be used only in multiple time-series designs.
    d. All of the above.
    e. None of the above.
    f. Both a and c, only are true.

13. Which of the following statements is/are true about non-equivalent comparison group designs?

    a. Selecting a comparison group that is very similar to the experimental group is very important in enhancing internal validity.
    b. Using switching replications can enhance internal validity.
    c. Using switching replications is likely to reduce internal validity.
    d. Both a and b are true.

14. A time-series design is used to evaluate whether a county's new family preservation demonstration program, which began in 2000, appears to be reducing out-of-home placements of children. Below are four different chronologically ordered annual out-of-home placement rates for five years before the program began and five years after it began. Which pattern best supports the notion that the program is causing the desired reduction?

	Program Years									
	1995	1996	1997	1998	1999	2000	2001	2002	2003	2004
a.	1000	950	900	850	800	750	700	650	600	550
b.	950	975	960	950	980	750	700	650	600	550
c.	850	980	700	850	800	700	900	850	950	750
d.	700	980	700	950	750	700	900	750	950	700

a. Pattern a best supports the notion that the program is causing the desired reduction.
b. Pattern b best supports the notion that the program is causing the desired reduction.
c. Pattern c best supports the notion that the program is causing the desired reduction.
d. Pattern d best supports the notion that the program is causing the desired reduction.

15. What role can qualitative research methods play as part of experimental or quasi-experimental studies?

a. None; experimental or quasi-experimental studies should be purely quantitative.
b. They control for threats to internal validity.
c. They can help us anticipate, avoid, or alleviate practical pitfalls in implementation.
d. They can help us develop possible explanations for unexpected, puzzling findings.
e. Both c and d, only, are true.

16. Which of the following statements is/are true about implementing experiments and quasi-experiments in service-oriented social work practice agencies?

    a. If the study design has high internal validity, we can be fairly certain that practitioners will implement the tested intervention in the intended manner.
    b. A good, logical design ensures that control group members will not be influenced by the tested intervention.
    c. A good, logical design ensures that cases will be assigned to treatment conditions in the intended manner.
    d. All of the above.
    e. None of the above.

EXERCISE 11.1

Suppose you conduct an experimental evaluation of an outpatient substance abuse treatment program. Suppose 100 clients are randomly assigned, half to an experimental group and half to a control group. Of the 50 experimental group clients, 30 completed your services as well as all your testing, and 20 dropped out without finishing the services or completing the posttests. All 50 control group clients completed all testing. The improvement among your 30 experimental group clients was much better than the improvement among your control group clients. In fact, 100 percent of your experimental group clients improved, while only 60 percent of your control group clients improved. Would you therefore infer that your program is effective? Why or why not?

EXERCISE 11.2

If you were to replicate the study in Exercise 11.1, what steps would you take to minimize attrition? What would you do to minimize the potential for experimenter expectancies, experimental design characteristics, or measurement bias to influence the results?

EXERCISE 11.3

Suppose you want to conduct an evaluation of the effectiveness of a parent education program for substance abusing parents referred for child neglect. In the first phase, the program tries to change undesirable attitudes about child rearing and teaches parents child rearing skills. It does not address substance abuse issues until the second phase.

1. Design an internally valid nonequivalent control group quasi-experiment for evaluating the effectiveness of Phase 1 in the above program, and explain why you think it would have adequate internal validity. Also identify its limitations from the standpoint of internal validity.

2. Design an internally valid simple time-series study for evaluating the effectiveness of Phase 1 in the above program, and explain why you think it would have adequate internal validity. Also identify its limitations from the standpoint of internal validity.

3. Design an internally valid multiple time-series study for evaluating the effectiveness of Phase 1 in the above program, and explain why you think it would have more internal validity than either of the above designs.

EXERCISE 11.4

Suppose you want to strengthen your nonequivalent control group quasi-experiment for evaluating the effectiveness of Phase 1 in the above program evaluation.

1. Describe how you would use multiple pretests to strengthen the design, and explain why you think that would strengthen its internal validity.

2. Describe how you would use switching replications to strengthen the design, and explain why you think that would strengthen its internal validity.

EXERCISE 11.5

Suppose you work in a state mental health planning agency and want to evaluate the impact of a statewide case management program that began in 1995. The program's aim is to reduce the number of inpatient days spent in state hospitals for mental illness. Design a simple time-series evaluation of the program's impact. Explain why it would be scientifically credible, and identify its limitations from the standpoint of internal validity.

EXERCISE 11.6

Develop two hypothetical graphs of simple time-series data to illustrate the difference between statistical regression and the passage of time as threats to internal validity.

DISCUSSION QUESTIONS

1. Explain why random assignment to groups is the ideal way to try to make groups comparable.

2. Discuss at least four practical pitfalls often encountered in social work practice settings, and the ways they may adversely influence the carrying out of your experiment or quasi-experiment.

3. Discuss mechanisms that can be helpful in attempting to anticipate, avoid, or alleviate each of the pitfalls you have identified above.

4. Discuss the role of qualitative research techniques in attempting to anticipate, avoid, or alleviate each of the pitfalls you have identified above.

5. Explain why assessing the fidelity of an intervention being evaluated is important, and describe ways to assess intervention fidelity.

CROSSWORD PUZZLE

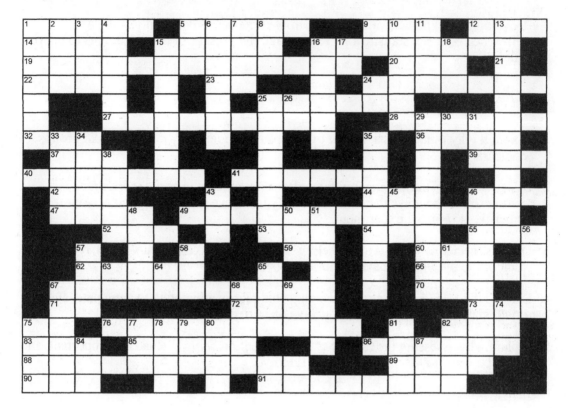

ACROSS

1 CLIENTS PARTICIPATING IN A QUASI-EXPERIMENT, OR CONTAINERS
5 Steerer
9 Fuel
12 Flood vehicle
14 Norwegian king
15 Show me the ______!
16 WHAT WE DO WITH QUASI-EXPERIMENTAL OR EXPERIMENTAL DESIGNS IN SOCIAL WORK
19 WE CAN STRENGTHEN THE VALIDITY OF NON-EXPERIMENTAL DESIGNS BY USING ______ DEPENDENT VARIABLES
20 Diamond ______ (Mae West role)
22 ______ ager
23 Approve
24 PRACTICAL PROBLEM TO AVOID OR ALLEVIATE IN CARRYING OUT EXPERIMENTS OR QUASIEXPERIMENTS
25 Sartre's country
27 USE ______ REPLICATIONS TO STRENGTHEN THE VALIDITY OF NON-EXPERIMENTAL DESIGNS
28 To wet thoroughly; to saturate
32 Psychadelic drug of the 1960s
35 Sicilian mountain
37 Meadow
39 Summer in France
40 Net player in tennis
41 Exhibit gaudily
42 Nixon's wife
44 Who to call when injured badly in a car accident (abbrev.)
46 Something to have on the farm, but not on "The Simpsons"
47 Mine ______ have seen the glory
49 ONE PITFALL TO AVOID IN AN EXPERIMENT OR QUASI-EXPERIMENT IS ______ OF THE CONTROL CONDITION
53 ______-hoo (attention getter)
54 Refrain syllable for a tune
55 Graduate degree for compassionate helpers who we hope will be evidence-based
59 Football lineman (abbrev.)
60 Short snooze
62 ______-EXPERIMENTAL DESIGNS
66 Run after
67 TYPE OF RESEARCH METHODS HELPFUL IN IDENTIFYING IMPLEMENTATION PROBLEMS IN EXPERIMENTS OR QUASI-EXPERIMENTS
70 Unit of corn
71 Tucson educational institute
72 Broadway hit of the late 1960's
73 Picnic pest
75 ______-annually (twice a year)
76 TYPE OF DESIGN INVOLVING MULTIPLE MEASUREMENT POINTS
82 Honest ______
83 Female reproductive cells of animals
85 Small restaurants
86 TYPE OF TIME-SERIES DESIGN INVOLVING ONLY ONE GROUP
88 AN ACTIVITY OFTEN NEEDED TO OBTAIN PARTICIPANTS IN AN EXPERIMENT OR QUASI-EXPERIMENT
89 Go up
90 Able was I ______ I saw Elba
91 ONE WAY TO AVOID CONTAMINATION OF THE CONTROL CONDITION IS TO LOCATE IT IN A ______ AGENCY OR BUILDING FROM THE EXPERIMENTAL CONDITION

DOWN

1 TYPE OF GROUP IN AN EXPERIMENT OR QUASI-EXPERIMENT
2 Balm for damaged skin
3 Capable of sound reasoning
4 EXTRANEOUS THINGS THAT CAN COINCIDE WITH THE INTERVENTION PERIOD
5 Hawaiian food
6 Bill for services
7 Plumbing problem
8 Popeye's girlfriend Olive ______
9 Abbreviation for Jimmy Carter's state
10 United in a formal relationship
11 Something not to wear on casual Fridays
12 Dinner ______ Eight
13 SWITCH THESE TO GET MORE VALIDITY IN YOUR NON-EXPERIMENTAL DESIGN
15 USE ______ PRETESTS TO GET MORE VALIDITY IN YOUR NON-EXPERIMENTAL DESIGN
16 ______ AGENCY STAFF MEMBERS IN DESIGNING YOUR RESEARCH
17 Burlington's state (abbrev.)
18 TV's funny alien
24 Not an iMAC, but politically correct
25 A DESIRABLE ATTRIBUTE FOR THE INTERVENTION YOU EVALUATE
26 Hospital worker
29 SOMETHING TO ANTICIPATE BY STAFF IN YOUR CASE ASSIGNMENT PROTOCOL
30 ______ tu Brutus?
31 Direction from St. Louis to Detroit
33 IF TIME-SERIES DATA HAVE THIS BEFORE THE INTERVENTION, IT SUGGESTS THAT PASSAGE OF TIME MIGHT BE THE EXPLANATION
34 Stall; put off
35 THE OPPOSITE OF ATTRITION
38 Change
43 Healthy bean or type of sauce
45 Damage
46 WHAT EXPERIMENTAL AND COMPARISON GROUPS SHOULD BE IN A NON-EQUIVALENT COMPARISON GROUPS DESIGN
48 Plant leaf
50 Internet service company (abbrev.)
51 Nurtured
56 Take away by force
57 Water; color
58 Command to Fido
61 Word of surprise
63 Tuscaloosa school (abbrev.)
64 Word of agreement in Juarez

DOWN

65 Impostor
67 Shake
68 Not those
69 XXVIII divided bi iv
74 Once named (before marriage)
75 Sleep inducing professor
77 Hospital area for critically ill
78 Primary
79 Newt
00 Big truck
81 Italian money
82 Church section
84 Unreturnable tennis serve; or to score 100% on an exam
87 University in Boston emphasizing technology (abbrev.)

CHAPTER 12

Single-Case Evaluation Designs

OBJECTIVES

1. Explain the logic of single-case evaluation designs in the evaluation of practice effectiveness.

2. Identify the chief advantages and disadvantages of using single-case evaluation designs instead of group designs to evaluate practice.

3. Discuss the ways that single-case evaluation designs can be used as part of the assessment and monitoring of client problems.

4. Identify practical constraints that can limit the practitioner's ability to conduct rigorous single-case design evaluations.

5. Discuss special problems in measurement and data gathering when practitioners use single-case designs to evaluate their practice.

6. Identify the alternative ways practitioners can gather single-case evaluation design data, and discuss the advantages and disadvantages of each alternative.

7. Explain triangulation and its advantages.

8. Discuss the importance of the baseline phase and identify alternative baseline patterns and their implications.

9. Identify and describe alternative single-case evaluation designs and explain their advantages and disadvantages.

10. Interpret the visual significance and meaning of alternative graphed data patterns in single-case evaluation design results.

11. Discuss the implications of ambiguous data patterns and what to do when they are encountered.

12. Interpret aggregated results of multiple single-case evaluation practice evaluations.

13. Discuss the important role replication can play in the interpretation of single-case evaluation findings.

14. Discuss ethical controversies that apply specifically to practice evaluation using single-case evaluation designs.

15. Be able to employ single-case evaluation designs in your own professional practice.

PRACTICE-RELEVANT SUMMARY

Single-case evaluation designs are time-series designs (discussed in Chapter 11) that can be used to evaluate practice with a single case, such as an individual, a family, or a group. Many social work educators these days believe that single-case evaluation methodology is one of the most relevant research topics for future practitioners, since practitioners can implement these designs themselves, in their own practice, in evaluating their effectiveness with specific cases or in conducting assessment and monitoring.

The key concept in the logic of single-case evaluation designs is the repeated measurement of the target problem many times before and after an intervention begins and seeing whether improvement in the target problem consistently coincides with the onset of the intervention being evaluated.

When you decide to use a single-case evaluation design to evaluate your practice with a particular case, an early challenge involves identifying the appropriate target problem(s) and then operationally defining it. Because any one operational indicator may fail to detect client improvement, the principle of triangulation is commonly employed. *Triangulation* involves the use of two or more indicators or measurement strategies when confronted with a multiplicity of measurement options, all of which have different flaws.

Subsequent decisions must be made about who should conduct the measurement. Should the client self-monitor? Or should someone else do it, such as the practitioner or a client's significant other? Each option has its own unique advantages and disadvantages, and, again, the principle of triangulation can be employed. The same applies to decisions about sources of data, such as available records, interviews, self-report scales, and direct behavioral observations.
If a self-report scale is used, its reliability, validity, and sensitivity to subtle changes become relevant, as does its applicability to frequent repeated measurement in the context of a clinical relationship and setting. Client self-monitoring is very commonly used to measure client progress. This approach is often the most feasible in terms of practitioner resources; moreover, many target problems, such as the frequency of negative thoughts, cannot be measured by anyone other than the client. But self-monitoring is highly vulnerable to client bias and research reactivity. The latter occurs when the process of observing and recording the data influences change in the target problem.

One way to minimize bias and reactivity is through the use of unobtrusive observation, which means observing and recording behavioral data in ways that by and large are not noticeable to the people being observed. Unobtrusive observation, however, is very difficult for practitioners to conduct. Data gathered through direct observation can be quantified in terms of frequency, duration, and/or magnitude.

Once you have developed your measurement strategy, the next big challenge involves obtaining an adequate baseline. The baseline is the phase of repeated measures that are gathered before the intervention begins. Baselines are control phases. The graphed pattern of data collected during the baseline phase will be compared to the graphed pattern of data collected during the intervention (experimental) phase. To have a reasonable chance of finding a visually significant improvement in the graphed data pattern after the onset of intervention, the baseline phase ideally should have several attributes. It should involve many measurement points (between five and ten at a minimum). The chronological graphed data pattern should be stable, not fluctuating wildly. Finally, the pattern should not reflect a trend of dramatic improvement to the degree that suggests that the problem is nearing resolution before intervention even begins. (It's great for the client if this happens, of course, but it obviates the utility of the single-subject design and perhaps also the need to apply the intervention to the already dramatically improving target problem.)

When a baseline does not have the above three attributes, it probably should be extended until it does have them. The realities of practice, however, may not let you wait that long. Under these conditions, you simply do the best you can do and hope that the overall data pattern (after the intervention phase is completed) has some utility. In some situations you may even have to obtain a retrospective baseline, which relies on available records or the memory of the client or significant others. When you rely on memory you should use specific, identifiable events that are easy to recall and that go back no more than several weeks.

There are a variety of alternative single-case evaluation designs to choose from. The realities of practice, however, probably will lead you to select the simplest design: the *AB design*. This design includes only one baseline phase (A) and one intervention phase (B). The advantage of this design is its simplicity and the fact that it will often be the only one that practice constraints will permit. However, because it has the potential to detect only one visually significant coincidence in the data pattern (from A to B), it offers less control for history than the alternative designs. Nevertheless, the potential to detect one visually significant shift has enough value to warrant using the AB design when it is the best you can do. Moreover, if the results of an AB design can be consistently replicated in subsequent AB designs involving the same intervention with similar clients and similar target problems, the threat of history becomes farfetched.

The most common alternatives to the AB design build replication into the same study with the same client and thus provide increased control for history within the one study. One alternative is the *ABAB design,* which assumes that if you withdraw the intervention and then reintroduce it you can see if the target problem gets worse (or slows its rate of improvement) during the second baseline (the second A) and then begins to steadily improve again when intervention is reintroduced (during the second B phase). Two major problems with this design are: (1) that practitioners may be unwilling to withdraw an intervention that appears to be working, and (2) improvement on some target problems is irreversible, even when intervention is withdrawn.

Another common alternative is the *multiple-baseline design,* which involves staggering the application of the intervention to different target problems, settings, or individuals. This increases control for history by providing more than one time point at which a dramatic coincidence can occur. Although this design avoids the problems inherent in ABAB designs, it does not get around the possibility that when the intervention is applied to the first target problem or setting its effects may generalize over into other target problems or settings.
Sometimes practitioners will set out to use an AB design, but after finding no improvement during B will try out a different intervention during an added-on (C) phase. If that intervention doesn't appear to be effective, they may then add on a D phase, during which they try a third type of intervention. The results of an ABC or ABCD design should be interpreted with caution. If only the last intervention tried (the C in ABC or the D in ABCD) yields improvement, it is plausible that an extraneous event eventually occurred to cause the improvement or that the last intervention might not have worked had it not been preceded by the previous interventions, which alone were not enough. Replication with subsequent clients, in which the interventions are introduced in varying sequences, will help you sort this out.

In single-case evaluation research, replication enhances both internal and external validity. It enhances internal validity by adding more possibilities to observe consistent unlikely coincidences that help us sort out the plausibility of history (that is, extraneous events) as the cause of changes in the target problem. It enhances external validity by increasing the number and diversity of cases and contexts with which the intervention has been tested.

Single-case evaluation studies also can be enhanced by incorporating qualitative research methods. Qualitative interviews with the client and significant others can help alleviate ambiguity in data patterns by identifying the possible occurrence of extraneous events. Qualitative interviews can also facilitate the planning of single-case evaluation studies by improving our understanding of the target problem, how to measure it, and how best to intervene. Interviews additionally help in identifying what parts of the intervention clients perceive to be most helpful, and why, and they can be used with significant others to corroborate client-reported data. Videotaping or audiotaping intervention sessions can aid in assessing intervention fidelity. Event logs completed by clients or significant others help us assess the location and timing of target problems, mediating circumstances, and extraneous events bearing on drawing causal inferences from outcome data patterns.

Many social work education programs emphasize single-case evaluation designs in their research and practice curricula and urge students to use these designs in their eventual practice. I hope you will use these designs in your practice, but you should not set out to do so wearing rose-colored glasses. Be prepared to encounter practical obstacles to your use of these designs, obstacles such as client crises that do not allow time for developing adequate baselines, heavy caseloads that do not leave you ample time to plan or conduct this type of practice evaluation, clients who do not follow through on self-monitoring, or colleagues and supervisors who do not understand, appreciate, or support this "research stuff." You also should be prepared to encounter data patterns that are ambiguous and that therefore do not offer clear implications for practice. I say this not to discourage you from doing this sort of practice evaluation, but to help prepare you for the difficulties and frustrations it will entail. By expecting these problems, perhaps you will be less disappointed and more persistent when you experience them.

REVIEW QUESTIONS

1. The main feature of single-case evaluation designs that can help practitioners infer whether their intervention appears to be the real cause of improvement in the target problem is:

   a. Having an A phase and a B phase
   b. Having many multiple measurement points before and after intervention begins
   c. The opportunity to see if improvement occurs at any point
   d. The feasibility of these designs

2. Which of the following is ***NOT*** an appropriate aim of a practitioner using a single-case evaluation design with one particular case?

   a. To identify during assessment precipitating conditions influencing the target problem
   b. To know when a lack of progress may call for changing the intervention
   c. To generalize about the practitioner's or the intervention's effectiveness with other cases
   d. None of the above; they are all appropriate aims

3. To evaluate the effects of an environmental change, the client self-monitors his negative thoughts that have tended to lead to angry outbursts. Which of the following should be considered by the practitioner doing a single-subject evaluation with this client?

   a. Research reactivity
   b. Social desirability bias
   c. The obtrusiveness of the observation
   d. The possible use of self-monitoring at some point as a clinical tool
   e. All of the above

4. To increase the likelihood that your results are truly reflective of the target problem, and are not being influenced by measurement procedures, you should:

   a. Measure unobtrusively
   b. Use direct observation
   c. Use self-report scales
   d. Use interviews

5. If you are using a single-case evaluation design to evaluate an intervention with an abusive parent, which of the following indicators of effectiveness would be the *least* appropriate, given the number of data points needed?

    a. Number of positive parenting behaviors
    b. Number of incidents of severe physical abuse
    c. Number of negative comments to the child
    d. Amount of time spent playing with the child

6. Which of the following statements is/are true about baselines in single-case evaluation designs?

    a. They should be no longer than a few measurement points.
    b. They should be stable.
    c. They should show that the target problem is clearly improving.
    d. All of the above.

7. A practitioner obtains the following data in a single-subject evaluation of her effectiveness in using play therapy to reduce a child's nightmares.

Number of nightmares: A phase: 3 3 2 2 1 1 0 0 0 B phase: 0 0 0 0 0 0 0 0 0

What should the practitioner conclude from these data?

    a. The intervention is effective with this client.
    b. The intervention is ineffective with this client.
    c. Maturation or the passage of time appears to be a plausible explanation.
    d. None of the above.
    e. Only a and c.
    f. Only b and c.

8. Suppose that in the above evaluation the practitioner obtained the following results: Number of nightmares: A phase: 2 2 2 2 2 0 0 0 B phase: 0 0 0 0 0 0 0 0 0

What should the practitioner conclude from these data?

    a. The intervention is effective with this client.
    b. The intervention is ineffective with this client.
    c. History appears to be a plausible explanation.
    d. None of the above
    e. Only a and c.
    f. Only b and c.

9. Suppose that in the above evaluation the practitioner obtained the following results: Number of nightmares: A phase: 2 2 3 2 2 3 2 2 B phase: 1 0 1 0 0 0 0 0 0

   What should the practitioner conclude from these data?

   a. It is plausible that the intervention is effective with this client.
   b. The intervention is not effective with this client.
   c. History cannot be entirely ruled out.
   d. None of the above.
   e. Only a and c.
   f. Only b and c.

10. Suppose you use an ABAB design to evaluate the effectiveness of a group intervention aimed at helping a particular child improve her social skills. Your outcome indicator is the number of friends she plays with after school each day, and you obtain the following results:

    A_1: 0 0 0 0 0 B_1: 1 1 2 2 2 A_2: 2 2 2 2 2 B_2: 2 2 2 2 2

    What should you conclude from these data?

    a. It is plausible that the intervention is effective with this client.
    b. The intervention is not effective with this client.
    c. History cannot be entirely ruled out.
    d. None of the above.
    e. Only a and c.
    f. Only b and c.

11. Suppose you conducted a multiple baseline study to evaluate the intervention in question 10. In this study you introduce three girls from the same school to the group at different points, and you obtain the following results regarding the number of friends each plays with after school each day:

	Baseline	Intervention
Girl 1	0 0 0	1 1 1 2 2 2 2
Girl 2	0 0 0 1 1	1 2 2 2 2
Girl 3	0 0 0 1 1 1 1	2 2 2

    What should you conclude from these data?

    a. It is plausible that the intervention is effective with generalization of effects.
    b. The intervention does not appear to be effective with these clients.
    c. History is a plausible explanation.
    d. None of the above.
    e. Only a and c.
    f. Only b and c.

12. Suppose you used the same intervention as in questions 10 and 11, but before starting the group intervention you tried a social skills intervention with the client in an individual context. Suppose your ABC design yielded the following results regarding number of friends she plays with after school each day:

    A: 0 0 0 0 0 0 B: 0 0 0 0 0 0 C: 1 1 1 2 2 2

    What should you conclude from these data?

    a. It is plausible that the group intervention is effective with this client.
    b. The group intervention does not appear to be effective with this client.
    c. The individual intervention may be a necessary precursor to the group intervention.
    d. None of the above.
    e. Only a and c.
    f. Only b and c.

13. In single-case evaluation, replication can:

    a. Reduce ambiguity in the meaning of specific outcomes
    b. Enhance external validity
    c. Help in sorting out different alternative plausible explanations for particular data patterns
    d. All of the above

EXERCISES 12.1 to 12.8

Below are eight hypothetical data patterns for AB design findings in eight unrelated hypothetical practice evaluations of an intervention attempting to reduce an undesirable behavior. Develop an AB design graph for each pattern, interpret the findings, and discuss alternative explanations and whether and why the findings are ambiguous or clear-cut.

EXERCISE 12.1: A: 3 2 2 3 2 2 3 3 0 0 B: 0 0 0 0 0 0 0 0 0 0

EXERCISE 12.2: A: 1 1 1 1 1 1 3 4 4 4 B: 4 3 1 1 1 1 1 1 1 1

EXERCISE 12.3: A: 4 4 4 4 4 4 3 4 5 4 B: 4 5 4 4 3 4 4 1 0 0

EXERCISE 12.4: A: 7 4 6 3 5 3 5 2 4 1 B: 4 1 4 0 3 1 3 0 2 0

EXERCISE 12.5: A: 2 1 2 1 2 2 7 8 7 8 B: 2 1 2 0 1 2 8 2 1 1

EXERCISE 12.6: A: 3 4 3 4 3 4 3 4 3 3 B: 6 8 5 1 0 0 1 0 0 0

EXERCISE 12.7: A: 7 7 7 6 6 6 5 5 4 4 B: 3 3 3 2 2 2 1 1 0 0

EXERCISE 12.8: A: 5 5 4 4 6 5 4 5 6 5 B: 2 1 2 1 0 1 1 0 1 0

EXERCISE 12.9

On a separate page prepare an event log to be completed by clients and/or significant others for a hypothetical single-case evaluation study you make up, based, if possible, on a real case you have worked with in your field practicum or elsewhere.

DISCUSSION QUESTIONS

1. Suppose the data in Exercises 12.1 to 12.8, above, represented eight separate studies on the same intervention with the same target problem. Discuss how you would aggregate the findings of the eight studies, and interpret the aggregate findings in terms of their implications for the effectiveness of the intervention.

2. Do you think that you are likely to conduct single-case evaluations as part of your professional social work practice? Why or why not?

3. Do you think single-case evaluation designs are applicable primarily to practitioners using behavioral interventions and not very useful for practitioners using nonbehavioral interventions? Why or why not?

4. Explain the core logic of single-case evaluation designs, and discuss with respect to that logic the relative degree of internal validity of AB designs with very few data points, AB designs with many data points, ABAB designs, and multiple-baseline designs.

5. Discuss the advantages of incorporating qualitative methods—such as interviews, videotaping or audiotaping, and event logs—as part of single-case evaluation studies.

CROSSWORD PUZZLE

ACROSS

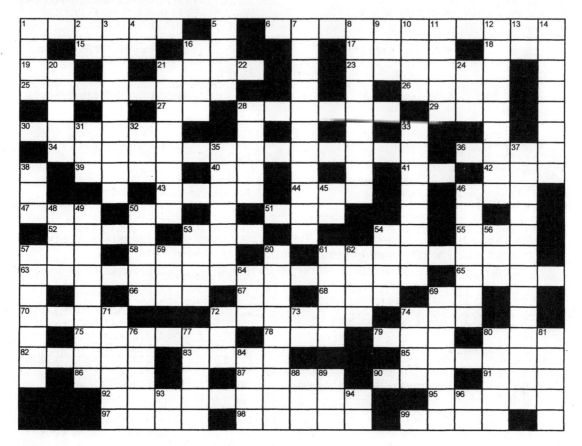

1 IDEAL BASELINE PATTERN
6 USE MORE THAN ONE MEASUREMENT OPTION
15 Pester
16 Excellent grades on two exams
17 Average
18 Nickname for Carter, Reagan, Clinton or George W. before prez.
19 Prosecutor (abbrev.)
21 Bibliography abbreviation
23 Straits or sea
25 TYPE OF VALIDITY NOT STRONG IN SINGLE-CASE DESIGNS
26 Not rich
27 Severe respiratory disease (abbrev.)
28 These are a few of my favorite ______
29 Direction from Philadelphia to Boston
30 Lure
34 ______ OF EFFECTS (possible explanation of some multiple baseline results)
36 Pub missile; or rush
39 Inert sign gas
40 Either_____
41 Where to find Jones Beach or SUNY Stony Brook (abbrev.)

DOWN

1 Agree with
2 ______ itsy bitsy spider
3 CONTROL PHASES IN SINGLE-CASE DESIGNS
4 T-shirt size (abbrev.)
5 Place for criminals
7 PROCESS THAT CAN HELP RESOLVE AMBIGUITY OR IMPROVE EXTERNAL VALIDITY IN SINGLE CASE DESIGN RESEARCH
8 ATTRIBUTE OF SOME SINGLE-CASE DESIGN RESULTS WITH UNSTABLE DATA PATTERNS
9 Once named
10 The world according to ______ .
11 Marriage
12 WHAT TO DO WITH THE RESULTS OF VARIOUS SINGLE-CASE DESIGN STUDIES
13 ______ sir, with love
14 A COMMON FUNCTION OF SINGLE CASE DESIGNS
16 ABBREVIATION FOR REVERSAL-WITHDRAWAL DESIGNS
20 Chopping

ACROSS

42 Informal summer shirt
43 MULTIPLE COMPONENT DESIGN
44 Poison ______
46 Dog, cat, or gerbil
47 Beginning of a kindergarten or pre-school song
50 ______ Smith (first Catholic nominee for president in the US)
51 Type of snake or wrap
52 Duke of ______ (Babbie's favorite song)
53 Devoured
54 Let it ______
55 ______ Paulo, Brazil
57 Feminine possessive or LBJ's dog
58 Peek-a-boo, ______ you
61 Supercuts staff
63 ______ OF EFFECTS (possible explanation of some reversal-withdrawal design results
65 Units of electrical current strength
66 Prefix often used regarding protecting the environment
67 Common abbreviation of highway signs
68 Bullfight cheer
69 Abbreviation to examine when purchasing vitamins
70 Walked on
72 Curt
74 Foot digit
75 DESIRABLE TYPE OF SIGNIFICANCE IN SINGLE CASE DESIGN GRAPHS
78 Take advantage of
79 Agassi's aim
80 Ocean crossed by Columbus (abbrev.)
82 Christopher ______ (disabled actor and stem cell research advocate)
83 SOCIAL DESIRABILITY ______ (likely problem in self-monitoring)
85 Mickey mouse's love
86 Gun a motor
87 Abundant
90 Obtain
91 Female reproductive cell
92 SELF MONITORING MAY CREATE THIS MEASUREMENT PROBLEM
95 ______ EFFECTS (may be problematic in multiple component designs)
97 Long, arduous journey
98 Stop from proceeding
99 Release

DOWN

21 TYPE OF VALIDITY ENHANCED BY HAVING MORE MEASUREMENT POINTS OR MORE BASELINES
24 IDEALLY, MEASUREMENT SHOULD BE ______-REACTIVE
28 A_2 IS THE ______ PHASE OF AN ABAB DESIGN
31 A DESIRABLE NUMBER OF BASELINE DATA POINTS
32 Head of a corporation (abbrev.)
33 ______ SUCCESSIVE COINCIDENCES INDICATE VISUAL SIGNIFICANCE
35 Finds
37 TYPE OF BASELINE WHEN A PROSPECTIVE BASELINE IS NOT POSSIBLE
38 Vegetable in a pod
45 State where Lee surrendered to Grant (abbrev.)
46 ______ OF TIME (something controlled for with multiple measurement points in baseline)
48 Ninety-nine bottles of ______ on the wall
49 ______ EFFECTS (possible problem in multiple-component design results)
50 Not dead
53 Flight or space prefix
54 Group of adjacent binary digits
56 Money machine (abbrev.)
57 MULTIPLE BASELINE DESIGNS PROVIDE MORE CONTROL FOR ______ THAN DO AB DESIGNS
59 Just a ______ (slang term for soon or wait)
60 SELF-MONITORING IS PARTICULARLY VULNERABLE TO THIS TYPE OF MEASUREMENT
61 IF THE BASELINE TREND HAS THIS, PASSAGE OF TIME MAY BE THE EXPLANATION
62 Cause to slant
64 Research ethics panel (abbrev.)
69 ONE MEASUREMENT OPTION IS TO HAVE THE CLIENT SELF-______
71 Turn aside; deflect
72 Nee Clay; "The Greatest"
73 Not them
74 SINGLE CASE DESIGNS ARE A TYPE OF ______-SERIES DESIGN
76 Cut
77 Toward the rear
80 Positively-charged electrode in a battery
81 Suspicious; wary; or LSD advocate
84 Dry
88 In good shape
89 Summer in Paris
93 First two in a vowel sequence
94 Twelve months in a ______ (abbrev.)
96 Musical tone or common abbreviation in memos

CHAPTER 13

Program Evaluation

OBJECTIVES

1. Identify the similarities and differences between program evaluation research and other forms of social work research.

2. Discuss the historical development of program evaluation.

3. Discuss the impact of managed care on program evaluation.

4. Describe the political aspects of program evaluation and their implications for objective scientific inquiry.

5. Compare the advantages and disadvantages of in-house evaluators and external evaluators.

6. Discuss political, ideological, and logistical factors that influence whether and how program evaluation is conducted or utilized.

7. Explain how evaluators can attempt to minimize stakeholder resistances to an evaluation and to maximize their utilization of it.

8. Describe quantitative and qualitative research methods used in process evaluations and in monitoring program implementation.

9. Discuss the functions of cost-effectiveness analysis and cost-benefit analysis and the complexities involved in them.

10. Discuss five alternative approaches to needs assessment and the advantages and disadvantages of each.

11. Differentiate the assessment of normative need and demand.

12. Describe the purpose of logic models in program evaluation.

13. Discuss the ways quantitative and qualitative research methods can be combined in program evaluation.

PRACTICE-RELEVANT SUMMARY

Program evaluation has become ubiquitous in social work practice, as funding sources today demand evidence regarding the return on their investments in various programs and as human service professionals seek to find better ways to help people and do not want to see scarce welfare resources squandered on programs that don't really help their intended target populations. Funding sources often require a program evaluation component as a prerequisite for approving grant applications and supportive evaluative data as a basis for renewing funding. This requirement has been a mixed blessing. It has fostered more research that could help us improve policies and programs and find better ways to help people. But it also has politicized the evaluation research process, since the findings of evaluation research can provide ammunition to the supporters or opponents of a program.

Vested interests can jeopardize free, scientific inquiry. Pressure may be exerted to design the research or to interpret its findings in ways likely to make the program look good. Sometimes program evaluation is conducted in the cheapest, most convenient way possible, guided by the belief that funding sources don't care about the quality of the research; they just want to be able to say that the programs they fund have been evaluated.

In your social work practice you will probably participate in, conduct, or utilize many program evaluations. When you do, you should not be naive about the potential influence of vested interests on the integrity or quality of evaluations. At the same time, however, you should not become so overly cynical that you dismiss all program evaluation as politically biased. People with vested interests often have sufficient integrity and professional concern for learning the best ways to help clients that they are able to put their vested interests aside and act in a manner that fosters the most objective, scientific evaluation possible.

One factor thought to influence an evaluation's vulnerability to the biasing influences of vested interests is whether the program evaluation is conducted by evaluators who work for the agency being evaluated. When they do, they are called *in-house evaluators*. In contrast, *external evaluators* work for external agencies, such as governmental or regulating agencies, private research consultation firms, or universities. Despite their vulnerability to political pressure, in-house evaluators may have certain advantages over external evaluators, such as greater access to program information and personnel and more knowledge about the program, its research needs, and potential obstacles to the feasibility of certain evaluation designs.

External evaluators also may be influenced by political considerations. In particular, they may want to get and stay in the good graces of the personnel of the program being evaluated, since those personnel often influence the decision about which external evaluators will be funded to conduct future evaluations of their services. Also, external sponsors of evaluations may be just as biased as in-house personnel. They may seek negative evaluation results to justify the cessation of funding of certain programs, or they may fret that negative results would make them (the sponsors) look bad and in turn threaten their own fundraising efforts. Whether or not program evaluation findings ultimately will be utilized often depends on whether they threaten or support deeply held beliefs or vested interests.

In addition to vested interests, another pragmatic factor influencing whether and how program evaluation studies are done is the logistics involved in their implementation. *Logistics* refers to getting subjects to do what they're supposed to do, getting research instruments distributed and returned, and other daily task details required to make a study feasible to carry out within the context of uncontrollable daily life in a particular agency. The logistical details of an evaluation project are often under the control of program administrators.

Steps have been suggested that program evaluators can take to prevent or minimize logistical problems and to promote the utility and ultimate use of their findings. To begin, they should learn as much as possible about stakeholders with vested interests in the evaluation. Evaluators should involve stakeholders in a meaningful way in planning the evaluation. Stakeholders include not only administrators and funders, but also service recipients and program personnel at all levels. Evaluators should share mutual incremental feedback with stakeholders throughout all phases of the evaluation. The cooperation of program personnel might be fostered further by assuring them that they will get to see and respond to a confidential draft of the evaluation report before it is finalized and distributed to other stakeholders. The evaluator can foster the utilization of the evaluation report by tailoring its form and style to the needs and preferences of those in a position to utilize it. Reports should be clear, succinct, cohesive, and carefully typed with a neat and uncluttered layout. When adapting the report to an audience of program personnel, do not present every peripheral finding and do not present negative findings bluntly and tactlessly. Couch negative findings in language that recognizes the yeoman efforts and skills of program personnel and that does not portray them as inadequate. Develop realistic, practical implications based on the findings.

While the foregoing steps are advisable, they are no guarantee that political or logistical pitfalls will be avoided. Your findings may be so negative that it is impossible not to threaten staff who are extremely fearful of losing precarious funding. When this happens, even if you follow all the recommended steps, stakeholders may still seek to discredit your evaluation. You may also find that the best-laid plans do not anticipate unforeseen logistical problems. Evaluation plans are unlikely to remain at the forefront of the minds of program personnel as they encounter unexpected difficulties in operating their programs and make program changes that impact the evaluation.

Program evaluation can have multiple purposes. It can assess the ultimate success of programs, problems in how programs are being implemented, or information needed in program planning and development. *Summative evaluations* are concerned with the first of the three purposes, involving the ultimate success of a program and decisions about whether it should be funded. *Formative evaluations* focus on obtaining information helpful in planning the program and in improving its implementation and performance. Summative evaluations will generally be quantitative in approach. Formative evaluations may use quantitative methods, qualitative methods, or both. These types or purposes of program evaluation are not mutually exclusive.

Evaluations of program outcome and efficiency may assess whether the program is effectively attaining its goals, whether it has any unintended harmful effects, whether its success is being achieved at a reasonable cost, and how the ratio of its benefits to its cost compares with the benefits and costs of other programs with similar objectives. This approach to evaluation is sometimes called the *goal attainment model of evaluation.* It involves operationally defining the formal goals of the program in terms of measurable indicators of program success, which serve as dependent variables in experimental and quasi-experimental designs that attempt to maximize internal validity within the feasibility constraints of the agency setting. The two major approaches to assessing the efficiency of a program are called cost-effectiveness analysis and cost-benefit analysis. In *cost-effectiveness analysis*, the only monetary considerations are the costs of the program itself; the monetary benefits of the program's effects are not assessed. In *cost-benefit analysis*, in addition to monetizing program costs, an effort is made to monetize the program's outcome.

The goal attainment model has been criticized by some for being overly concerned with formal goals, which are often stated in unreachable grandiose terms in order to secure funding or are stated so vaguely that different evaluators may not agree on how best to operationally define them. Evaluations focusing on a few operational indicators of success risk missing areas in which the program really is succeeding. Some argue that the evaluation of outcome therefore ought to be abandoned and replaced by evaluations of program processes. Others suggest keeping the goal attainment model but with some adjustments, such as measuring every conceivable indicator of outcome.

Some programs have unsuccessful outcomes simply because they are not being implemented properly. *Outcome evaluations* therefore should be supplemented by *evaluations of program implementation.* Evaluations of program implementation can have great value even without any evaluation of program outcome. If a program is not being implemented as planned, the need for changes may be implied without an outcome evaluation. But evaluations of program implementation are not necessarily concerned only with the question of whether a program is being implemented as planned. There are many other possible questions that examine how best to implement, as well as maintain, the program. Evaluations that focus on these questions are often called *process evaluations.* When programs are still in their infancy and have not yet had enough time to identify and resolve startup bugs and other problematic processes in implementation, outcome evaluations may be premature, and process evaluations may be more advisable. All of the methodologies covered in this book can be applied to evaluate program implementation. The most appropriate methodology to use depends on the nature of the research question. Although process evaluations can involve quantitative methods, they tend to rely heavily on qualitative methods such as open-ended qualitative interviewing or participant observation of staff or clients.

Evaluation also can be done before programs are implemented -- for the purpose of program planning. The most common form of this type of evaluation is called needs assessment. *Needs assessment* studies may assess the extent and location of the problems the program seeks to ameliorate as well as the target population's characteristics, problems, expressed needs, and desires. This information is then used to guide program planning and development concerning such issues as what services to offer, how to maximize service utilization by targeted subgroups, where to locate services, and so on.
Needs can be defined in normative terms or in terms of demand. When defining needs *normatively*, needs assessments compare the objective living conditions of the target population with what society deems acceptable or desirable from a humanitarian standpoint. If needs are defined in terms of *demand*, however, only the individuals who indicate that they feel or perceive the need themselves would be considered to be in need of a particular program or intervention.

Five techniques for conducting a needs assessment are: (1) the key informants approach, (2) the community forum approach, (3) the rates under treatment approach, (4) the social indicators approach, and (5) the community survey approach. The *key informants approach* utilizes questionnaires or interviews to obtain expert opinions from individuals presumed to have special knowledge about the target population's problems and needs as well as about current gaps in service delivery to that population. The prime advantage of the key informants approach is that a sample can be obtained and surveyed quickly, easily, and inexpensively. The chief disadvantage of this method is that information is not coming directly from the target population; the quality of that information depends on the objectivity and depth of knowledge underlying the expressed opinions.

The *community forum approach* involves holding a meeting in which concerned members of the community can express their views and interact freely regarding needs. The advantages of this approach include its feasibility, its ability to build support and visibility for the sponsoring agency, and its ability to provide an atmosphere in which individuals can consider the problem in depth and be stimulated by what others have said, thus taking into account things they might otherwise have overlooked. Its disadvantages include the questionable representativeness and objectivity of those who attend such meetings and of those who are the most vocal.

The *rates under treatment approach* attempts to estimate the need for a service and the characteristics of its potential clients, based on the number and characteristics of clients already using that service in a comparable community. The prime advantages of the rates under treatment approach are its quickness, simplicity, low cost, and unobtrusiveness. Its prime disadvantage is that it assesses only the portion of the target population that is already using services, and thus it pertains primarily to demand and may underestimate normative need. Additional disadvantages would be involved if the comparison community provides the service in a way that potential consumers find undesirable or has unreliable or biased records and data.

The *social indicators approach* examines aggregated statistics that reflect conditions of an entire population. Using social indicators is unobtrusive and can be done quickly and inexpensively, but there may be problems in the reliability of a particular existing database. The utility of this approach depends on the degree to which the existing indicators can be assumed to reflect future service utilization patterns accurately.

The most direct way to assess the characteristics and perceived problems and needs of the target group is to survey its members, through the *community survey approach*. The advantages and disadvantages of the direct survey approach parallel those in surveys in general. Of particular concern is the need to have high response rates and minimize measurement biases such as those connected to social desirability and acquiescent response sets. Because each of the five approaches to needs assessment has its own advantages and disadvantages, needs assessment studies ideally should combine two or more of the approaches to get a more complete picture of normative needs, felt needs, and demand for prospective services.

Some program evaluations have a comprehensive scope that covers methods and purposes associated with program planning, program processes and program outcomes. Such evaluations are enhanced by the development and use of logic models. A logic model is a graphic portrayal that depicts the essential components of a program, shows how those components are linked to short-term process objectives, specifies measurable indicators of success in achieving short-term objectives, conveys how those short-term objectives lead to long-term program outcomes, and identifies measurable indicators of success in achieving long-term outcomes. Different logic models might emphasize program theory, program activities, or program outcomes. Which logic model to choose will vary depending upon program needs and what seems to be most helpful for those involved in program management and evaluation.

REVIEW QUESTIONS

1. Which of the following statements is ***NOT*** true about program evaluation?

   a. It can apply qualitative as well as quantitative research methods.
   b. Although its rapid growth was been in the latter half of the 20th century, it dates back to earlier centuries.
   c. It is no more political than other forms of research.
   d. It is conceptually very similar to social work research.

2. Which of the following statements is true about program evaluation?

   a. It is always politically biased.
   b. It is almost never politically biased.
   c. Vested interests can impede the atmosphere for free, scientific inquiry.
   d. Funding sources always seek to obtain the most objective findings possible.

3. Which of the following is ***NOT*** an advantage of in-house evaluators (as compared to external evaluators)?

   a. Greater knowledge of the program
   b. Increased awareness of feasibility obstacles
   c. Greater independence and objectivity
   d. Greater likelihood of being trusted by program personnel

4. Which of the following statements is/are true about external evaluators?

   a. Future evaluation contracts are *not* influenced by the nature of the findings they report.
   b. Attacks on the credibility of their work are *not* motivated by the nature of the findings they report.
   c. Funding bodies sponsoring evaluations may have vested interests regarding the findings reported by the external evaluator.
   d. All of the above.
   e. None of the above.

5. In planning an evaluation, evaluators should:

   a. Minimize interaction with stakeholders who have vested interests in the outcome of the evaluation.
   b. Make sure stakeholders who have vested interests in the outcome of the evaluation are not involved in the planning of the evaluation.
   c. Keep program personnel, who ultimately might be one focus of the evaluation, out of the evaluation planning.
   d. All of the above.
   e. None of the above.

6. Summative evaluations of program success in goal attainment are more likely than other forms of evaluation to:

    a. Use experimental and quasi-experimental designs
    b. Use qualitative methods
    c. Be focused on the immediate informational needs of program administrators
    d. Ignore formal organizational goals

7. Which of the following statements is/are true about monitoring program implementation?

    a. Learning how well a program has been implemented can have an important bearing on the meaning of the results of a goal attainment evaluation.
    b. It may use quantitative as well as qualitative methods.
    c. It often involves process evaluation.
    d. All of the above.
    d. None of the above.

8. Which of the following statements is/are true about assessing the need for a particular program?

    a. The number of people who need a program may exceed the number who say they need it.
    b. The number who ultimately use the program will be accurately depicted by the number who say they will use it.
    c. We can be certain that the number of people who need a planned service in a community will be accurately depicted by the number who currently use the same service in a similar community.
    d. All of the above.
    e. None of the above.

9. In doing a cost-benefit analysis of a program:

    a. Complex principles of cost accounting are involved.
    b. We must go beyond purely economic considerations and must make value judgments about humanistic benefits.
    c. We ask whether monetized benefits exceed monetary costs.
    d. All of the above.
    e. None of the above.

10. Which of the following statements is true about the key informants approach to needs assessment?

    a. It utilizes experimental or quasi-experimental designs.
    b. Key informants are members of the target population, not practitioners.
    c. It is one of the most expensive, time-consuming approaches to needs assessment.
    d. A disadvantage is that the information is not coming directly from the target population.

11. Which of the following statements is true about the community forum approach to needs assessment?

    a. It utilizes rigorous survey designs.
    b. Its chief advantages are more pragmatic than scientific.
    c. Those who attend and speak at the forums have a high probability of being representative of the target population.
    f. It minimizes measurement bias.

12. Which of the following statements is true about the social indicators approach or the rates under treatment approach to needs assessment?

    a. The social indicators approach is obtrusive.
    b. The rates under treatment approach is obtrusive.
    c. The rates under treatment approach pertains primarily to demand and may underestimate normative need.
    d. The social indicators approach or rates under treatment approach ensures that the data are highly reliable.

13. Which of the following statements is true about the community survey or target group survey approach to needs assessment?

    a. It is an indirect way to assess need.
    b. It is the least expensive way to assess need.
    c. It is vulnerable to the disadvantage of low response rates or social desirability bias.
    d. If people say they will use a service, we can be very confident that they will use the service.

14. Which of the following statements is true about focus groups?

    a. They involve the use of quantitative research methods.
    b. Participants are typically chosen using probability sampling methods.
    c. Despite their advantages, they are expensive and time consuming.
    d. The group dynamics can bring out information that might not have emerged in a survey.

EXERCISE 13.1

Suppose you want to evaluate the effectiveness of a promising new form of child therapy to alleviate the harmful effects of traumatic experiences. To be certified to provide the new therapy, experienced practitioners must attend several weekend training workshops and ten sessions of monthly supervision. You arrange for half of the practitioners in a child guidance agency to obtain the training and supervision. Your plan is to see if the traumatized children assigned to the practitioners certified to provide the new therapy benefit more from treatment than comparable children assigned to the other practitioners.

1. What type of research design and measurement approach would you use to conduct the outcome evaluation?

2. What logistical problems would you be likely to encounter in implementing your design?

3. Who would be the stakeholders in your evaluation? What are their vested interests in the evaluation, and how might those vested interests potentially interfere with the rigor or implementation of your research design?

4. Identify the steps you would take to minimize resistance to the evaluation or the utilization of its results in the agency.

5. Describe how normative need versus demand might operate in assessing the need for the new therapy among children and their parents or guardians.

6. Discuss the importance of monitoring the implementation of the new service and how you would go about evaluating its implementation.

7. Discuss the difference in how you would evaluate the cost-effectiveness versus the cost-benefit of the new intervention. Identify difficulties in monetizing the benefits.

EXERCISE 13.2

Suppose you are a legislative aide specializing in social welfare policy for a United States senator. She is cautiously supportive of legislation to fund a series of expensive demonstration projects to test alternative ways to prevent child abuse, but only under the condition that each project be rigorously evaluated and that continued funding hinge on the evaluation findings. She envisions the funding going to the federal Office of Children bureaucracy, whose staff would administer the funding of the projects and of their evaluations. She asks you to advise her on the politics of program evaluation, how the politics may impact the evaluations, and how best to maximize the scientific integrity of the evaluation designs and their reports. What would you tell her, taking into account in-house versus external evaluators, vested interests, and the politics of evaluation? What would you recommend regarding her expectation that the federal bureaucrats will administer the evaluations?

EXERCISE 13.3

You are interested in starting a program to treat spouse abusers in an area that has not yet had such a program. But first you must document the need for the program, from a normative standpoint as well as from the standpoint of anticipating the likely level of utilization of the new program. Describe how you would assess this need, using each of the five approaches to needs assessment discussed in the text. Identify the advantages and disadvantages of each approach.

DISCUSSION QUESTIONS

1. Can all social work research be considered program evaluation research? Why or why not? If your answer is "no" identify, for discussion purposes, a social work research question that we would not be able to fit under the program evaluation rubric.

2. Do you agree with those who argue that evaluations should not focus on the attainment of formal organizational goals? Why or why not?

3. Discuss the value of combining quantitative and qualitative research methods in program evaluation and illustrate how it can be done.

CROSSWORD PUZZLE

ACROSS

1 _____ ASSESSMENT IS A COMMON FOCUS OF EVALUATION FOR PROGRAM PLANNING
4 A COMPREHENSIVE, YET RELATIVELY COSTLY APPROACH TO ASSESSING NEEDS IS TO CONDUCT A _____ SURVEY OF THE COMMUNITY
9 We're _____ to see the wizard
10 Cube root of one thousand
11 EVALUATING _____ ATTAINMENT CAN BE COMPLICATED BY THE INTENTIONALLY GRANDIOUS NATURE OF SOME ORGANIZATIONAL MISSION STATEMENTS
13 Going
16 Al from Tennessee
17 INVOLVING STAKEHOLDERS IN PLANNING AN EVALUATION MAY ENHANCE ITS EVENTUAL _____
20 Shirt size between Med and XL
21 ANALYZING _____ INDICATORS (ONE WAY TO ASSESS COMMUNITY NEEDS)
22 American playwright who wrote Tiny Alice and others
24 Lifted
25 Ernie's pal on Sesame Street
26 Greek vowel
27 Britain's Isle of _____
28 Type of poem
30 Sixth sense
32 _____ GROUPS INVOLVE PEOPLE IN A GUIDED DISCUSSION
35 Contingency word
36 Gab
37 ONE PURPOSE OF PROGRAM EVALUATION IS TO _____ PROGRAM IMPLEMENTATION
39 Monopoly purchase (abbrev.)
40 One third of a yd.
41 State south of WY
42 News service (abbrev.)
45 Traveler's place to stay
47 Francis Scott _____
48 _____ CARE: ONE HISTORICAL FORCE AFFECTING THE POLITICS OF PROGRAM EVALUATION
49 Clinton thought this word has multiple definitions
50 May honorees
52 _____ FORCES CAN BIAS PROGRAM EVALUATIONS
57 UCLA mascot or Boston hockey mascot
58 Goose's mate
61 _____ EFFECTIVENESS ANALYSIS (ONE WAY TO ASSESS PROGRAM EFFICACY)
62 Separate
63 South of MD and DC
64 Get together
66 STAKEHOLDERS MAY HAVE _____ INTERESTS IN AN EVALUATION
68 _____ UNDER TREATMENT APPROACH TO NEEDS ASSESSMENT
70 Clay as a lad
71 Flavor
72 Male or female

DOWN

1 Take your time!
2 Failing grade
3 EVALUATIONS OF PROGRAM _____ ASK WHETHER OUTCOMES ARE BEING ACHIEVED AT A REASONABLE COST
4 Gainsay
5 Gerund ending
6 Goad (on)
7 Not so warm
8 SOME NEEDS ASSESSMENTS SURVEY MEMBERS OF ____ GROUPS
10 Descriptive heading
12 He's to the left of the LT
14 Those most likely to be invited, or what Santa makes and then checks twice
15 lasso
18 Overly
19 Where Napoleon was exiled
23 COST-_______ ANALYSES ATTEMPT TO MONETIZE PROGRAM OUTCOMES
27 Give __ a break!
29 ONE WAY TO DEFINE NEED IS IN TERMS OF ____
31 A ____ EVALUATION IS A FORM OF MONITORING PROGRAM IMPLEMENTATION THAT CAN BE USED TO IDENTIFY AND IRON OUT BUGS IN A PROGRAM
32 ONE PRAGMATIC, YET SCIENTIFICALLY RISKY FORM OF NEEDS ASSESSMENT IS TO HOLD A COMMUNITY _______
33 Former Middle Eastern Alliance
34 Shoot, stem or twig broken from a plant
35 ANOTHER PRAGMATIC WAY TO ASSESS NEEDS IS BY INTERVIEWING KEY _______.
38 Dale and Trigger both loved him
43 Abbreviation in letters to Altoona, Reading or Scranton
44 ________ EVALUATORS ARE EMPLOYED FULL TIME BY THE AGENCY THEY EVALUATE
46 Wait till ___ year!
47 Common Korean surname
51 Ancient
52 Punctual
53 1.056 liquid quarts
54 Accepted or elected
55 _____ at the office!
56 Affectionate touch
57 Before A.D.
59 ___ Kneivel
60 Pre-television entertainment source
65 Tit for ___!
67 Strain or levy
69 Lineman who is eligible to catch passes (abbrev.)

CHAPTER 14

Sampling

OBJECTIVES

1. Define sampling and distinguish between the following terms: sample, population, and sampling frame.

2. Provide an example of how social workers commonly use sampling as part of their everyday practice.

3. Provide an example of sampling bias in social work practice.

4. Provide an example of a sampling frame that is biased with regard to a particular target population of concern to social workers.

5. Using a hypothetical example from social work practice, illustrate sampling error resulting from a sample size that is too small.

6. Describe the key feature of probability sampling, and explain how it safeguards against sampling bias.

7. Describe and illustrate the following major types of probability sampling and their functions: simple random sampling; systematic sampling; stratified sampling; and multistage cluster sampling.

8. Identify two reasons why nonprobability sampling techniques are often used in social work research and practice, and provide an example that would require the use of a nonprobability sampling technique.

9. Describe and illustrate the methods, functions, and risks for each of the following types of nonprobability sampling: purposive or judgmental sampling, quota sampling, reliance on available subjects, and snowball sampling.

10. Describe and illustrate how, despite the risks in availability sampling, some studies using it can provide useful tentative findings.

11. Provide an example of gender bias in sampling.

PRACTICE-RELEVANT SUMMARY

Sampling is the process of selecting observations. In research, the sampling process is selected in a deliberate, strategic manner in which the researcher decides whom or what to observe as a basis for generating new ideas, testing hypotheses, or generalizing about the characteristics of a population. In life outside of the research arena, we all conduct a less systematic, less conscious form of sampling as we make decisions in our daily lives based on incomplete sets of observations. We may, for example, ask our friends about their experiences with their automobiles as one basis for deciding what brand of car to buy. Or we may decide to see a movie that several people recommended. Chances are you decided to enter the field of social work based on an incomplete set of observations (that is, a sample) about this profession. As you amass more observations about social work in your classroom study and fieldwork, you will enlarge your sample and learn whether your original sample gave you a reasonably accurate portrayal of the profession.

Daily sampling decisions also are made in social work practice. Direct-practice decisions about recommended intervention plans, for example, may be made on an incomplete set of observations based on what segments of a client system say or do while in your office. This sample of observations may or may not give an accurate portrayal of how all the members of a client system function away from your office. Decisions about what services to offer may be made based on what is said at a community or agency meeting. The people who attend or are most vocal at that meeting may or may not present an accurate portrayal of the kinds of services that are most needed. Perhaps the people with the greatest needs are the least likely to attend the meeting or the most reticent about speaking up. Decisions about agency processes may be made based on client feedback. But perhaps only the most satisfied clients provide the feedback; perhaps the most dissatisfied ones don't bother, and therefore the feedback is misleadingly positive and fails to identify needed changes. As you gain experience in this (or any other) profession, you will probably encounter a few administrators who favor a form of sampling in which they only seek out the opinions of staff members who always agree with them. These administrators, and their sycophants, are probably unaware of the bias in this form of sampling, believing that they simply provide the best set of observations and that those outside the in-group are outside because they provide less valuable observations.

Daily practice decisions, therefore, can be faulty if they are based on a faulty sample of observations. Samples of observations can be faulty and consequently misleading if the sampling process is biased, as in the examples above. Faulty and misleading decisions can also result from a sample that is too small. It would be foolhardy to bet a large sum on the outcome of an election based only on the candidate your next-door neighbor favors. In social work practice it would be foolhardy to invest a great deal of time and other resources in developing a large new program based on what only a couple of people said they needed.

Scientific sampling procedures have been developed so that we can minimize the likelihood that the samples we select will be biased or too small. These procedures are a critical part of social research. They can also be applied in making practice decisions, and when they cannot be applied, practitioners should at least be mindful of the risks they take when they base decisions on unscientifically selected samples.

The key feature of scientific sampling is the use of *probability methods,* which make it possible for every member of a population to have an equal chance of being selected into the sample. These methods also make it possible to estimate the amount of sampling error that can be expected in a given sample size. *Random selection* is the key to this process. Random selection does not mean haphazard selection; it is a careful, precise process. In *simple random sampling,* for example, each unit of a population is assigned a number. A table of random numbers is used to generate a list of random numbers, and the units having those numbers are included in the sample. An acceptable alternative to simple random sampling, one that may be more practical to use, is *systematic sampling*. A systematic sample is drawn by selecting every *k*th unit in a population.

For even greater precision, and to ensure adequate numbers of small subgroups (ethnic minorities, perhaps) in the sample, *stratified sampling* can be used. With this method, rather than selecting our sample from one overall list of the total population, we begin by breaking that list down into lists of homogeneous subsets of the population. For example, we may break it down into six lists, one list for each of the following ethnic groups: African Americans, Asian Americans, Mexican Americans, Native Americans, Whites, and Others. Then we would randomly or systematically select the appropriate number of elements from each list.

Another sampling technique, *multistage cluster sampling,* is used when the members of a population cannot be easily listed, or when they are geographically so dispersed as to make it too costly to travel great distances to reach small numbers of selected elements. If the elements of the population are already grouped into clusters (churches, schools, and so on), a list of all clusters can be sampled using any of the three foregoing probability sampling techniques. After the clusters are selected in this way, elements within each cluster can be selected using the same techniques.

An important caveat in the use of probability sampling involves the distinction between populations and sampling frames. A sampling frame is the list of elements from which a probability sample is selected. Some limited sampling frames fail to include certain segments of the population. Thus, if you selected a probability sample of spouse abusers based on a sampling frame that lists only the spouse abusers receiving treatment for spouse abuse, your probability sample would not be representative of the population of spouse abusers, because those not in treatment would be excluded. If you sought to generalize only to the segment of the population of spouse abusers who are in treatment, your sampling frame would be fine. But using it to generalize to the entire population of spouse abusers would yield a biased sample, despite the use of probability sampling.

Another important caveat involves the possibility of non-response bias, which occurs when a substantial proportion of people in the randomly selected sample choose not participate in the study. There is no scientific or mathematical formula as to where the cutoff point is for deeming the refusal rate to be too high to still interpret your findings as if they were based on probability sampling. One way to estimate whether the refusal rate is too high is by examining whether your findings could have changed in a meaningful way had people who refused actually participated. This determination would assess the proportion of refusals. Is it large enough such that had the people refusing actually participated, and had they been unlike the actual participants in regard to the variables of your study, would have changed your findings to a meaningful extent?

Although it is important for you to understand the basics of probability sampling techniques and to utilize them when possible, you also should know that feasibility constraints frequently prevent the use of probability sampling in social work research and practice. Instead, practitioners and researchers often must *rely on their judgment to purposively* select a sample that seems representative or that seems to fit the purpose of the inquiry. Sometimes they simply *rely on available subjects* to whom they have easy and inexpensive access for data gathering. For some inquiries, such as in surveying the homeless or undocumented immigrants, subjects are hard to identify or find. Under these conditions, snowball sampling is used. This involves asking subjects you locate to guide you to other members of the target population, and then asking each additional subject you locate to help you find additional members whom they know. This is called *snowball sampling,* since subjects are accumulated gradually in a snowball fashion.

All of the foregoing sampling techniques that do not involve the use of probability methods—purposive (or judgment) sampling, reliance on available subjects, and snowball sampling—are called *nonprobability sampling procedures*. You probably will have to use these procedures frequently. When you do, it is important to be cautious and mindful of the risks inherent in not using probability techniques. To help offset these risks, sometimes a nonprobability technique called *quota sampling* is used. Using this technique, you select a specified proportion of subjects with specific characteristics (such as gender, ethnicity, and so on). Although using quotas may improve a nonprobability sample, it does not guarantee protection against sampling biases, as does probability sampling.

Sometimes you will encounter studies that make no effort to be representative of or generalize to a population. These studies often will be called *qualitative investigations*. Qualitative studies tend to be more exploratory in nature and seek to probe into deeper meanings among a very small sample. Rather than select samples that are representative, therefore, these studies select theoretically meaningful samples that conceivably may be unrepresentative. Rather than attempt to derive generalizable findings, these studies intend to generate tentative new insights or new hypotheses whose generality can be investigated in future studies. Qualitative studies should not be denigrated because they do not use probability sampling or because they eschew concerns about sampling error or representativeness, since they neither intend nor claim to accurately portray a population. Rather, the quality of the sampling (as well as other methodological features of qualitative studies) should be judged according to whether the study generates tentative new ideas or new ways of looking at things. A qualitative study using nonprobability sampling that gives us a fresh new tentative perspective on a problem, or which helps us understand more deeply its possible meanings to or influences on people, can be just as valuable (if not more so) than a study that uses probability sampling to accurately portray the extent of an already-known phenomenon.

Thus, although probability sampling is less risky than nonprobability sampling from the standpoint of generalizing accurately to a population, some good studies use nonprobability sampling. Rather than think you must always use probability sampling, you should understand when certain sampling techniques are more appropriate than others, the functions of each technique, how feasibility constraints bear on the choice of a sampling procedure, and the risks inherent when samples are too small or vulnerable to bias.

Regardless of whether you are using probability or nonprobability sampling techniques, you should be careful to avoid gender bias — a bias that has become increasingly evident with the advent of feminism. We should never generalize to both genders when one gender is not adequately represented in the research sample. Likewise, you should avoid cultural bias, such as when certain minority groups are inadequately represented in the sample but generalizations are made to the entire population

REVIEW QUESTIONS

1. Which of the following statements about sampling is ***NOT*** true?

   a. It is the process of selecting some elements of a population from a larger set of elements.
   b. It makes little difference which sampling method is used; they all provide reasonably accurate information.
   c. Large populations, in the millions, can be accurately portrayed with samples of less than 2000.
   d. All of the above statements are true.
   e. None of the above statements is true.

2. Sampling error can result from:

   a. Samples that are too small
   b. Biased sampling procedures
   c. Biased sampling frames
   d. All of the above

3. In general, sampling error decreases as:

   a. The sample size increases
   b. The population ages
   c. The standard deviation increases
   d. All of the above
   e. None of the above
   f. Only a and b are true

4. You want to generalize to the nation's population of spouse abusers in treatment. You handpick five treatment programs for your sample because you believe them to be highly representative of the population. You have selected:

    a. A cluster sample
    b. A purposive or judgmental sample
    c. A quota sample
    d. A snowball sample
    e. A simple random sample

5. Which of the following statements is ***NOT*** true about probability sampling?

    a. It enables every member of a population to have an equal chance of being selected into the sample.
    b. It will always be perfectly representative of the population.
    c. It enables us to estimate the degree of sampling error in our data.
    d. It is the best way to avoid conscious or unconscious sampling bias.
    e. All of the above statements are true.
    f. None of the above statements is true.

6. To assess client satisfaction, a social worker in a large family service agency sends a questionnaire to all 1000 clients who completed or dropped out of services during the past two years. Five hundred clients respond to the survey. Which of the following statements is true about this sampling procedure?

    a. It was random, since the social worker exerted no influence over who responded and therefore the response pattern was haphazard.
    b. The sample was probably representative, since such a large proportion of the population responded.
    c. It was not particularly vulnerable to sampling bias.
    d. All of the above are true.
    e. None of the above is true.

7. A social worker attempts to generate new insights about adult survivors of childhood sexual abuse by conducting in-depth interviews with those survivors she is able to identify and locate. She begins by attending a small self-help group for adult survivors and then asking the members who agree to be interviewed to identify other survivors who might agree to be interviewed. She continues this process with each new interviewee. Which of the following statements is true about this sampling procedure?

    a. It is called snowball sampling.
    b. In light of the circumstances and purpose of the study, it can be more appropriate to use than probability sampling.
    c. It is highly vulnerable to sampling error.
    d. All of the above are true.
    e. None of the above is true.

8. To assess the need in a small and very poor town for parent education classes on child nurturance, a social worker randomly selects telephone numbers from the phone book and then interviews the mother in each home where small children reside. Which of the following statements is/are true about this sampling procedure?

    a. It uses probability sampling techniques.
    b. It involves gender bias.
    c. Its sampling frame might be biased against the very poor.
    d. All of the above.
    e. None of the above.
    f. Only b and c are true.

9. You want to conduct a nationwide study interviewing spouse abusers in spouse abuse treatment programs. You want to minimize sampling error and maximize the representativeness of your sample. You have no population list, but you do have a list of all spouse abuse treatment programs. You have limited travel funds and want to conduct your interviews with as little travel as required for a representative sample. You should:

    a. Conduct cluster sampling
    b. Randomly select a sample of treatment programs, then randomly select participants in the selected programs
    c. Conduct simple random sampling
    d. Conduct nonprobability sampling
    e. None of the above
    f. Only a and b
    g. Only b and c

10. You want to assess client satisfaction with your large statewide agency's services. You want to make sure that enough members of certain small minority subgroups are included in the sample. You want to minimize sampling error and maximize the representativeness of your sample. You should use:

    a. Cluster sampling
    b. Stratified sampling
    c. Systematic sampling
    d. Quota sampling
    e. Purposive sampling

11. To learn more about spouse abusers in treatment in general you interview every spouse abuser in treatment in your agency. You have interviewed:

    a. The population
    b. A nonprobability quota sample
    c. A nonprobability sample that relied on available subjects
    d. A probability sample
    e. A snowball sample

EXERCISE 14.1 TO 14.4

Below and over the next few pages is a made-up list of 100 fictional names of fictional service recipients. Beside each name is the person's fictional ethnicity, their fictional level of satisfaction with services, and whether (in this fictional depiction) they would reply to a mailed questionnaire about their satisfaction with services. This list is to be used in Exercises 14.1 to 14.4.

Name	Ethnicity[1]	Satisfaction[2]	Reply[3]
00. H. Aaron	W	10	Yes
01. A. Adler	W	10	Yes
02. A. Ant	W	10	Yes
03. E. Babbie	W	10	Yes
04. E. Banks	AfA	9	Yes
05. B. Bradley	W	9	Yes
06. J. Carter	W	9	Yes
07. C. Cielo	H	9	Yes
08. C. Chan	AsA	8	Yes
09. W. Clinton	AfA	8	Yes
10. J. Cobb	NA	8	Yes
11. C. Coolidge	W	8	Yes
12. V. Corleone	W	8	Yes
13. G. Costanza	W	8	Yes
14. L. Doone	W	8	Yes
15. D. Dors	W	8	Yes
16. D. Duck	W	8	Yes
17. J. Edwards	W	8	No
18. B. Eden	W	8	Yes
19. G. Estevan	H	8	Yes
20. D. Evans	W	7	Yes
21. C. Evert	W	7	Yes

	Name	Ethnicity[1]	Satisfaction[2]	Reply[3]
22.	P. Ewing	AfA	7	Yes
23.	F. Fabio	W	7	Yes
24.	F. Fannon	W	7	Yes
25.	J. Ferrer	W	7	Yes
26.	R. Fingers	W	7	Yes
27.	J. Fischer	W	7	No
28.	L. Fishburne	AfA	7	Yes
29.	G. Gamble	AfA	7	Yes
30.	J. Garcia	H	7	Yes
31.	C. George	NA	6	Yes
32.	F. Gump	W	6	No
33.	P. Gunn	W	6	No
34.	N. Hale	W	6	Yes
35.	M. Ham	W	6	Yes
36.	M. Hammer	AfA	6	No
37.	H. Hidalgo	H	6	Yes
38.	A. Hirt	W	6	No
39.	D. Ho	AsA	6	Yes
40.	H. Hoover	W	6	Yes
41.	B. Hogan	W	6	Yes
42.	Mr. Hyde	W	6	No
43.	L. Ito	AsA	6	Yes
44.	J. Jackson	AfA	6	Yes
45.	M. Jackson	AfA	6	Yes
46.	Dr. Jeckyll	W	6	No
47.	T. Jefferson	W	6	Yes
48.	S. Jobs	W	6	Yes

	Name	Ethnicity[1]	Satisfaction[2]	Reply[3]
49.	A. Jolson	W	6	No
50.	J. Joplin	W	6	Yes
51.	C. Kramer	W	6	No
52.	K. Kong	AsA	5	No
53.	L. Lau	AsA	5	Yes
54.	Ledbelly	AfA	5	Yes
55.	R.E. Lee	W	5	No
56.	J. Lemon	AfA	5	Yes
57.	J. Lennon	W	5	No
58.	A. Loos	AsA	5	Yes
59.	L. Lovett	AfA	5	Yes
60.	L. Luciano	W	5	No
61.	Mr. Lucky	W	5	No
62.	C. Manson	W	5	No
63.	R. Martin	H	5	Yes
64.	C. Marx	W	5	No
65.	G. Marx	W	5	No
66.	H. Marx	W	5	No
67.	K. Marx	W	5	No
68.	Z. Marx	W	5	No
69.	W. Mays	AfA	4	No
70.	M. McGuire	W	4	Yes
71.	M. Monroe	W	4	No
72.	M. Mouse	W	4	No
73.	M. Munson	NA	4	No
74.	C. Neal	AfA	4	Yes
75.	N. Nee	AsA	4	No

	Name	Ethnicity[1]	Satisfaction[2]	Reply[3]
76.	N. Neff	AfA	4	No
77.	W. Nelson	W	4	Yes
78.	N. Nolte	W	4	Yes
79.	H. Newton	AfA	3	No
80.	R. Nixon	AfA	3	Yes
81.	O. North	AfA	3	No
82.	P. Ochs	NA	3	No
83.	O. Ojeda	H	3	No
84.	A. Oliver	AfA	3	No
85.	L. Olivier	AfA	3	No
86.	M. Osmond	AfA	3	Yes
87.	P. Pan	AsA	3	No
88.	P. Parker	AfA	2	No
89.	B. Parks	NA	2	Yes
90.	O. Paz	H	2	No
91.	J. Peron	H	2	No
92.	S. Rhee	AsA	2	No
93.	S. Sosa	AfA	2	No
94.	L. Steffens	AfA	2	No
95.	S. Sue	AsA	2	No
96.	M. Tamayo	H	1	No
97.	R. Valens	H	1	No
98.	J. Williams	AfA	1	No
99.	O. Winfrey	AfA	1	No

[1]Ethnicity codes: W = White, not Hispanic; AfA = African American; NA = Native American; AsA = Asian American; H = Hispanic.

[2]Level of satisfaction with services from 1 (lowest satisfaction) to 10 (highest satisfaction).

[3]Would they reply to a mailed questionnaire?

Mean level of satisfaction for entire list = 5.49

Number of names in each ethnicity category (the number is the same as the percentage, since the total number is 100) and their mean satisfaction level:

White	50	mean = 6.54
African American	25	mean = 4.36
Hispanic	10	mean = 4.40
Asian American	10	mean = 4.60
Native American	5	mean = 4.60
TOTAL	100	mean = 5.49

Exercises 14.1 to 14.4 involve the use of the box in Appendix B of the text that displays a Table of Random Numbers and the accompanying box that explains how to use the table of random numbers. (The list ranges from 00 to 99, instead of 1 to 100, so that you need only use two digits from the random numbers table.)

EXERCISE 14.1

1. Select a simple random sample of 20 names from the above list. Briefly explain the procedure you used to select the 20 names.

2. How many members in your sample are from each of the five categories of ethnicity in the above list? How does that compare to their percentages above?

3. Add up the 20 satisfaction scores of the 20 names you randomly selected. Divide the sum by 20 to find the average (mean) satisfaction score of your sample. How close did your sample's mean come to the overall mean of 5.49 from the list? Briefly explain.

4. To what do you attribute the closeness or discrepancies between the proportions of ethnic groups in your sample and the proportions of ethnic groups in the list of 100? To what do you attribute the closeness or discrepancy between the mean satisfaction level of your sample and the overall mean of 5.49 from the list? Briefly explain.

EXERCISE 14.2

1. Repeat Exercise 14.1, but select a systematic sample (beginning with a random start) of 20 names instead of a simple random sample. Briefly explain the procedure you used to select the 20 names.

2. Compare the results with those in Exercise 14.1. Discuss the similarities and differences from the standpoint of sampling error and from the standpoint of whether the two sampling methods are essentially interchangeable.

3. Add the mean satisfaction scores of your two samples of 20 names each (the mean from Exercise 14.1 added to the mean of Exercise 14.2). Divide the sum by 2 to obtain a mean of the two means. Does the latter mean come closer to the overall mean of 5.49? Briefly explain why or why not.

EXERCISE 14.3

1. Using the same list of 100 names, select a stratified sample of 20 names, stratifying by ethnicity. Select 10 Whites, 5 African Americans, 2 Hispanics, 2 Asian Americans, and 1 Native American. Briefly explain the procedure you used to select the 20 names.

2. Add up the 20 satisfaction scores of the 20 names in your stratified sample. Divide the sum by 20 to find the average (mean) satisfaction score of your sample. How close did your sample's mean come to the overall mean of 5.49 from the list? How does the accuracy of your stratified sample's mean compare to the accuracy of the

means from the simple random sample and from the systematic sample? Is that what you expected? Why or why not? Briefly explain why the stratified sample's mean was or was not closer than the other two means to the overall mean of 5.49.

EXERCISE 14.4

Examine the fourth column of the list of 100 names. Notice that it indicates whether clients would reply to a mailed questionnaire. Fifty-five would reply, and 45 would not.

1. If your sample consisted only of the 55 names who responded, what type of sample would that be?

2. What would the advantages and disadvantages of that sample be compared to the ones you selected in Exercises 14.1 to 14.3?

3. If you calculate the mean scores of those who would and would not reply, you would find that the 55 respondents have a mean satisfaction level of 6.67, whereas the mean for the 45 who would not reply is 4.00. How does the accuracy of the means of the samples you drew in Exercises 14.1 to 14.3 compare to the accuracy of the 6.67 mean of the above fictionalized sample of 55 respondents to a mailed questionnaire? What does this imply for what you would do later on in your professional practice if you ever need to conduct a client satisfaction survey?

EXERCISE 14.5

1. Discuss the conditions under which selecting a purposive sample would be warranted.

2. What would be the risks?

EXERCISE 14.6

1. Discuss the conditions under which selecting a snowball sample would be warranted.

2. What would be the risks?

3. Briefly describe how you would go about selecting a snowball sample of women who have been battered by their mates but have not reported the abuse, have not sought services, and continue to live with the batterer.

DISCUSSION QUESTIONS

1. Your supervisor assigns you to conduct a needs assessment study to ascertain the extent of need in your agency's geographic area for new services not yet provided but that could be developed and offered by your agency. She suggests that you prepare a form asking about need for the new services that current clients can voluntarily fill out and drop in a box while they wait for their appointments. How would you react to her suggestion? Would you suggest an alternative sampling procedure you believe would yield better, more representative information? If so, identify and briefly describe the alternative procedure you would propose. Briefly explain your rationale for agreeing with her suggestion or for proposing the alternative procedure.

2. Although a large number of professional social workers are members of the National Association of Social Workers (NASW), many others are not. Your state chapter of NASW decides to survey social workers in your state to see if they adequately understand legal and ethical codes regarding dual relationships with clients. As an active member of the chapter who has expertise in research methods, you are appointed to chair a committee to conduct the survey. The members of your committee suggest that your sample be randomly selected from the statewide NASW membership list. They argue that because the sample would be random, it would be free from bias. Remembering your research methods text's discussion about the difference between populations and sampling frames, you feel compelled to tactfully point out a potential bias in their suggested procedure, despite the fact that it involves probability sampling. Briefly state your response and specify alternative or additional sampling procedures that you would suggest.

3. You have a limited amount of travel money and time to conduct face-to-face interviews with eighth-graders about their exposure to substance abuse. However, your agency wants your study to be statewide and your sample to be representative of eighth-graders in the state

   a. If you decided to use a probability sampling procedure, which would it be? Briefly describe how you would implement it.

   b. If you decided to use a nonprobability sampling procedure that you felt would have the best chance of any nonprobability sampling procedure of yielding a representative sample, which nonprobability sampling procedure would you choose? Briefly describe how you would implement it. You have a limited amount of travel money and time to conduct face-to-face interviews with eighth-graders about their exposure to substance abuse. However, your agency wants your study to be statewide and your sample to be representative of eighth-graders in the state.

4. Conceptualize and describe a hypothetical example of gender bias in selecting a sample for a social work research study connected to assessing or intervening with a particular problem. Explain how it is biased and the undesirable practical implications of that bias.

5. You have been assigned to conduct a survey to assess the social service needs of undocumented immigrants from Mexico who reside in the United States and are worried about being deported back to Mexico. What special sampling challenges would this assignment pose? How would cultural competence help you deal with these obstacles?

CROSSWORD PUZZLE

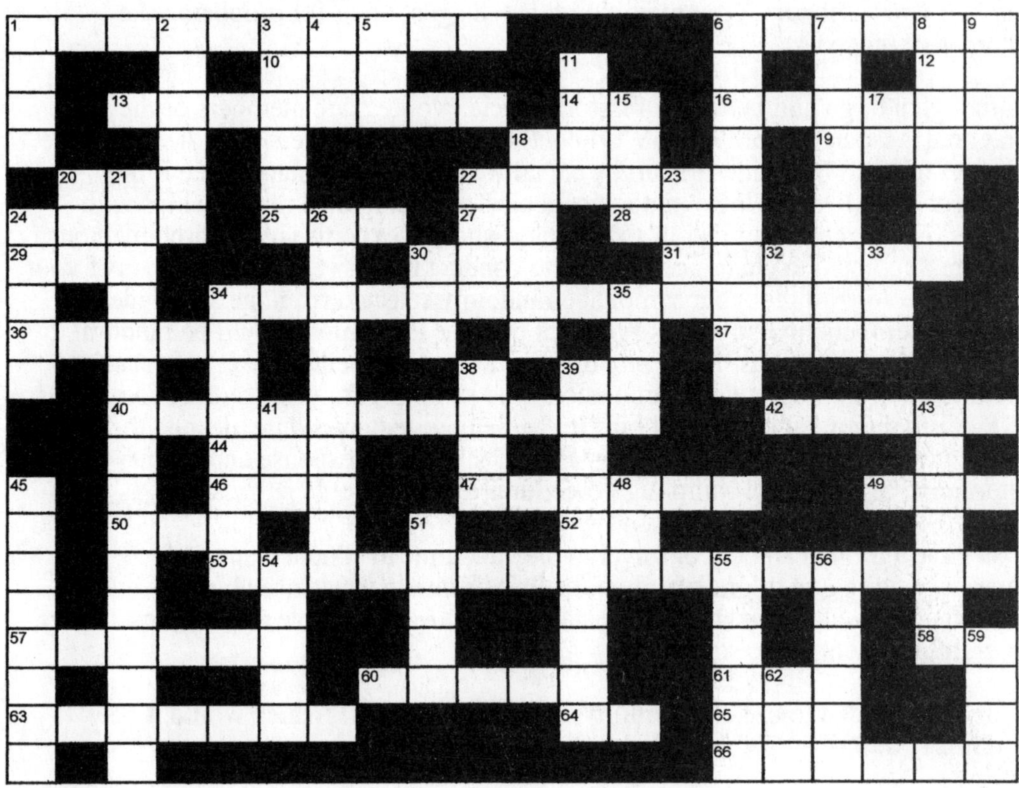

ACROSS

1 PURPOSIVE OR ______ SAMPLING
6 Evening meal
10 Owed
12 Yes or ______?
13 TYPE OF SAMPLING COMMONLY USED IN QUALITATIVE RESEARCH
14 Record album
16 Rigorous
18 Korean auto
19 Uncontaminated
20 Type of poem
22 TYPE OF RANDOM SAMPLE
24 Dyad
25 Dept. of Public Safety acronym
27 "______ You Like It"
28 Goal
29 No ______ and or buts
30 Donkey or fool
31 Cruel person
34 IN ORDER TO GENERALIZE TO A POPULATION, YOUR SAMPLE SHOULD BE ______
36 Damn
37 Concept
39 ______ what?!
40 TYPE OF SAMPLE THAT PERMITS ESTIMATES OF THE AMOUNT OF SAMPLING ERROR
42 ______ me if you can
44 Old pro
46 Former Ugandan dictator ______ Amin
47 Yassir ______
49 Three men in a ______ (nursery rhyme)
50 SAMPLING INTERVAL FOR SELECTING 100 CASES FROM A SAMPLING FRAME OF 1000 CASES
52 Offensive lineman in football (abbreviated)
53 FEATURE OF GOOD PROBABILITY SAMPLES
57 KEY ATTRIBUTE OF ALL PROBABILITY SAMPLES
58 Second musical note
60 SAMPLING ______ (LIST OF SAMPLING UNITS)
61 Immature flower
63 Walks unsteadily
64 First musical note
65 Anger
66 Irregular weather system causing flow of warm air

DOWN

1 ______ the Baptist
2 A POSSIBLE FORM OF SAMPLING BIAS
3 King who abdicated
4 Knob
5 Hot or cold drink
6 EFFICIENT ALTERNATIVE TO SIMPLE IN RANDOM SAMPLING
7 TYPE OF SAMPLING USING HANDPICKED ELEMENTS BASED ON YOUR KNOWLEDGE OF THE POPULATION
8 Encipher
9 Mechanical routine
11 Thin
15 Daddy
17 Home of the Hoosiers (abbrev.)
18 Slang term for face
20 Lummox
21 TYPE OF STRATEFIED SAMPLE FOR INCLUDING LARGER PROPORTIONS OF CASES FROM SMALL MINORIT GROUPS
22 Talk back impudently
23 Mona ______
24 Part of puzzle or pie
26 ALL OF THE ELEMENTS FROM WHICH A SAMPLE IS DRAWN
30 Democrat opponent of D.D.E. in 1952 and 1956
32 Acted
33 Red, Bering, or Dead
34 Deleting
35 Helen's home
38 Deceased jazz singer ______ Fitzgerald
39 TYPE OF RANDOM SAMPLING USED TO ENSURE SELECTION OF ELEMENTS FROM SMALL GROUPS
41 Place to sleep
43 MULTISTAGE ______ SAMPLING
45 African American, Asian American, Mexican American, or Native American

CHAPTER 15

Survey Research

OBJECTIVES

1. Identify two advantages and two disadvantages of using surveys as a mode of observation.

2. Identify two types of surveys commonly conducted in social work agencies.

3. Identify two advantages of using self-administered questionnaires in surveys.

4. Describe three methods for promoting higher response rates in mailed surveys.

5. Describe the function and process of monitoring mailed questionnaires.

6. Prepare an effective cover letter for a mailed survey.

7. Discuss the importance of non response in mailed surveys and identify response rates that are generally considered adequate, good, and very good.

8. Identify four advantages of interviews over questionnaires.

9. Describe five general rules for survey interviewing.

10. Identify three advantages and two disadvantages of telephone surveys, as compared to face-to-face surveys.

11. Discuss the advantages and disadvantages of online surveys.

PRACTICE-RELEVANT SUMMARY

Surveys are a data collection method in which a sample of respondents is interviewed or administered questionnaires. Surveys have been conducted since ancient times and are one of the most frequently used modes of observation in social work and the social sciences. Surveys offer an expedient way to collect data describing populations. Surveys can be used for exploratory and explanatory as well as descriptive purposes. They can be cross-sectional or longitudinal. Individuals are the most common units of analysis, but not the only ones.

Due largely to the feasibility of surveys, and their relevance to some important concerns of social work agencies, social work practitioners—particularly those in administrative or planning positions—often find themselves involved in conducting surveys. Common foci of agency surveys are the satisfaction of their clients with the services they have received and the needs of current and prospective clients for new services being planned.

The use of self-administered questionnaires is one of the most expedient ways to conduct a survey. Self-administered questionnaires are relatively inexpensive and take relatively little time to administer. Another advantage is that they give respondents complete anonymity, which might be important when sensitive topics are covered. The mailed survey method is the one most commonly used with self-administered questionnaires.

A key factor influencing the representativeness—and hence the value—of mailed surveys is the response rate. Several methods can be used to encourage higher response rates. One is the use of a self-mailing questionnaire requiring no return envelope. If that is not feasible, you can use stamped, self-addressed return envelopes. A cover letter should explain the importance of the survey, express the endorsement of esteemed sponsors, guarantee anonymity to respondents and explain how they were selected, and indicate how long the questionnaire takes to complete. Shorter questionnaires are more likely to be returned than longer ones.

It is important to monitor the returns of questionnaires. As the rate of return starts dropping off, a follow-up mailing should occur. It is a good idea to plan on two follow-up mailings, two or three weeks apart. It is best to send a new copy of the questionnaire with each follow-up letter of encouragement. The higher the response rate, the greater the likelihood that the sample is representative of the population. No strict, precise standards exist to help you determine whether your response rate is acceptable. Rules of thumb, however, are commonly used, which depict 50% as an adequate response rate, 60% as a good response rate, and 70% as a very good response rate.

Interviews offer some advantages over self-administered questionnaires. One is that they decrease the likelihood of obtaining incomplete questionnaires or of respondents tossing questionnaires into the wastebasket. Another is the opportunity they provide for explaining words that respondents do not understand. This decreases the number of "don't know" and "no answer" responses. Interviews also make observing social situations and probing into unexpected responses possible.

Interviewers should dress in a fashion similar to that of the people being interviewed. They should be neat and clean. They should have a pleasant demeanor. They should be familiar with the questionnaire, be able to read items naturally and smoothly, follow the question wording exactly, and record responses exactly. They should know how to probe, in a neutral fashion, when asking open-ended questions or when inappropriate replies are given to close-ended questions. Interviewers should be trained thoroughly and supervised, and they should be given specifications to help explain and clarify difficulties that may arise with specific items.

Interview surveys can be conducted face to face or by telephone. During the Depression era telephone interviews were found to be dubious because there were many more poor people without telephones. This produced biased samples—most notoriously in 1936, when a telephone survey predicted that Alf Landon would win a landslide victory over Franklin Roosevelt in the presidential election. Today, however, only about 3% of all households are without telephones. Class-related biases connected to unlisted numbers can be avoided by using random-digit dialing. Hence there is much less class bias in telephone surveys nowadays. Telephone interviews are more acceptable today and offer some important advantages over face-to-face interviews. They are cheaper and quicker, since no travel is involved. They avoid the problem of how to dress and may be safer for interviewers. Not having to face the interviewer in person may facilitate more honesty in giving socially disapproved answers. On the other hand, telephone interviews also have some disadvantages. They may increase suspicion among some respondents, especially those who have become alienated by the proliferation of manipulative telephone sales solicitations. Reluctant respondents may find it easier to stop the interview by hanging up. And if they have an answering machine, they may use the answering machine to screen calls and thus may not even answer in the first place. In the future, telephone survey samples may be biased according to how people use their answering machine, and fax surveys may be used more often, since they may produce higher response rates.

The new technology of survey research includes the use of the Internet and the World Wide Web. The main advantage of online surveys is that they can quickly and inexpensively be sent to very large numbers of prospective respondents anywhere in the world. The main disadvantage concerns the representativeness of the respondents. People who use the internet, and who are most apt to respond to online surveys, are likely to be younger, more affluent and more highly educated than the rest of your target population.

Surveys have some disadvantages as compared to alternative modes of observation. Their need for standardization can result in inflexibility, which can limit the opportunity to assess deeper meanings and unique social situations. Survey data, therefore, can appear superficial and artificial. Moreover, surveys only assess what people say, which may not match what they do. These disadvantages can be offset by combining a qualitative inquiry with a survey.

Surveys have some special strengths that other modes of observation may lack. They make it feasible to gather data from a large sample and generalize to a large population (assuming proper sampling and survey procedures are used). A weakness of surveys can also be a strength. Their standardization and inflexibility can make surveys less vulnerable to biases in observation and data collection than some other modes of observation. This is accomplished by requiring that questions be asked the same way with all respondents and that inappropriate meanings not be imputed to responses.

REVIEW QUESTIONS

1. Which of the following is a disadvantage of survey research in data collection?

   a. Increased flexibility
   b. Greater vulnerability to bias
   c. Reduced feasibility to obtain large samples
   d. All of the above
   e. None of the above

2. Social work agencies commonly conduct surveys to:

   a. Assess client satisfaction with or needs for services
   b. Determine whether services are causing desired outcomes
   c. Assess the deeper meanings of client problems or needs
   d. All of the above

3. Which of the following is *not* an advantage of using self-administered questionnaires in surveys?

   a. Lowered costs
   b. Less reluctance by respondents to answer questions about sensitive issues
   c. Less non response bias
   d. Less time required to collect data

4. Higher response rates in mailed surveys can be promoted by:

   a. Using self-mailing questionnaires requiring no return envelopes
   b. Enclosing cover letters explaining the importance and sponsorship of the survey
   c. Using shorter questionnaires
   d. Having follow-up mailings
   e. All of the above

5. A 50% response rate to a mailed survey is generally considered:

   a. Too small
   b. Adequate
   c. Good
   d. Very good

6. Which of the following is *not* an advantage of interviews over questionnaires?

   a. Higher response rates
   b. Fewer items unanswered
   c. More opportunity to probe into unexpected responses
   d. Less reluctance by respondents to answer questions about sensitive issues

7. Which of the following is *not* a good rule for survey interviewing?

   a. Dress as you usually dress; don't try to dress like your respondents.
   b. Don't read questionnaire items verbatim; rephrase questions in your own words.
   c. Summarize or paraphrase respondent answers that could be worded more clearly or with better grammar.
   d. When probing into unclear responses, ask if the respondent meant what you think they meant.
   e. All of the above (they are all things *not* to do).
   f. None of the above (they are all good rules).

8. Which of the following is *not* an advantage of telephone surveys over face-to-face surveys?

   a. They are cheaper and quicker.
   b. They avoid the problem of how to dress.
   c. They may facilitate more honesty in giving socially disapproved answers.
   d. They make it harder for respondents to prematurely terminate the interview.
   e. None of the above; all are advantages.

9. Which of the following statements is true about survey response rates?

   a. A demonstrated lack of response bias is more important than a high response rate.
   b. Anything less than 80% is not considered a good response rate.
   c. If people don't respond to your first mailing, they probably will not respond to follow-up mailings.
   d. All of the above.
   e. None of the above.

10. Which of the following is true about the use of new technologies for surveys?

   a. Computer assisted telephone interviewing (CATI) *increases* interviewing time.
   b. The spread of telephone answering machines has improved the amount and representativeness of data collected by telephone surveys.
   c. A strength of online surveys is their representativeness.
   d. All of the above.
   e. None of the above.

EXERCISE 15.1

Prepare a cover letter for a hypothetical survey on consumer satisfaction in your agency.

EXERCISE 15.2

Prepare several open-ended questions about student satisfaction with their social work courses. Form a group of three students and take turns interviewing each other with the questions you've prepared. Have a third person observe and critique each interview, then engage in a three-way discussion of each interview. Focus on how well you utilize neutral probes in this exercise.

EXERCISE 15.3

Repeat Exercise 15.2, this time focusing on how well you record responses. Both the interviewer and the observer should record responses. Compare each pair of recordings, and discuss how to improve each of the recordings from the standpoint of the principles discussed in Chapter 15.

DISCUSSION QUESTIONS

1. How do you react when you receive telephone calls asking you to respond to a telephone survey? Under what conditions do you choose to respond or not respond? What have interviewers said or done that influenced you to respond, not respond, or perhaps abort the interview?

2. How do you react when you receive Email messages asking you to respond to a survey? Under what conditions do you choose to respond or not respond?

3. Suppose you conducted a mailed survey on a sensitive topic and, despite implementing all the recommended efforts to maximize response rates, were only able to obtain a 25% response rate. How would you characterize the value of your data, and what issues would you consider in forming your judgment? What additional steps could you take to assess the value of your data?

4. Make a list of at least four research questions that might be of great interest to social workers in a particular agency. Include at least one question that would best fit each of the following survey modalities: a mailed survey, a face-to-face interview survey, and a telephone survey. Also include at least one question that would best be addressed by a modality other than a survey. Discuss why each question best fits the particular modality you've identified for it.

CROSSWORD PUZZLE

ACROSS

1 PARTICIPANT IN A MAIL SURVEY
9 Someone who doesn't belong
14 Next to
16 At any time
17 Killer whale
18 Deity
16 Ending of an email address to Rubin or Babbie
20 ______ Lib
21 PREFIX FOR AN OFTEN UNWELCOME FORM OF MARKETING
22 HIGH TECH BUT RISKY FORM OF SURVEY
24 Least good
26 Indefensible or unjust
27 I am, you are, it ______
28 ______, humbug!
29 I ______ ______! (Reply to professor using too many examples)
30 AN INTERVIEWER SHOULD BE WELL ______ IN APPEARANCE
33 Tasty Mexican munchies
36 Natural resource obtained by drilling
37 Dreaded respiratory disease (abbrev.)
38 SOMETHING THAT CAN BE DONE IN AN INTERVIEW BUT NOT IN A MAIL SURVEY
41 Grand ______ home run
43 Between primary and tertiary
47 Genetic material used in cloning or in crime labs
49 Calm, central part of hurricane
50 Relative of an ave.
52 Male human
53 Sixth letter, failing grade
55 AN INTERVIEWER USUALLY SHOULD ______ IN A FASHION SIMILAR TO THAT OF THE PEOPLE WHO WILL BE INTERVIEWED
58 Albacore or chunk light
60 American corporation that owns NBC and which makes electrical appliances
61 I ______ Sam; Sam I ______
63 New Deal program in Tennessee
64 Get ______ with it already!
65 Hot and bubbling
66 The Steelers play in the Southwestern part of this state
67 Without hesitation
69 INEXPENSIVE TYPE OF SURVEY
70 ______ the beginning
71 Tip ______ the iceberg
72 ______ Rogers (abbrev.)
73 CIA forerunner during WWII
75 Interviewers will do this
76 Freudian term for biological urges
79 TYPE OF SURVEY THAT DOESN'T REQUIRE PROPER GROOMING
82 ONE ADVANTAGE OF MAIL SURVEYS
85 Either ______
86 Hewing tool
87 Television and entertainment company (abbrev.)
89 INTERVIEW SURVEYS GENERALLY HAVE ______ RETURN RATES
90 ______ Palmas
92 ______ arm and a leg

DOWN

1 STAMPED, SELF-ADDRESSED ______ ENVELOPE
2 Not odd
3 ______-ADMINISTERED QUESTIONNAIRE
4 Practice what you ______
5 WHAT SOMEONE MAY DO IF YOUR MAILED QUESTIONNAIRE IS TOO LENGTHY, IF THERE IS NO COVER LETTER, OR IF THEY DON'T CARE ABOUT THE PURPOSE OF THE SURVEY (two words)
6 ______ Spock
7 Environmental prefix
8 Nickname for Nanette
9 ______ THE RATE OF RETURN OF A MAILED SURVEY
10 Bad day in March for Julius Caesar
11 INTERVIEWS HAVE ______ MISUNDERSTOOD QUESTIONS THAN MAIL SURVEYS
12 Altar words uttered often by Liz Taylor and Henry VIII
13 Prefix for turbine
14 What to do in a tub
15 Three ft.
24 WWII American soldier
23 COVER ______
25 GROUPS PARTICIPATING IN SURVEYS THAT MAY REPRESENT POPULATIONS
29 60 TO 70 PERCENT IS A ______ RESPONSE RATE
30 Adrenal ______
31 Beast of burden
32 INTERVIEWERS SHOULD HAVE A PLEASANT ______
34 Casey ______ the bat
35 Dan Rather's network
39 Hospital employee who provides TLC
40 Clam ______
42 All in favor say ______
44 SOME ONLINE SURVEYS ARE SENT VIA ______
45 Where to find L.A.
46 ______ Olde Gifte Shoppe
48 ONE WEAKNESS OF SURVEYS IS VULNERABILITY TO ______
50 YOU SHOULD PUT THIS ON YOUR RETURN ENVELOPES
51 Large horn
54 INTERVIEWERS SHOULD BE VERY ______ WITH THE QUESTIONNAIRE
56 ______ Peron
57 Overeat
59 Din
60 When not in Greece, where you can find Athens and a school of social work (abbrev.)
62 Narcissist's obsession
66 A TELEMARKETING POLITICAL TECHNIQUE DISGUISED AS A SURVEY IS CALLED A ______ POLL
67 SURVEY METHODS CONDUCTED FACE TO FACE OR BY PHONE
68 ______ you wanna dance?
73 You'll need this if you want some canned foods
74 ______ what?!

ACROSS

93 TYPE OF LETTER ACCOMPANYING MAILED SURVEYS
94 Spanish assent
96 Chip partner
97 Yield
99 For example (abbrev.)
101 Where to find SUNY Stoney Brook (abbrev.)
103 INTERVIEW PROBES SHOULD BE ______
105 RANDOM ______ DIALING
107 Initials of 20th century poet
109 Type of code found in a penitentiary
110 Snail-like
111 Greek letter or common airport abbreviation
112 Stage of sleep when dreams occur (abbrev.)
113 In a strange manner
114 POPULAR RESEARCH METHOD FOR GENERALIZING FROM A SAMPLE TO A POPULATION
115 RESULT OF A LOW RESPONSE RATE TO A SURVEY

DOWN

77 Snoop Doggy ______
78 He wrote "The Raven"
79 INTERVIEWERS SHOULD BE CAREFULLY ______ TO FOLLOW QUESTION ORDER AND WORDING EXACTLY
80 UCLA's city
81 WHEN ADMINISTERING STANDARDIZED QUESTIONNAIRES, INTERVIEWERS SHOULD RECORD RESPONSES ______
82 A brief interjection seeking clarification or repetition
83 Organization for Gretzky and Lemieu (abbrev.)
84 ______ Doubtfire
85 ______ Glory
88 Mediocre grade
91 How not to save
93 Jailbird's abode
95 QUESTIONS OR STATEMENTS ON A SCALE
98 100 yard ______
100 Third musical note
102 Call ______ ______ day
104 Airline with a hub at O'Hare
105 Women's patriotic organization (abbrev.)
106 ______ whiz
107 Prefix associated with three
108 Black or Red ______
109 Place that accepts mail (abbrev.)

CHAPTER 16

Analyzing Available Records: Quantitative and Qualitative Methods

OBJECTIVES

1. Define unobtrusive observation and distinguish it from obtrusive observation.
2. Identify the advantages of unobtrusive observation and illustrate its application to a social work research question.
3. Describe content analysis and illustrate its use in investigating research questions about social work practice.
4. Provide an example of content analysis in social work in which the unit of analysis differs from the unit of observation.
5. Illustrate how sampling techniques are applied in content analysis.
6. Distinguish manifest and latent content coding and provide examples of each.
7. Provide an example in which a quantitative count of manifest content categories would not translate into a precise depiction of the degree to which a particular concept characterizes content.
8. Identify three guidelines for counting and record keeping in content analysis.
9. Distinguish qualitative and quantitative approaches to content analysis and provide an example of each in social work.
10. Identify the strengths and weaknesses of content analysis.
11. Explain why social workers seeking to analyze existing statistics should be concerned with, and should inquire as to, their reliability and validity.
12. Provide an example of analyzing existing statistics to research social welfare policy, and identify three sources of existing statistics for policy research.
13. Discuss how to find sources of data available for analyzing existing statistics.
14. Distinguish qualitative historical/comparative methods, such as *verstehen* and hermeneutics, from quantitatively oriented longitudinal methods.
15. Identify three sources of historical/comparative data.

16. Distinguish primary and secondary sources of historical/comparative data, and discuss the cautions that are advisable in working with each type of source.

17. Discuss the importance of corroboration in historical research.

PRACTICE-RELEVANT SUMMARY

Observation in social work practice and research tends to be obtrusive—that is, it tends to be conducted with the awareness of the people being assessed that they are being observed. Obtrusive observation can yield misleading information, because it may influence what people say or do. Obtrusive observation also involves collecting data in the present and can be relatively time consuming. To avoid some of these problems, you might wish to conduct unobtrusive analyses of available records, such as agency documents, case records, media reports, professional literature, and so on. This will enable you to study phenomena that have already occurred, which may save you time and will not involve the people being assessed in the measurement process.

One prime unobtrusive method is *content analysis,* which can be applied to available records or virtually any other form of human communication. It consists primarily of coding and tabulating the occurrences of certain forms of content that are being communicated. Content analysis has been an important source of social work practice knowledge, such as when a content analysis of excerpts from practitioner-client sessions identified the core conditions of a helping relationship (that is, empathy, warmth, genuineness, and so on).

Sampling is an important feature of content analysis: virtually any conventional sampling technique can be employed. One reason for the importance of sampling in content analysis is the complexity involved, since the unit of analysis often differs from the unit of observation.

Content analysis is essentially a coding operation and involves logical issues in conceptualization and operationalization as were discussed in Chapter 6. An important distinction in this connection is between manifest and latent coding. *Manifest coding* is a strictly quantitative method for counting the number of times certain words are used. *Latent coding* is more qualitative; it assesses the overall meaning of a passage or document. Quantitative counts of manifest content categories do not translate into precise depictions of the degree to which a particular concept characterizes a document's content. For example, if one agency's board meeting minutes mention cultural diversity twice as often as a second agency's, that doesn't necessarily mean that the first agency's commitment to cultural diversity is double the second agency's commitment.

When conducting a quantitative content analysis, it is important to use numerical codes that clearly distinguish between your units of analysis and your units of observation. Usually it is important to record the base from which the counting is done. Thus, rather than just say that *cultural diversity* was mentioned 20 times in one document and 10 times in another, you should also indicate the word length of each document. Issues of *validity* and *reliability* are noteworthy in content analysis. In quantitative content analysis, the number of times a word or phrase appears may not be a valid indicator of the degree to which a document has a particular attribute. Qualitative content analysis may be better at tapping underlying meanings, but different coders might have different judgments about the latent meaning of content.

Existing statistics provide another source for unobtrusive research. There are many sources for existing statistics in social work research, such as those issued annually by government and private agencies dealing with social problems. A challenge is to find existing data that cover what you are interested in. Often the data may pertain in some way to your interest but might not be an exact, valid representation of the variables you want to draw conclusions about. You should also look into potential biases or carelessness in the way the statistics were originally gathered and reported. Don't assume that because they are official documents, they are necessarily reliable or valid.

Historical/comparative analysis, which is usually done qualitatively, is a method for tracing developments over time and comparing developmental processes across cultures. A main focus is on seeking to discover common patterns that recur in different times and places. In social work research, for example, one can see recurring patterns over time in welfare policy reform efforts and mental health policy reform efforts. Noble reforms proposed in ways that would cost taxpayers more money fail again and again because they get adopted and implemented with insufficient public funding to implement critical features of the proposed reforms.

Endless sources are possible for historical/comparative analysis, such as letters, diaries, lectures, newspapers, magazines, agency documents and annual reports, and so on. *Primary sources* provide firsthand accounts by someone present at an event. *Secondary sources* describe past phenomena based on primary sources. People who author primary sources may depict events in a biased manner, due to their vested interests, and historical/comparative researchers should vigilantly consider and look into this possibility. A prime way to handle this problem is by looking for corroboration across multiple sources.

Historical/comparative research involves primarily fluid, qualitative interpretive methods, such as *verstehen* and hermeneutics, which do not contain easily listed steps to follow. The historical/comparative researcher seeks to detect patterns in voluminous details and to take on, mentally, the circumstances, views, and feelings of those being studied and to interpret their actions appropriately.

REVIEW QUESTIONS

1. When we conduct unobtrusive observation:

    a. People are aware that they are being observed.
    b. We can influence what our subjects say or do.
    c. We collect data only in the present time.
    d. All of the above.
    e. None of the above.

2. Which of the following is an example of unobtrusive observation of cultural diversity in an agency?

    a. Count the proportion of staff, board members, and clients of each background as depicted in agency documents and client records.
    b. Interview staff about their views regarding cultural diversity.
    c. Obtain the consent of administrators and practitioners to attend agency meetings to observe how often cultural diversity is discussed.
    d. All of the above.

3. A content analysis is conducted of individual client case records to see if agencies that have provided more in-service training on cultural diversity appear to provide services that are more ethnically sensitive than agencies offering less in-service training on cultural diversity. Which of the following statements is true about this content analysis?

    a. Individual case records are the units of observation.
    b. Individual agencies are the units of analysis.
    c. In-service training records are the units of analysis.
    d. None of the above.
    e. Both a and b, only, are true.

4. In the content analysis in question 3 above, the researcher read each session's progress notes and made an overall assessment of whether it reflected ethnic sensitivity. The researcher was doing:

    a. Latent content coding
    b. Manifest content coding
    c. Quantitative coding
    d. Reliability coding

5. An agency administrator, concerned about the extent to which her staff are taking their clients' ethnicity into account when providing services, conducts a content analysis of staff progress notes and finds that staff with social work degrees mentioned the client's ethnicity 100 times, whereas staff with other degrees mentioned it 50 times. The administrator was correct in concluding:

   a. Social workers are twice as likely as other staff to take ethnicity into account.
   b. Other staff are half as likely as social workers to take ethnicity into account.
   c. Ethnicity was mentioned more times in social workers' progress notes than in the progress notes of other staff.
   d. All of the above.

6. If textbook A on social work practice mentions client ethnicity 100 times and textbook B mentions it 90 times, then:

   a. Textbook A emphasizes ethnicity more than textbook B.
   b. Textbook A devotes a greater proportion of content to ethnicity.
   c. Both a and b are true.
   d. Neither a nor b is necessarily true.

7. As compared to latent coding, manifest coding in content analysis:

   a. Has an advantage in terms of validity
   b. Is less suitable for tapping underlying meanings
   c. Has a disadvantage in terms of reliability
   d. Has less specificity
   e. None of the above

8. Which of the following is/are true about using existing statistics issued in official agency statistical reports?

   a. We can be reasonably certain that their reliability and validity are high.
   b. The data may have been collected in a careless fashion.
   c. Biases may have influenced the way data were collected and reported.
   d. We can be reasonably certain that the data are almost never grossly inaccurate.
   e. Both a and d, only, are true.
   f. Both b and c, only, are true.

9. In conducting a historical/comparative analysis of an agency's commitment to cultural diversity, a social worker finds that the agency's administrative minutes and letters written by the agency's executive director during the last decade express much more commitment to increasing cultural diversity in the agency than do letters and minutes from the past. Which of the following statements is/are true about this example?

    a. The minutes and letters are secondary sources.
    b. It is safe to conclude that the agency has increased its cultural diversity during the last decade.
    c. Other types of sources of data reflecting the agency's commitment to cultural diversity should be compared to the above sources to check for inaccuracies due to biases.
    d. All of the above.

10. Which of the following statements is *not* true about historical/comparative research, such as *verstehen* and hermeneutics?

    a. It involves a series of specific procedures that should be followed precisely.
    b. It involves primarily fluid, qualitative interpretive methods.
    c. It involves the detection of patterns in voluminous details.
    d. It involves seeking to mentally take on the views and feelings of those being studied.
    e. None of the above; they are all true.

EXERCISE 16.1

Conduct a content analysis of the chapters you have read so far in the Rubin and Babbie textbook, based on the book's latent content, to determine the extent to which the book values qualitative methods and quantitative methods equally or the extent to which it values one more than the other. I suggest you begin by skimming each chapter quickly to jog your memory, jotting brief notes as to what you would conclude about the research question in light of what you recall was said about the relative importance of qualitative or quantitative methods in each chapter. Then consider your notes qualitatively in terms of what you think the book's overall, underlying message is about the relative importance of the two sets of methods.

EXERCISE 16.2

Once you have completed the above qualitative analysis of latent content, conduct a quantitative analysis of the same chapters with regard to their manifest content concerning the same research question. Begin by formulating a sampling plan, such as rereading every 10th or 20th page of the chapters you have already completed. Alternatively, you may want to just reread the "Main Points" listed at the end of each chapter. You will also need to conceptualize the words or phrases you will look for and count to indicate how much content on qualitative methods is in the book versus how much content on quantitative methods there is. Then proceed with your counting, recording your findings and conclusions below. Also identify below your sampling procedure and the words or phrases you looked for. (Writing this down now will be useful when you compare your findings with those of your classmates in Exercise 16.4.)

EXERCISE 16.3

Compare your conclusions in the above two exercises. Were they the same? Discuss why you think they were or were not the same. Which of the two content analyses do you think is the more valid for this particular book and *Study Guide*? Why?

EXERCISE 16.4

Compare your results and conclusions for the above two content analyses with those of your classmates. Was there more agreement among you with one approach (manifest versus latent) than the other? What do you think explains the consistency or inconsistency of results and conclusions across the students performing this exercise? What does this suggest regarding the reliability and validity of the two approaches?

DISCUSSION QUESTIONS

1. Explain why content analyses that examine both manifest and latent content may reach more valuable conclusions than content analyses restricted to only one of the two types of content.

2. Suppose you studied trends in the frequency of reported spouse abuse and reported service utilization connected to spouse abuse by analyzing two sets of existing statistics: one issued annually by a government agency and one issued annually by the National Organization for Women (NOW). In what ways, if any, do you think the government agency statistics might differ from the NOW statistics, and why? What does this imply about issues regarding the reliability and validity of existing statistics?

3. Suppose your colleague conducted the study in question 2 above and found a huge increase in the frequency of reported spouse abuse and reported service utilization connected to spouse abuse beginning in 1995 (coinciding with the start of the infamous O. J. Simpson trial). Suppose your colleague concluded that spouse abuse is on the rise, as is seeking services connected to it. After reading a rough draft of her preliminary report, which she gave you in the hope of getting your feedback, what would you say to your colleague regarding whether her conclusions about the increase are warranted in light of the validity of the statistics she used as a measure of the rate of actual spouse abuse? What does this imply about potential pitfalls in relying on existing statistics and how to handle those pitfalls?

4. Five years ago the ultraconservative newspaper (the only newspaper in your small, politically conservative city) published a scathing editorial attacking your agency for its efforts to help poor teenagers with unwanted pregnancies to secure abortions. The editorial urged elected officials to cut off your agency's public funding. Now, a social work doctoral student, for her dissertation, is conducting a historical/comparative analysis of possible changes in your agency's philosophy about abortion services, based on the content of the agency's annual reports and on letters written by the agency's executive directors. She tentatively concludes that the agency's philosophy has changed in the aftermath of the editorial, and that the agency now has become less supportive of the criticized abortion services. She shares her tentative conclusions with you because you are her friend and you have been a service provider at the agency for ten years. Based on your direct experience in providing services, you believe her conclusions are wrong. What would you advise her as to the risks inherent in relying on the accuracy of only one type of primary source, the reasons her sources may be biased and misleading, and additional sources she should obtain and analyze for corroborating evidence?

CROSSWORD PUZZLE

ACROSS

1 Type of word processing font
6 UNOBTRUSIVE MEASURES ARE ______ LIKELY TO AFFECT BEHAVIOR THAN OBTRUSIVE MEASURES
10 Couch potato's entertainment
12 SECONDARY SOURCES DESCRIBE ______ PHENOMENA
13 Raison de ______
14 Debt abbreviation
16 ______ ANALYSIS IS A METHOD FOR STUDYING HUMAN COMMUNICATION
17 A PROCESS FOR TRANSFORMING RAW DATA INTO STANDARDIZED QUANTITATIVE FORM
19 Most populous continent
20 Newfangled television gimmick
23 Read a manuscript for the purpose of suggesting improvements
24 HERMENEUTICS INVOLVES MENTALL TAKING ON THE ______ AND ______ OF THE PARTICIPANTS (WITH 22 DOWN)
25 To be or not ______ be
26 AN ______ TYPE IS A CONCEPTUAL MODEL COMPOSED OF THE ESSENTIAL QUALITIES OF A SOCIAL PHENOMENON
28 The ______ Sullivan Show
29 ______ you like it
30 ______ Miserables
31 ______ Folly (Alaska purchase)
33 TYPE OF CONTENT REQUIRING RESEARCHER'S JUDGEMENTS
35 Former Jr.
36 Cry of discovery
38 Mr. ______ (old TV show)
39 Green tropical fruit
42 Abominable snow men
43 Nuisance
44 Loser twice to DDE

DOWN

2 New stock offerings (abbreviated)
3 TYPE OF CONTENT THAT IS DIRECTLY VISIBLE
4 Como ______ usted?
5 French holy woman (abbrev.)
6 ONE TYPE OF PRIMARY SOURCE
7 Spielberg's cute alien
8 Jr.'s dad
9 TYPE OF SOURCE THAT MIGHT REPEAT THE MISTAKES OF A PRIMARY SOURCE
10 Ocean movements
11 No longer valid
15 ______ OF ANALYSIS (CONNECTED TO ECOLOGICAL FALLACY)
16 Woman's name
18 Car in an old rock song
21 State represented by Lincoln in congress (abbrev.)
22 SEE 24 ACROSS
24 Type of steak
27 Kaput
29 Paler
32 MISSING ______
34 Edge
37 Fool
40 ______ the people
41 He ______ risen

CHAPTER 17

Qualitative Research: General Principles

OBJECTIVES

1. Compare and contrast the following qualitative research paradigms: naturalism, grounded theory, participatory action research, and case studies.

2. Describe the use of ethnography and give an example of how it could be used to study a social work research problem.

3. Describe the use of grounded theory and give an example of how it could be used to study a social work research problem.

4. Discuss how the use of grounded theory and ethnography can overlap.

5. Discuss how the aims of sampling in qualitative research differ from the aims of sampling in quantitative research, and describe the purpose and illustrate the use of snowball sampling, deviant case sampling, intensity sampling, critical incidents sampling, maximum variation sampling, homogeneous sampling, and theoretical sampling.

6. Describe the case study method and illustrate how it may be applied to a social work research topic.

7. Describe the use of client logs and give an example of how they can be used in single-case evaluations.

8. Discuss the key strengths and weaknesses of qualitative research, particularly as they pertain to depth of understanding, subjectivity, generalizability, and research ethics.

9. Identify three key threats to the trustworthiness of qualitative research studies.

10. Describe how each of six strategies is commonly used to enhance the trustworthiness of qualitative research studies.

PRACTICE-RELEVANT SUMMARY

Many social workers whose practice involves policy analysis and advocacy have been concerned about the ways that certain welfare reform policies may be impacting mothers and children who are at risk for losing their eligibility for welfare benefits. What will the mothers resort to in order to survive (assuming that a shortage of jobs that they qualify for and a shortage of affordable child care will make it hard for them to become legitimate wage earners)? What impact will this have on their ability to mother their children? What impact will the deterioration in mothering and the loss of subsistence resources have on the children? Will they become homeless? Will they be starving and freezing on the streets? Will they and their mothers increasingly resort to crime? What impact will all this have on the type of adults they become, assuming they live that long?

It is perhaps impossible to anticipate all, or even most, of the important ways that welfare reform legislation can change the lives of the needy. What research methods can social workers use to study this phenomenon and inform the public about the impact of the legislation? Experiments will be difficult, since we don't control the independent variable, which is the variation in welfare policy. Surveys are possible to use, but is it reasonable to expect an acceptable level of participation in a survey? More important, perhaps, can we foresee the future ways welfare reform may impact the lives of welfare recipients well enough to know all the questions we should ask and how we should ask them? Neither experimental nor survey findings, moreover, are apt to tug at the heartstrings of many voters who believe that welfare is a central cause of many social ills. Other kinds of findings are needed to do that, findings that help the reader walk in the shoes of good people who are suffering. Social work practitioners seeking such findings should see the relevance of learning about *qualitative research methods*, since these methods help us study new phenomena that we cannot adequately anticipate.

One qualitative research paradigm geared to producing findings that build empathy for the plight of people through observations that cannot, and perhaps should not, be reduced to numbers is *participatory action research.* With this paradigm, the researcher serves as a resource to those being studied—typically, disadvantaged groups—as an opportunity for them to act effectively in their own interest. The disadvantaged participants define their problems, define the remedies desired, and take the lead in designing the research that will help them realize their aims.

Most of qualitative inquiry is based on the *grounded theory* paradigm. This approach is an inductive process of seeking patterns in one set of observations and then engaging in a constant comparison process of seeking different types of cases and observations and constantly modifying working hypotheses until a point is reached when new types of cases and observations no longer alter the findings.

In qualitative research the emphasis is on observing everyday life as it unfolds in its natural environment. It is also often called *ethnography* or *ethnographic research,* since it often involves studying a culture from the point of view of the inhabitants of that culture. Key elements in an ethnographic research strategy include establishing generic propositions, being open to inquiring about anything, trying to see the world through the eyes of the people you seek to understand and gain deep familiarity with their subjective experiences and interpretations, attempting to understand them from their own perspective, constantly aiming for new observations and new analyses, and balancing the use of observations and theoretical elaboration in presenting data.

Qualitative researchers typically use nonprobability sampling techniques that incorporate aspects of *quota sampling* and *purposive sampling*. *Snowball sampling* is also commonly used; this approach begins by identifying a few relevant subjects and expands the sample through referrals from those subjects. *Deviant case sampling* is useful, too, since important insights can be gained from studying people who do not fit the usual pattern. *Intensity sampling* helps prevent a distorted portrayal of the phenomenon by selecting cases that are more or less intense than usual but not so unusual that they would be called deviant. Another useful strategy is *critical incidents sampling,* studying events in which something of special importance seemed to happen. *Maximum variation sampling* calls for studying a phenomenon under heterogeneous conditions to capture its diversity. *Homogeneous sampling,* on the other hand, is a strategy for studying those subjects or events thought most likely to evince a particular construct of interest. When using grounded theory, *theoretical sampling* comes into play, as described above with regard to the constant comparison method of grounded theory.

A *case study* is an idiographic examination of a single individual, family, group, organization, community, or society. Sources of evidence might include existing documents, observations, and interviews. The rationale for using the case study method typically is the availability of a special case that seems to merit intensive investigation. The application of the case study method that is perhaps of greatest interest to social workers is when the case being studied is an individual, group, or family engaged in social work treatment. Such case studies might involve the use of *client logs,* which are particularly useful to practitioners employing single-case evaluations in their own practice. Qualitative logs are journals that clients keep of events that are relevant to their problems.

The chief strength of qualitative research is the depth of understanding that it permits. Another key advantage is its flexibility. It also can be relatively inexpensive, although this is not always the case. The chief weaknesses of qualitative research are its vulnerability to the subjectivity of the researchers and those being observed and its limited generalizability. Field research, by bringing researchers into direct and often intimate contact with their subjects, also can raise ethical concerns dramatically.

Standards for evaluating qualitative studies have been developed to examine the potential for research reactivity, researcher biases and respondent bias. Strategies to minimize these problems include prolonged engagement, triangulation, peer debriefing and support, negative case analysis, member checking, and auditing.

REVIEW QUESTIONS

1. Qualitative research methods are more appropriate than quantitative methods for:

   a. Studying new phenomena that we cannot anticipate
   b. Developing a deeper understanding of meanings
   c. Situations that require a flexible research approach
   d. All of the above
   e. None of the above

2. The grounded theory method:

   a. Starts with theory, then seeks observations to confirm it
   b. Is an inductive process for letting theory emerge from observational patterns
   c. Excludes methods involving observations or interviews
   d. Is a geological social work method

3. Which of the following is a term often used to characterize qualitative research?

   a. Ethnography
   b. Grounded theory
   c. Naturalism
   d. All of the above
   e. None of the above

4. Which of the following is *not* a common sampling technique frequently employed in qualitative research?

   a. Snowball sampling
   b. Deviant case sampling
   c. Intensity sampling
   d. Critical incidents sampling
   e. Stratified random sampling

5. Which of the following is a chief strength of qualitative research?

   a. Depth of understanding
   b. Tightly structured methods
   c. Measurement objectivity
   d. Generalizability

6. Which of the following is/are a true about the trustworthiness of qualitative research?

   a. Participant observation ensures that research reactivity will be avoided.
   b. Participant observation ensures that researcher biases will be avoided
   c. Shorter interviews or observation periods ensure that respondent biases will be avoided.
   d. Lengthy engagement ensures that going native will be avoided.
   e. All of the above.
   f. None of the above.

7. Which of the following is/are a true about the case study method?

    a. It is an idiographic examination of a single individual or a group.
    b. Sources of evidence might include existing documents, observations, and interviews.
    c. It might involve life history interviews.
    d. All of the above.
    e. None of the above.

8. Which of the following is/are a true about participatory action research?

    a. The researcher should avoid trying to help those being studied.
    b. The researcher serves as a resource to those being studied.
    c. Participants are kept out of the research design process.
    d. All of the above.
    e. None of the above.

9. Which of the following is/are true about purposive sampling in qualitative research?

    a. It can be used to select a sample of deviant cases.
    b. It can be used to try to obtain a representative sample.
    c. It can be used to select a sample of critical cases.
    d. All of the above.

EXERCISE 17.1

Write down the potential threats to the trustworthiness of the findings for each of the following hypothetical situations. Compare your answers with those of your classmates and discuss any differences you encounter.

a. A 22-year-old social worker who continues to grapple with issues connected to her perception that her parents were overprotective of her tends to interpret the behavior of the troubled adolescents she observes in terms of their reactions to parental overprotection.

b. A young social worker seeking to understand the culture of residents in a juvenile correctional facility begins to see the world through the eyes of the residents, which includes disregarding the viewpoints of the security staff and other authority figures, based exclusively on the horror stories he hears about them from the residents.

c. A social worker who recently had to place her elderly parent in a nursing home becomes angry when conducting observations of staff-resident interactions in a study of nursing home care. She begins to focus exclusively, and in a moralistic manner, on staff inadequacies.

d. A social worker observing social behavior in a prison cafeteria observes that all the white prisoners eat on one side of the room and all the African American prisoners eat on the other side. He therefore concludes that the prison staff members practice racist segregation.

e. Another social worker interviewing the prisoners in situation d, above, learns that each group prefers to eat on its own side of the room. Based on this, she concludes that racism is not a problem among the prison staff.

EXERCISE 17.2

Practice the preparation of a client log by preparing one for yourself. Use it to monitor the occurrence of a behavior you would like to change (for example, smoking, overeating, and so forth). Record critical incidents and related information as described in the "Client Logs" section of Chapter 17. Compare your log with the logs of your classmates.

EXERCISE 17.3

Suppose you wanted to use the grounded theory method to develop an in depth understanding of how and why social work practitioners differ in regard to evidence-based practice. Summarize what you would do and the sampling methods you would employ .

DISCUSSION QUESTIONS

1. Do you think you would have a preference regarding doing qualitative versus quantitative research? If so, which approach would you prefer and why? Be sure to consider methodological issues as well as your own style in formulating your answer.

2. Discuss how ethnographic researchers can attempt to adopt the points of view of the people they are studying, while at the same time preserving their scientific objectivity and analytic stance.

3. In light of the superior generalizability of findings based on probability sampling techniques, discuss the reasons nonprobability sampling techniques are usually preferable when conducting qualitative research.

4. Briefly describe the functions of six strategies to minimize the influence of research reactivity, researcher biases and respondent bias in qualitative studies.

CROSSWORD PUZZLE

ACROSS

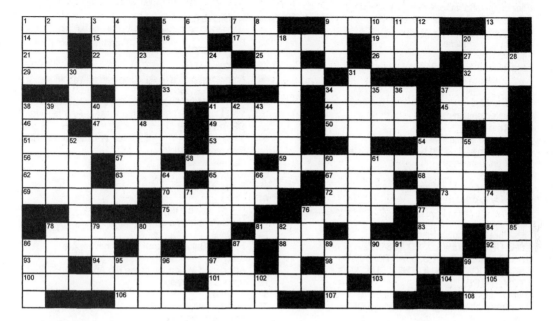

1 Large container
5 Sign on some doors
9 Foreign
14 Male pronoun
15 "______ the Hop" (1950's rock song)
16 Professor's scientific helper (abbrev.)
17 ______ OF UNDERSTANDING IS ONE STRENGTH OF QUALITATIVE RESEARCH
19 Unable to accomplish
21 12 step program (abbrev.)
22 (WITH 5 DOWN): A QUALITATIVE METHOD THAT ATTEMPTS TO DERIVE THEORY FROM PATTERNS OR THEMES AMONG OBSERVATIONAL DATA
25 ______ T of "The A Team" (I pity the fool who can't get this abbreviation)
26 Hot season in Cannes
27 Small black and white sea bird belonging to the puffin family
29 ONE STRATEGY IMPACTING THE RIGOR OF QUALITATIVE STUDIES
32 Give it a ______!
33 The first two initials on Mickey Mantle's cap
34 MANY QUALITATIVE STUDIES CAN BE TERMED ______ STUDY RESEARCH
37 "Here Comes the ______" (Beatles tune)
38 What yellow jackets might do to you when disturbed
41 "Sock ______ ______ me!"
44 A triple crown winner may be this after retirement
45 John's dance partner in "Pulp Fiction"
46 Double ______ nothing!
47 Answer to some exam questions

DOWN

1 Converse informally
2 ______ Window (Hitchcock classic)
3 Bye bye
4 QUALITATIVE METHOD INVOLVING NATURALISTIC OBSERVATIONS AND HOLISTIC UNDERSTANDINGS OF CULTURES OR SUBCULTURES
5 SEE 22 ACROSS
6 This bird catches the worm
7 QB's goal
8 Half
9 Cry of discovery
10 Frost
11 Consume
12 Direction from Nashville to Boston
13 THE FIELD ______ IS FOR RECORDING OBSERVATIONS
18 (With 59 ACROSS): STRATEGY IMPACTING THE RIGOR OF QUALITATIVE STUDIES INVOLVING REPEAT INTERVIEWS AND/OR LENGTHY OBSERVATION
20 One statistic; a single piece of information
23 Abbreviation often used instead of i.e.
24 "Secrets of the ______ … sisterhood"
28 St. north of TN and south of OH
30 XXVII divided by IX
31 TYPE OF QUALITATIVE OBSERVATIONS
34 Losing side for R.E. Lee
35 Earth's star
36 5 PM in NYC during Sept.
37 THE USE OF _____ METHODS CAN BE BOTH A STRENGTH AND A LIMITATION OF QUALITATIVE RESEARCH

ACROSS

49 Bright gas
50 Eller in "Oklahoma" or Em in "Wizard of Oz"
51 Something to fold in poker (2 words)
53 Body part of Dracula or snakes
54 Alphabetical sequence
56 First woman
57 Less than FT work
58 ______ Whom the Bell Tolls
59 SEE 18 DOWN
62 Gun an engine
63 Rabbit step or teen dance
65 King of the ______
67 Winna in the Thrilla in Manilla
68 Good card to have in the hole or up your sleeve
69 Oily or untrustworthy
70 Lousy car
72 ___ is just a bowl of cherries
73 Get ready to drive
75 Test
76 Yesteryear
77 Salsa that is not hot or medium
78 TYPE OF SAMPLING USED IN SOME QUALITATIVE STUDIES, STARTING WITH ONE PARTICIPANT AND THEN BUILDING FROM THERE
81 Fuss
83 Dehydrated athlete might get this in the OR
84 State east of AL
86 Very small amount
88 QUALITATIVE RESEARCH MEASURES, THOUGH TAPPING MORE DEPTH OF MEANING, ARE OFTEN LESS _______ THAN SURVEY MEASURES
92 Three ft
93 Important early presidential primary st.
94 Laid back
98 Sherlock's find
100 Refrains from doing (2 words)
101 Hauled
103 Blair Witch Project St.
104 Happy New _____!
106 Astounding
107 Bro's sib
108 JFK's predecessor

DOWN

38 Becomes less intoxicated
39 Take a trip
40 Highest degree
41 NATURE OF CONVERSATIONAL INTERVIEWS
42 Russian ______ ______ (Famous restaurant in New York City)
43 2000 pounds
48 Archaic preposition regarding something being given to somebody
52 ______ CASE SAMPLING CAN SOMETIMES YIELD INSIGHTS INTO "NORMAL" PATTERNS OF BEHAVIOR
54 "Now ______ ______ believer" (Words from an old Monkees hit song)
55 Genuflect
60 Festival
61 Present
64 Cop a ______
66 ______ apple a day....
71 Laxative brand name
74 Anxious
76 Famous Baltimore poet who is nevermore
77 5280 feet
78 Arty district in London or the Big Apple
79 Vikings used these
80 Look out ______!
82 Mild expletive
85 Admire or worship
86 500 mile car race or inexpensively produced movie
87 First man
89 Boys
90 Aid to the poor in olden times
91 Blossom
95 Bambi's aunt
96 Devoured
97 Common environmental prefix
99 Marry
102 Second musical note
105 After BC, or source of magazine revenue

CHAPTER 18

Qualitative Research: Specific Methods

OBJECTIVES

1. Identify the steps involved in preparing to undertake direct observation in the field.
2. Describe the dilemma involved in attempting to balance the competing aims of maintaining objectivity and adopting an alien point of view in qualitative research.
3. Contrast and identify the advantages and disadvantages of observing as a complete participant, as a participant-as-observer, and as a complete observer.
4. Identify the tools and strategies field researchers employ to manage the challenging process of recording observations and maximizing the quality of the recorded notes.
5. Discuss the ways qualitative interviewing differs from survey interviewing, and identify the differences between the following three forms of qualitative interviewing: informal conversational interviews, interview guides, and standardized open-ended interviews.
6. Describe the use of the life history method and give an example of how it could be used to study a social work research problem.
7. Describe the use of focus groups and give an example of how they can be used to study a social work research problem.
8. Describe the advantages and disadvantages of focus groups.
9. Define and contrast the emic and etic perspectives in participant observation.
10. Identify the do's and don'ts of note taking when engaging in participant observation or qualitative interviewing.

PRACTICE-RELEVANT SUMMARY

Qualitative research often involves participant observation in naturalistic settings. The term *field* refers to those settings. The qualitative researcher prepares for the field by reviewing literature on the group to be studied, discussing the group with informant members of the group, and developing rapport with group members.

Participant observation can be conducted on a continuum from complete participant to complete observer, with less extreme options of participant-as-observer and observer-as-participant in between. At one extreme, the complete participant may be best able to fully grasp what it's like to be the people under study but may also be most vulnerable to affecting what is being studied and to lose one's own sense of identity and analytic stance. At the other extreme, complete observers preserve their sense of identity and analytic stance and are less likely to affect what is being studied but are also less likely to develop a full appreciation of what is being studied. When operating toward the complete-participant end of the continuum, researchers should try to achieve a difficult balance between adopting the points of view of the people they are studying and being able to step outside those viewpoints and analyzing them from the standpoint of an objective social scientist.

In addition to direct observation, qualitative research relies heavily on open-ended interviewing that tends to be unstructured. At one extreme are completely unstructured *informal conversational interviews* that contain no predetermined questions and in which you can use your social work listening, probing, and attending skills to subtly direct the flow of the conversation to stay on track and help you develop a richer understanding of things relevant to your research. At the other extreme are *standardized open-ended interviews,* in which open-ended questions are written out in advance precisely as they are to be asked during the interview. In between the two extremes is the *interview guide* approach, which lists the topics and issues to be covered in outline form and allows the interviewer to adapt the sequencing and wording of questions to each particular interview.

Other qualitative methods frequently mentioned in the literature that may employ interviewing include life histories and focus groups. With the *life history* method, researchers ask open-ended questions to discover how the participants in a study understand the significant events and meanings in their own lives. *Focus groups* are often used for needs assessment, or for collecting other forms of program evaluation data. They consist of people who engage in a guided discussion of a specified topic. Focus group participants are typically chosen by means of purposive sampling or reliance on available subjects. They offer the advantage of being inexpensive, generating speedy results, and offering flexibility for probing. In addition, the group dynamics that occur in focus groups can bring out aspects of the topic that evaluators may not have anticipated and that may not have emerged in individual interviews. The disadvantages of focus groups include their questionable representativeness and the potential for group dynamics to create pressures for people to say things that may not accurately reflect their true feelings or their prospective actions. Another disadvantage is that the data emerging from focus groups are likely to be much more voluminous and less systematic than structured survey data. Analyzing focus group data, therefore, can be difficult, tedious, and subject to the biases of the evaluator.

In all forms of qualitative interviewing, respondent answers to interview questions should be recorded as fully as possible. Verbatim recording is ideal, with a tape recorder when applicable. Additional penciled notes should be recorded in a notebook at the scene of action or as soon as possible afterward. Notes should include both exact descriptions of what happened and your interpretations of them. Since you will be unable to write down everything you observe, you should use your judgment to record the most important things. You should take notes in stages, beginning with sketchy notes at the scene of action and then rewriting them in more detail as soon as you are alone. Notes should be retyped each night, with multiple copies made for cutting and pasting later. Notes should be organized into files containing a chronological record, historical and biographical files, a bibliographical file, and analytic files. Many types of analytic files can be created in a continuous, flexible process.

REVIEW QUESTIONS

1. The complete-participant strategy of observation has the advantage of:

    a. Helping the researcher fully grasp what it's like to be the people under study
    b. Helping the research avoid affecting what is being studied
    c. Helping researchers preserve their sense of identity and analytic stance
    d. All of the above
    e. None of the above

2. Researchers using the complete-participant strategy of observation are less likely to:

    a. Develop a full appreciation of what is being studied
    b. Affect what is being studied
    c. Preserve their sense of identity and analytic stance
    d. Encounter ethical constraints

3. Complete-participant researchers should:

    a. Never step outside the viewpoints of their subjects
    b. Never adopt the viewpoints of their subjects
    c. Try to both adopt the viewpoints of their subjects and be able to step outside them
    d. Avoid the standpoint of the objective social scientist

4. The qualitative researcher prepares for the field by:

    a. Reviewing literature on the group to be studied
    b. Discussing the group with informant members of the group
    c. Developing rapport with group members
    d. All of the above
    e. None of the above

5. Which of the following is *not* true about qualitative interviewing?

    a. It tends to be less structured than quantitative interviewing.
    b. It tends to be open-ended.
    c. It may involve informal conversational interviews that contain no predetermined questions.
    d. It never involves asking questions precisely as they are written out in advance.

6. When recording qualitative data, you should:

    a. Record responses to interview questions verbatim
    b. Describe what happens as well as your interpretations of what you observe
    c. Record at the scene of action and rewrite your notes in more detail as soon as you are alone
    d. All of the above
    e. None of the above

7. Which of the following is/are true about focus groups?

    a. They are often used for needs assessment.
    b. Their participants may not be representative of the target population.
    c. Group dynamics may bias responses.
    d. All of the above.
    e. None of the above.

8. Which of the following is/are advantages of focus groups?

    a. They are inexpensive.
    b. They offer flexibility for probing.
    c. Group dynamics may generate unanticipated aspects of the topic.
    d. All of the above.
    e. None of the above.

9. Which of the following is/are true about the life history method?

    a. It is commonly used in feminist studies.
    b. Closed-ended questions are used more than open-ended questions.
    c. Objective accuracy is emphasized.
    d. All of the above.
    e. None of the above.

10. Which of the following is/are true about informal conversational interviews?

    a. They typically are well planned.
    b. Questions should arise spontaneously during the course of the interview.
    c. Because these interviews are informal, the use of professional interviewing skills should be avoided.
    d. At the outset, it is important for interviewers to show how well they understand the interviewee's situation.

EXERCISE 18.1

In the social work courses you are taking this semester, observe and take field notes on the social interactions among social work students and their instructors ten minutes before and ten minutes after your next class session in each course. The focus of your inquiry should be on the nature of verbal and nonverbal communication among students and between students and instructors and on how the communication varies depending on such factors as the instructor's presence or absence, who is communicating with whom, and the instructor's subject area (that is, research, policy, practice, and so on).

Follow the guidelines in Chapter 18 in the section on "Recording Observations," including separate notes on empirical observations and on interpretations of them. Then develop your research conclusions and write them below. Have your classmates share their conclusions with each other after they all finish the exercise. Do their conclusions agree? Disagree? To what do you attribute any disagreements? (Enter your conclusions about disagreements below as well.)

EXERCISE 18.2

Prepare a set of about ten open-ended questions about student satisfaction with your social work education program. Conduct a structured interview with one or more other social work students, asking the questions exactly as you have written them out. Have another student in your class independently conduct informal conversational interviews with the same students. Both you and the other interviewer should independently record and analyze your interview data as recommended in Chapter 18. After each of you has completed your data analysis and written your conclusions, compare the similarities and differences in your conclusions and brainstorm with each other as to explanations for why the two different interview methods yielded similar or different conclusions. In your discussion, be sure to consider potential limitations that might account for some of your conclusions or some of the differences between the two sets of conclusions. Then engage the same students in a focus group discussion of the same topic. In what ways is the information generated by the focus group similar and different from the above two sets of conclusions?

DISCUSSION QUESTIONS

1. Discuss the difficulty involved in balancing the emic and etic perspectives and how qualitative researchers attempt to achieve that balance.

2. Discuss the advantages and disadvantages of the three alternative forms of qualitative open-ended interviewing (informal conversational interviews, interview guide approach, and standardized open-ended interviews).

3. Suppose you were interviewing social work practitioners in an effort to develop an in-depth understanding of their views about evidence-based practice? Which of the above three open-ended interviewing approaches would you use? Explain the reasons for your choice.

4. Describe how you would take notes in the interviews in number 3, above.

CROSSWORD PUZZLE

1	2	3	4	■	5		6	7	8	9		
10				11		■	12				■	■
13					■	■	14				■	15
16					17	18		■	■	19	20	
■		■	21				■	■	22			
■	■	23		■	24		■	25				
■	26			27			28	■	29			
30			■		■	■	31	32	■	33		■
34					■	35				■		■

ACROSS

1 PERSPECTIVE INVOLVING TRYING TO ADOPT THE BELIEFS, ATTITUDES AND OTHER POINTS OF VIEW SHARED BY THE CULTURE BEING STUDIED
5 THE COMPLETE ____ IS LESS LIKELY TO AFFECT WHAT IS BEING STUDIED BUT ALSO LESS LIKELY TO DEVELOP A FULL APPRECIATION OF WHAT IS BEING STUDIED
10 Girl's name
12 Type of molding or arch
13 Caesar's "Veni"
14 Shakespeare's Othello was one
16 THE _____ PARTICIPANT IS MOST VULNERABLE TO AFFECT WHAT'S BEING STUDIED AND TO GOING NATIVE
19 Abbreviation for a certain amount of heat
21 Keep your ____ on the prize
22 When repeated, a Hawaiian fish
23 Like a St. but probably less busy than an Ave.
24 This might be your job title if you help your professor with research
25 Despised
26 WITH 29 ACROSS, AN INTERVIEWING METHOD FOR DISCOVERING STUDY PARTICIPANTS UNDERSTAND THE SIGNIFICANT EVENTS AND MEANINGS IN THEIR LIVES
29 See 26 Across
30 Network that airs Nova
31 Are you with __ or against…?
33 ___ Barker (Notorious mobster of yesteryear)
34 _____ GROUP (PEOPLE WHO ENGAGE IN A GUIDED DISCUSSION OF A SPECIFIC TOPIC)
35 QUALITATIVE INTERVIEWS EMPHASIZE THE USE OF ___-ENDED QUESTIONS

DOWN

1 A PERSPECTIVE THAT CONTRASTS WITH 1 ACROSS
2 A town or county in Georgia
3 Islamic religious leader
4 Happy ____
5 Middle of boat?
6 "____ like it hot"
7 Type of trip
8 Antique car
9 AN IDEAL WAY TO RECORD INTERVIEW RESPONSES
11 Depend (on)
15 THE INTERVIEW _____ APPROACH LISTS TOPICS TO BE COVERED IN OUTLINE FORM
17 First name of a famous architect (Rhymes with the first name of an obese fictional detective and a fiddling Roman emporor)
18 Ruler of old
20 Chew _____ (schmooze)
22 Undesirable prefix
23 Record album (British)
26 "Curb Your Enthusiasm" channel
27 Feature of sports bars
28 Slang expression meaning "okay"
30 ___ Chang's (chain of China bistros)
32 Opposite of NW

CHAPTER 19

Qualitative Data Analysis

OBJECTIVES

1. Describe alternative ways one can look for patterns in research data.
2. Describe and compare case-oriented analysis, cross-case analysis, and conversation analysis.
3. Describe the constant comparative method used in the grounded theory method.
4. Describe semiotics.
5. Describe the coding process in qualitative analysis, and define open coding.
6. Illustrate the use of memos in qualitative data analysis, including a comparison of code notes, theoretical notes, and operational notes as well as elemental, sorting, and integrating types of memos.
7. Describe the purpose and process of concept mapping.
8. Discuss the use of computers in qualitative analysis.

PRACTICE-RELEVANT SUMMARY

Although direct social work practice and qualitative research differ in various key ways, they share some similarities that attract many social workers to qualitative methods. Both endeavors commonly employ intensive, open-ended and probing interviews with fewer people than the number who participate in most quantitative studies. Both report what is said and observed in those interviews in detail-rich, narrative forms unlike the statistical emphases of most quantitative studies. Both tend to emphasize an idiographic and inductive approach, focusing more on individual differences and the influences of differing social contexts than do nomothetic quantitative studies. Both commonly attempt to gain an empathic sense of what things mean and what the world looks like from the from the individual's perspective, perhaps delving deeply into the life history of the individual. Both appreciate naturalistic inquiry; for example, social work practitioners understand the utility of home visits. In light of the above commonalities, social work practitioners might feel comfortable with some of the data processing and data analysis methods commonly employed in qualitative research. For example, direct social work practitioners commonly use qualitative techniques such as memoing in their clinical record keeping. You may want to keep these similarities in mind as you read this summary of the qualitative data analysis methods discussed in Chapter 19. [1]

Six different ways of seeking patterns in research data are: 1) *frequencies*; 2) *magnitudes*; 3) *structures*; 4) *processes*; 5) *causes*; and 6) *consequences*. In qualitative studies, these patterns are commonly sought via *cross-case analysis*. Two strategies for cross-case analysis are *variable-oriented analysis* and *case-oriented analysis*. The focus of variable-oriented analysis is on interrelations among variables among people who carry those variables. The focus of case-oriented analysis is *idiographic*, looking at all factors concerned with an individual case and seeking a complete, in-depth understanding of that individual case. But since one case is insufficient to develop a theory, in cross-case analysis additional cases are examined in the same idiographic manner, as the researcher looks for *patterns* and tries to explore why some cases fit one pattern while other cases fit another pattern. Ways to look for patterns include using the *grounded theory method* (as discussed in Chapter 17) and *content analysis* (discussed in Chapter 16) of various forms of communication such as *conversation analysis* and *semiotics* (the science of signs).

The key process of qualitative data processing is *coding according to concepts*. With *open coding*, the codes emerge throughout the process of collecting and closely examining the data. As we code, we use a technique called *memoing*, in which we write memos to ourselves and our collaborators. The memos might include *code notes* that identify code labels and their meanings, *theoretical notes* about things like deeper meanings and relationships that seem to be emerging, or *operational notes* about methodological issues. *Elemental memos* involve a detailed rendering of a specific matter. *Sorting memos* develop key themes that bring together a set of related elemental memos. *Integrating memos* tie together sorting memos into a larger, theoretical context. The relationships among concepts that emerge in qualitative data analysis can be displayed in graphical form, in a process called *concept mapping*.

Computers are increasingly being used among researchers analyzing qualitative data. Word processing programs can facilitate finding passages containing key words. Database and spreadsheet programs also help. There are now a large number of software programs created specifically for qualitative data analysis.

---

1 The ideas conveyed in the first paragraph of this summary were drawn from Padgett, D. K. (1998). "Does the Glove Really Fit? Qualitative Research and Clinical Social Work Practice." *Social Work*, 43, 4, July, 373-381. Padgett also cites the following source for some of these ideas: Gilgun, J. (1994). "Hand into Glove. The Grounded Theory Approach and Social Work Practice Research. In E. Sherman & W. J. Reid (Eds.), *Qualitative Research in Social Work* (pp. 115-125). New York: Columbia University Press.

REVIEW QUESTIONS

1. In looking for patterns in qualitative data on caregiver burden, we can examine:

    a. frequencies as to how often the caregiver receives respite.
    b. magnitudes as to the degree of stress experienced.
    c. structures regarding different types of caregiving.
    d processes about the stages of caregiver burden.
    e. All of the above.
    f. None of the above.

2. If we look for interrelations among several variables across people who carry those variables what type of cross-case analysis strategy are we using?

    a. Variable-oriented analysis.
    b. Case-oriented analysis.
    c. Semiotics.
    d. Idiographic.

3. Which of the following statements is/are true about case-oriented analysis?

    a. It is idiographic.
    b. It looks at all factors concerned with an individual case.
    c. It seeks a complete, in-depth understanding of an individual case.
    d. All of the above.
    e. None of the above.

4. In cross-case analysis, the researcher:

    a. turns from the first case to others, seeing if the variables that were important in the first case are important in others.
    b. looks for other important variables when subsequent cases are unlike the first one.
    c. might explore why some cases seem to reflect one pattern while others reflect another.
    d. All of the above.
    e. None of the above.

5. Which of the following statements is/are true about the grounded theory method?

    a. It is similar to cross-case analysis.
    b. It begins with observations rather than hypotheses.
    c. It employs the constant-comparative method.
    d. All of the above.
    e. None of the above.

6. Which of the following statements is/are true about semiotics?

    a. It employs content analysis.
    b. It focuses on symbols and meanings associated with signs.
    c. It is considered a social science.
    d. All of the above.
    e. None of the above.

7. Which of the following statements is/are true about qualitative coding?

    a. The concept is the organizing principle.
    b. A given code category can be applied only to text materials of the same length.
    c. Standardization is necessary.
    d. All of the above.
    e. None of the above.

8. Which of the following statements is/are true about open coding?

    a. Questions are asked about the phenomena as reflected in the data
    b. Data are broken down into discrete parts, closely examined, and compared for similarities and differences.
    c. Codes emerge throughout the process of collecting and closely examining the data.
    d. All of the above.
    e. None of the above.

9. In analyzing the data from qualitative interviews of Asian American battered women, you write a note to yourself wondering why the more recently battered women, who seem to be less acculturated, appear to take much longer to disclose the battering and to seek help from their social support network than do the other battered women. Your note is an example of:

    a. memoing.
    b. a code note.
    c. a theoretical note.
    d. an operational note.
    d. All of the above.
    e. None of the above.
    f. a and c, only, are correct.
    g. a and b, only, are correct.
    h. a and d, only, are correct.

10. The following exemplifies:

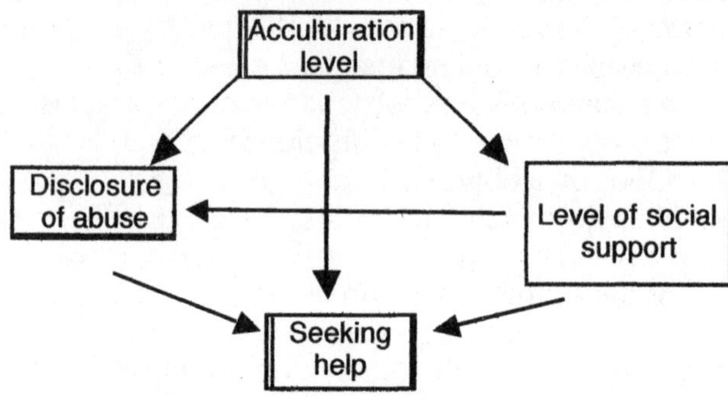

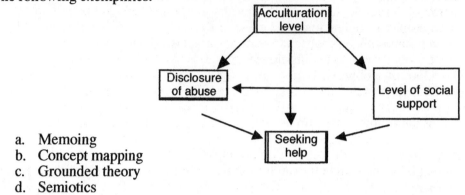

   a. Memoing
   b. Concept mapping
   c. Grounded theory
   d. Semiotics
   e. Coding

11. NUD*IST is:

   a. a cold Alaskan.
   b. someone who eats salad without dressing.
   c. a computer program for analyzing qualitative data.
   d. None of the above.

12. The computer can be used in analyzing qualitative data for:

   a. finding passages of narrative that contain the same words.
   b. sorting passages to gather all those dealing with the same concept.
   c. simultaneously analyzing several interviews from different interviewers.
   d. All of the above.
   e. None of the above; computers are used only for quantitative data analysis.

EXERCISE 19.1

Suppose you want to conduct a cross-case analysis of how social workers in your agency depict their orientations to direct practice. Below are the statements of four social workers. Identify the key concepts you might code in each statement.

Social Worker #1: "I stress the importance of the worker-client relationship and the need to forge an empathic, trusting therapeutic alliance. Long-term treatment is my preference. I like to try to cure people of their symptoms and change their personalities. I focus on early childhood attachment problems that have not been resolved. Although I emphasize attachment issues from early childhood, I recognize the need to address also such things as the here and now influence of family systems dynamics, cultural diversity, economic stress and community forces. I also recently attended a workshop on crisis intervention."

Social Worker #2: "I take an ecological/social change/social systems approach. I stress intervening in the client's social environment and helping them obtain resources, services and safety. I seem to be most effective with clients who have been oppressed by society or victimized by someone. I'd rather change social systems that are influencing the client than change the client. I don't believe in blaming the victim. I also like to engage in social action activities to make social policies more humane and to protect the rights and improve the plight of the oppressed. Nevertheless, to be effective I recognize the importance of developing a close, trusting worker-client relationship based on empathy and other relationship building skills."

Social Worker #3: "I take a feminist approach. Most of my clients are women who are victims of battering who have been victimized in some other way by our male dominated society. I eschew focusing on their psychological or childhood attachment issues, and believe that that is just blaming the victim. I also eschew dealing with family systems dynamics. Instead, I try to help battered women leave their abusers and find safety. My interventions are largely short-term and crisis intervention oriented. One of my strengths is my empathy for the plight of these women and the strong, trusting relationships I build with them."

Social Worker #4: I take a cognitive-behavioral approach. I recognize that many faulty cognitions and dysfunctional behaviors stemming from childhood issues. But rather than focus on long-term resolution of those issues, I focus on dysfunctional emotions connected to irrational beliefs in the here and now and on the need to restructure cognitions and learn better coping skills and parenting skills. Rather than focusing on long-term personality change and dealing with unresolved issues stemming from childhood, I deal in the present with specific skills, cognitions, and behaviors that can be changed in the short term through behavior modification and cognitive therapy techniques. Of course, to do this well I have to take the following things into consideration: current forces in the social environment, cultural issues, and forging a strong therapeutic alliance with each client.

EXERCISE 19.2

Using open coding and memoing, identify the patterns you observe across the above four statements. What concepts tend to fit the practice orientations of all four social workers? What concepts tend to differentiate their practice orientations?

DISCUSSION QUESTIONS

1. Based on what you have read in Chapter 19 (as well as in previous chapters) do you agree with those who deem qualitative research as more labor intensive than quantitative research? Why or why not?

2. Assuming that some day you were going to do research, and in light of the similarities between direct social work practice methods and qualitative research methods, do you think you would prefer doing qualitative research more than quantitative research? Why or why not?

3. Describe and differentiate the alternative forms of memoing in qualitative data analysis.

CROSSWORD PUZZLE

ACROSS

1 THESE ARE USED IN PREPARING DATA FOR PROCESSING
5 Exploited
9 All purpose physician
11 Metal ingredient
12 THERE ARE SEVERAL COMPUTER ______ DESIGNED FOR ANALYZING QUALITATIVE DATA
16 Educational lobby (teacher's organization)
17 Abbreviation for an expensive diagnostic procedure for orthopedic or neurological problems
18 Consumed
20 WITH 78 ACROSS: ONE APPROACH FOR DISCOVERING PATTERNS IN QUALITATIVE DATA
24 Legume in a pod
25 How do ______ ______? (2 words: common question after dressing for a big occasion)
26 Fraternity letter
27 Mild marital conflict
28 WITH 74 ACROSS: ONE AIM OF QUALITATIVE DATA ANALYSIS
31 At home
32 Diamond ____
33 WITH 13 DOWN: ANOTHER METHOD FOR DISCOVERING PATTERNS IN QUALITATIVE DATA
34 Addict may risk this (abbrev.)
35 Can. prov. With Niagra Falls
36 I ______ Sam
37 United (2 words)
40 Grunt of disgust
42 Eleventh US President
45 Poet's initials
46 Military medal (abbrev.)
48 Winnie the ______
50 Peak
52 Biblical you
55 Twelve mos.
56 ONE TOOL FOR PREPARING QUALITATIVE DATA FOR ANALYSIS
57 Eye for ______ eye
58 Where FDR, HST, JFK, LBJ, and Michael Jordan once roamed
60 Arafat's organization
61 IN ANALYZING DATA, WE SEEK TO DISCOVER POSSIBLE CAUSAL ______
63 Dizzy, John, or Howard
64 Celebrated, honored
67 Big ten school (abbrev.)
68 PROCESSING QUALITATIVE DATA IS AS MUCH ______ AS SCIENCE
69 Aide in monster movies
71 Title for 21 down
73 ______ cup or man
74 SEE 28 ACROSS
78 SEE 20 ACROSS
80 Live
81 Concerns of many college students (abbrev.)
82 Native American tribe

DOWN

1 WITH 14 DOWN: METHOD USING DIAGRAMS TO EXPLORE GRAPHICALLY RELATIONSHIPS IN QUALITATIVE DATA
2 Nabisco cookie treat
3 College administrator
4 Terry Bradshaw or Mean Joe Greene
6 Talks
7 Where to go when you break your leg at midnight (abbrev.)
8 Realm
9 ______ and bear it
10 Keystone state (abbrev.)
13 SEE 33 ACROSS
14 SEE 1 DOWN
15 Undetectable quality
19 Devour
21 ____ Corleone (Brando and DiNiro both played him)
22 ______ Calhoun (deceased 1950's actor)
23 ______ of Sam
27 Idler
29 Cry of discovery
30 Beat, rhythm
38 ANOTHER APPROACH FOR DISCOVERING PATTERNS IN QUALITATIVE DATA
39 QUALITATIVE RESEARCHERS ARE LIKELY TO USE ______ CODING
41 Caleb, Hale, or Bond
43 Measure of electrical resistance
44 Mein ______ (Hitler's book)
47 Unwanted mark
49 Commanding
51 Nat or Natalie
53 Sturdy tree
54 Not honored (but should be)
59 Brief snooze
62 NAME OF ONE COMPUTER PROGRAM FOR ANALYZING QUALITATIVE DATA (sans the asterisk)
63 ______ PROCESSING
65 Freudian self
66 Bird of peace
70 T______ (Jurassic Park menace)
72 Not fooled by
74 Prefix meaning defective
75 Be for he or she
76 Pedro's assent
77 Brazil tourist spot
79 Man of ______ Mancha

CHAPTER 20

Quantitative Data Analysis

OBJECTIVES

1. Explain the difference between nominal and other levels of measurement and give an example of a variable at the nominal level of measurement.

2. Explain the difference between ordinal and higher levels of measurement (that is, interval or ratio) and give an example of a variable at the ordinal level of measurement.

3. Identify the criteria for ratio-level measurement and give an example of a variable at that level.

4. Explain how variables at higher levels of measurement can be collapsed to lower levels and provide an example of this process.

5. Identify the functions of coding.

6. Identify the attributes of good code categories.

7. Be able to construct a codebook.

8. Identify the functions of data cleaning and describe two ways to clean data codes.

9. Interpret a univariate distribution of data.

10. Calculate and interpret the three measures of central tendency.

11. Understand and interpret the role of measures of dispersion.

12. Interpret the standard deviation.

13. Differentiate continuous and discrete variables, and select the appropriate calculation for each.

14. Construct and interpret collapsed response categories.

15. Recognize how the inclusion of qualitative findings can enhance the interpretation of descriptive statistics and how the inclusion of descriptive statistics can enrich a qualitative study.

PRACTICE-RELEVANT SUMMARY

No matter how much you may dislike or fear statistics, there is no escaping them. You may encounter them less as a direct practitioner of social work than as an accountant, but encounter them you will, and this chapter will help you deal with them when you must.

Some day, for example, you may be asked to present data summarizing the characteristics of clients in your unit or agency. Your decisions about how to analyze and present your findings will be influenced by the levels of measurement of your variables. Some variables, for example, only measure qualitative categories (gender, ethnicity, and so on). Others measure quantitative aspects of a variable (how much of something). Measures using only qualitative categories are at the *nominal* level of measurement.

Quantitative measures in social work are usually either at the ordinal or ratio level. *Ordinal* measures only can tell whether something has more or less of something than another thing; they cannot provide information on precisely how much more or less that is. Thus, a measure telling you that some clients were very satisfied with services, while others were moderately satisfied, is an ordinal measure. A *ratio* measure can provide precise differences, and its information can be used arithmetically because it employs an absolute zero point. Thus, a measure that tells you how many days a child has been in foster care is a ratio measure.

If the purpose of your report is solely descriptive, chances are you will undertake a univariate analysis, which examines one variable at a time (in contrast to a bivariate analysis, which examines two variables in relation to one another). To make your presentation manageable, you will probably construct a frequency distribution, which reports the number and percentage of cases in each attribute of each variable. To make your presentation even more manageable, you might collapse response categories of attributes into grouped categories of attributes, called *marginals*, and then report the raw numbers and the percentages of the marginals.

To further summarize the data, you would present measures of central tendency and dispersion. If you have *continuous variables* (variables at the interval or ratio level of measurement), you could present all three measures of central tendency: the mean, the median, and the mode. The *mean* is calculated by summing the values and then dividing the sum by the number of cases. The *median* is the middle value in the distribution. The *mode* is the most frequent value. If you have *discrete variables* (variables at the nominal or ordinal level of measurement), you would be restricted to the mode unless you violated some technical assumptions (which is often done).

Measures of central tendency don't give the whole picture, however. An average age of 45, for example, could come from an agency where half the cases are 10 years old and the other half are 80 years old. To depict how spread out the values are, you can present *measures of dispersion.* The range shows the distance separating the highest from the lowest value. The *interquartile range* is the range of scores for the middle 50% of cases. The *standard deviation* gives a sense of how far each case, on average, is from the mean. In a normal curve (a bell curve), 68% of the cases fall between one standard deviation above and below the mean. The standard deviation is calculated by subtracting the mean from each score, squaring the difference, summing the squares, dividing the sum of squares by the number of cases, and then finding the square root of the dividend.

Before your computer software will do any of the foregoing calculations for you, you must first *develop codes* that the computer can understand. There are two ways to develop codes. One involves using a coding scheme developed before analyzing your data. The second involves examining the data from a number of cases to determine the best categories to use in coding the data. Which approach to use depends on whether you are able, in advance, to anticipate all the responses likely to be relevant to your analysis. You will also need to develop a codebook, which describes the locations of variables and identifies the attributes of each variable and the code assigned to each attribute.

Various options exist for *entering your data* into your computer. One method used is to pre-code your data collection instrument, so that data can be entered directly on your computer keyboard as you examine each completed data collection instrument. When you use this direct data entry method, it is essential that data collection instruments be edited carefully before data entry to check for problems in the way data were recorded on the instrument. An even more direct data entry method, resources permitting, is to have telephone interviewers record data directly into the computer while they are conducting their telephone interviews. Another expedient method is to use optical scanning sheets, in which a machine reads black pencil marks on special code sheets.

Regardless of which data entry method you use, and no matter how carefully your data have been entered, some errors are inevitable. Consequently, data entry should be followed by a *data cleaning* phase before any data analyses are conducted. A simple form of cleaning data is called *possible-code cleaning*. Using possible-code cleaning, you examine the distribution of responses to each item in your data set and look to see if some responses exist for codes you didn't use (such as codes for categories other than male or female for a gender variable).

Conducting a qualitative inquiry can enhance the interpretation of descriptive statistics by providing insights into their potential meanings. Likewise, the inclusion of descriptive statistics can enrich a qualitative study, since counting some things is an inescapable part of detecting patterns or developing a deeper understanding of the phenomenon being studied.

REVIEW QUESTIONS

1. An instrument that assesses emotional disorder is at what level of measurement?

   a. Nominal
   b. Ordinal
   c. Ratio
   d. Not enough information to know

2. A measure that indicates exactly how many times in the last week a child saw his parent become inebriated would be at what measurement level?

   a. Nominal
   b. Ordinal
   c. Ratio
   d. Not enough information to know

3. What level of measurement would you have if you asked a child whether his parent became inebriated very often, often, sometimes, rarely, or never?

   a. Nominal
   b. Ordinal
   c. Ratio
   d. Not enough information to know

4. What level of measurement would you have if you asked a child whether the single parent he lives with is his mother or father?

   a. Nominal
   b. Ordinal
   c. Ratio
   d. Interval

5. Which of the following statements is true about coding?

   a. It is possible to develop a coding scheme before analyzing your data.
   b. One coding option involves examining the data from a number of cases to determine the best categories to use in coding the data.
   c. You will always be able to anticipate all the codes likely to be relevant to your analysis.
   d. All of the above.
   e. Only a and b are true.

6. A codebook should:

   a. Describe the locations of variables
   b. Identify the attributes of each variable
   c. Indicate the code assigned to each attribute
   d. All of the above

7. Which of the following statements is/are true about data processing?

   a. Once data have been originally entered, you should assume that no incorrect data are in the data set.
   b. After data entry, data can be cleaned by examining distributions of responses and looking for responses with illegitimate codes.
   c. Computers cannot be relied on to produce correct results if the data entered into them are in error.
   d. All of the above.
   e. None of the above.

8-10: The following information was found in a codebook:

Column	Variable	Codes-Categories
1	Gender	1 = Female 2 = Male
2	Ethnicity	1 = White, not Hispanic 2 = White Hispanic 3 = Hispanic, not White 4 = African American 5 = Asian American 6 = Native American 7 = Other 9 = Not answered
3	Relationship to nursing home resident	1 = Husband 2 = Wife 3 = Son 4 = Daughter 5 = Other 9 = Not answered

8. Which of the following statements is true about a person with the following data entered in columns 1 through 3: 142?

   a. It is a female African American wife of a nursing home resident.
   b. It is the 142nd person in the data set.
   c. It is a male African American husband of a nursing home resident.
   d. It is a female Native American daughter of a nursing home resident.

9. Which of the following statements is true about a person with the following data entered in columns 1 through 3: 252?

   a. The person is male.
   b. The person is a resident's wife.
   c. The person is Native American.
   d. There is an error in the data entry.

10. Which of the following statements is true about a person with the following data entered in columns 1 through 3: 386?

   a. The person did not report their gender.
   b. Their ethnicity is "other."
   c. They have no relationship to the resident.
   d. There are errors in the data entry.
   e. All of the above.

11-15: Below are the ages of the nine children on your caseload at a child guidance center:

3 3 3 3 4 8 9 10 11

11. 6 is the:

   a. Mean
   b. Median
   c. Mode
   d. Range

12. 4 is the:

   a. Mean
   b. Median
   c. Mode
   d. Range

13. 3 is the:

   a. Mean
   b. Median
   c. Mode
   d. Range

14. 8 is the:

   a. Mean
   b. Median
   c. Mode
   d. Range

15. Which of the following statements is true about the above distribution of ages?

   a. It is from a continuous variable.
   b. It is from a discrete variable.
   c. It contains no dispersion.
   d. The data are grouped into collapsed response categories.
   e. All of the above.

EXERCISE 20.1

Develop a codebook for the following questionnaire:

1. Gender

   ☐ Female
   ☐ Male

2. Age: __ __

3. Student status in social work program:

   ☐ Undergraduate
   ☐ First-year master's degree student
   ☐ Second-year master's degree student
   ☐ Doctoral degree student

4. Satisfaction with social work education you have received so far at this program:

   ☐ Very satisfied
   ☐ Satisfied
   ☐ Dissatisfied
   ☐ Very dissatisfied

5. Have you ever read the Rubin and Babbie text, Research Methods for Social Work?

   ☐ Yes
   ☐ No

6. Did you enjoy reading the Rubin and Babbie text, Research Methods for Social Work?

   ☐ Yes
   ☐ No
   ☐ Not applicable, I didn't read it.

EXERCISE 20.2

Which of the variables above in Exercise 19.1 is/are at the nominal level of measurement? ordinal level of measurement? ratio level of measurement?

EXERCISE 20.3

The number of timeouts during the 10 sessions of play therapy for each of the 20 children in your play therapy groups is listed below:

0	16	20	4	0
3	17	18	0	1
0	5	2	1	0
3	2	3	0	5

1. Construct a univariate frequency distribution with grouped data in four collapsed response categories, showing the percentages for each collapsed category.
2. Calculate the mean and state what it indicates.
3. Calculate the median and state what it indicates.
4. Calculate the mode and state what it indicates.
5. Discuss the advantages and disadvantages of the above three measures of central tendency you have calculated in terms of how well they summarize the distribution.

EXERCISE 20.4

Suppose you conceptualize a measure to assess whether a client's problem can be considered acute or chronic and, if chronic, the degree of chronicity. Suppose your measure is simply the number of times the client has been previously placed in some form of institutional care for the problem. Show three different ways to report (or categorize) that number. Each way should be at a different level of measurement. Start with the ratio level, then the ordinal level, and then the nominal level.

DISCUSSION QUESTIONS

1. Describe how you would go about cleaning your data using possible-code cleaning.

2. Why is it important to report both the mean and the median? Why won't reporting just one suffice?

3. Provide a hypothetical example of how combining descriptive statistics with a qualitative inquiry can enrich the qualitative inquiry as well as the interpretation of the descriptive statistics.

CROSSWORD PUZZLE

ACROSS

1 AVERAGE SUSCEPTIBLE TO EXTREME VALUES
4 Thumb a ride
8 Pindar product
9 THINGS TO BE ENTERED AND CLEANED
10 MEASURES OF _____ GIVE A SUMMARY INDICATION OF THE DISTRIBUTION OF CASES AROUND AN AVERAGE VALUE
11 Drew Barrymore was a child when she befriended him
12 Vegan's no no
13 3.14159
14 NBC Owner
15 WITH 9 DOWN: COMMONLY USED MEASURE OF DISPERSION
18 Yoko
19 ALTERNATIVE TO THE MEAN
21 Elevator button
23 Small donkey
24 Record
26 _____ YOUR DATA TO CHECK FOR CODING OR ENTRY ERRORS
27 Pedro's the
28 _____ cabin
29 NUMBER ASSIGNED TO AN ATTRIBUTE OF A VARIABLE
31 Former oil company, now called Exxon
32 He usually runs faster than a QB or a FB
33 LEVEL OF MEASUREMENT FOR GENDER
37 ABBA song (Call for help)
40 The Terminator
41 "_____ Couple"
43 Andy Roddick's shirt size
44 James' Sopranos co-star
45 ___ Fleming (Agent 007 author)
47 Common first names in Latin America
49 The Buckeyes
50 Ocean front suburban area east of NYC
51 Squeal on an accomplice
52 Three ft.
53 Crafty

DOWN

1 MOST COMMON VALUE
2 Archie Bunker's wife
3 Two time loser to DDE
4 Fabled loser to Tortoise
5 _____ girl!
6 Follow
7 What Orion did
9 SEE 15 ACROSS
13 JFK's boat in WWII
14 _____ DATA ARE CREATED THROUGH THE COMBINATION OF ATTRIBUTES OF A VARIABLE
15 Mono or hifi successor (sound system)
16 WHEN CONSTRUCTING TABLES, CONSIDER HOW TO HANDLE "_____ KNOWS"
17 _____ idea whose time has come
19 Think over
20 Pull
22 Soccer legend
23 Before A.D.
25 Past
29 Baby's bed
30 Very unpleasant
31 Wind blowing from Texas to New Mexico
34 LEVEL OF MEASUREMENT FOR A LIKERT SCALE
35 Humility
36 "Free _____"
38 Exclamation of surprise or pleasure
39 Appear
42 Aromas
46 Greek letter
48 Help

CHAPTER 21

Inferential Data Analysis: Part 1

OBJECTIVES

1. Explain the role of chance as a possible explanation for some observed correlations between variables in a sample.

2. Explain the role of statistical significance testing as a basis for refuting chance.

3. Discuss the role of theoretical sampling distributions in the concept of statistical significance.

4. Define statistical significance.

5. Discuss the criteria for selecting a significance level.

6. Define the critical region in a theoretical sampling distribution.

7. Define and identify when to use one- and two-tailed tests of significance.

8. Discuss the role of the null hypothesis and how it compares to the research hypothesis.

9. Define Type I and Type II errors and discuss the importance of each in social work research.

10. Discuss the impact of sample size on statistical significance, and how that bears on assessing relationship magnitude and considering substantive significance.

11. Interpret measures of association and their role in inferential data analysis.

12. Calculate and interpret the z-score approach to effect size.

13. Explain how the concepts of statistical significance, relationship magnitude (or effect size), and substantive significance are different, and how each gets considered as part of interpreting inferential data.

14. Discuss the bases for considering whether effect sizes are strong, medium, or weak, and the influence of value judgments on variations across studies in the substantive significance of the same effect size.

PRACTICE-RELEVANT SUMMARY

Just as there is no escaping descriptive statistics, there is no escaping inferential statistics -- at least not if you ever want your practice to be guided by your utilization of research that tests hypotheses relevant to social work.

Beyond *utilizing* research, someday you are likely to be asked to present data indicating the impact your unit or agency is having on some desired aim. Some of the folks asking for such data are likely to know about inferential statistics and the role chance might play in accounting for outcomes that on the surface might seem to suggest that your unit or agency is successfully achieving its aims. If and when you are faced with this situation, your practice will be more effective (that is, you will be better equipped to present your unit's or agency's data in an informed, persuasive manner) if you are able to include inferential data analysis procedures in your report -- procedures that will inform your audience of the likelihood that chance (or sampling error) accounts for your findings. These procedures will also give your audience hard data indicating the strength of your unit's or agency's impact, data that can be used as a basis for discussing the ultimate value (that is, the substantive significance) of the impact you are having.

The first step in the inferential data analysis process is to ascertain the probability that chance, or sampling error, accounts for your findings. In any study of any independent and dependent variables, even when there is no relationship in the population between those variables, there is a good chance of obtaining findings that show some relationship between those variables in your sample, although that relationship might be quite weak. The process of assessing the probability that chance explains your findings involves testing to see if the relationship you have observed is statistically significant. *Testing for statistical significance* means calculating the probability, or odds, of finding due to chance a relationship at least as strong as the one you have observed in your findings.

All of the methods for calculating statistical significance, no matter how different their mathematical assumptions and formulas may be, ultimately yield the same thing -- a probability between 0 and 1.0 that the observed relationship was obtained simply due to chance. Tests of statistical significance ascertain that probability by using theoretical sampling distributions. *Theoretical sampling distributions* show what proportion of random distributions of data would produce relationships at least as strong as the one observed in your findings. The theoretical sampling distribution thus shows the probability that observing the relationship you observed was due to the luck of the draw when and if no such relationship really exists in a population or in a theoretical sense.

The probability that the observed relationship could have been produced by chance is compared to a pre-selected level of significance. If that probability is equal to or less than that level of significance, the finding is deemed statistically significant and the plausibility of the null hypothesis (chance) is refuted.
Traditionally, social scientists, including social work researchers, have settled on .05 as the most commonly used cutoff point to separate findings not deemed significant

from those that are. However, a higher or lower level can be justified depending on the research context. Findings that fall in the zone beyond the cutoff point, and that are therefore considered statistically significant, comprise the critical region of the theoretical sampling distribution. The cutoff point is called the *level of significance*. When it is set at .05, it is signified by the following expression: $p \leq .05$. This means that any probability equal to or less than .05 will be deemed statistically significant. Researchers usually just report it as less than .05 ($p < .05$) because the probability rarely equals .05 exactly. A probability that is even a tiny bit above .05 would be considered to be greater than .05 -- outside of the critical region -- and therefore statistically not significant.

Hypotheses that do not specify whether the predicted relationship will be positive or negative are called *nondirectional hypotheses*. When testing nondirectional hypotheses, we must use two-tailed tests of significance. *Two-tailed tests of significance* place the critical regions at both ends of the theoretical sampling distribution. When testing directional hypotheses we can use *one-tailed tests of significance*. These locate the critical region of significant values at one, predicted end of the theoretical sampling distribution.

When we refer to chance as a rival hypothesis, we call it the null hypothesis. The *null hypothesis* postulates that the relationship being statistically tested is explained by chance -- that it does not really exist in a population or in a theoretical sense -- even though it may seem to be related in our particular findings. Thus, when our findings are shown to be statistically significant, we reject the null hypothesis because the probability that it is true -- that our results were caused by chance -- is less than our level of significance. Whenever we reject the null hypothesis, we are supporting the plausibility of our research hypothesis (assuming that we are predicting that two variables are related and that we are not seeking to show that they are unrelated). Conversely, whenever we fail to reject the null hypothesis, we are failing to support our research hypothesis.

Every time we make a decision about the statistical significance of a tested relationship, we risk making an error. If we decide to reject the null hypothesis, we risk making one type of error. If we do not reject the null hypothesis, we risk making another type of error. *Type I* errors occur when we reject a true null hypothesis. *Type II* errors occur when we accept a false null hypothesis. Social scientists tend to accept a much lower risk of making a Type I error than a Type II error. But just because so many social scientists conform to this convention does not mean that Type I errors are necessarily more serious than Type II errors, especially when human suffering is at stake. Deciding which type of error is more serious requires making value judgments, and the choice will vary depending on the nature and context of the research question.

The larger our sample, the less sampling error we have. Therefore, increasing sample size reduces the risk of a Type II error. However, with very large samples, weak and not particularly meaningful relationships can become statistically significant. When we assess statistical significance, we ask only one question: "Can a relationship be inferred to exist in a theoretical sense or in a broader population?" We do not assess how strong the relationship is. Significance levels do *not* indicate the relative strength of a relationship. A relationship significant at the .001 level is not necessarily stronger than one significant at the .05 level. A weak relationship can be significant at the .001 level if the sample size is very large, and a stronger relationship might be significant at the .05 level but not at a lower level if the sample size is not large.

Measures of association, such as correlation coefficients and analogous statistics (phi, rho, Cramer's V, gamma, eta, and so on), assess how strong a relationship is. Which measure of association should be used depends primarily on the level of measurement of your variables. The stronger the relationship, the closer the measure-of-association statistic will be to 1.0 or - 1.0. The weaker the relationship, the closer it will be to zero. Many measures of association are based on a *proportionate-reduction-of-error* (PRE) model and tell us how much error in predicting attributes of a dependent variable is reduced by knowledge of the attribute of the independent variable. Many measure-of-association statistics can be squared to indicate the proportion of variation in the dependent variable that is explained by one or more independent variables.

Statistics that portray the strength of association between variables are often referred to by the term *effect size*. This term is particularly common in clinical outcome research. Effect-size statistics might refer to proportion of dependent variable variation explained or to the difference between the means of two groups divided by the standard deviation (that is, the z-score). Effect-size statistics portray the strength of association found in any study, no matter what outcome measure is used, in terms that are comparable across studies. Thus, they enable us to compare the effects of different interventions across studies using different types of outcome measures. *Z-score effect sizes* of about .5 to .7 are generally considered to be medium or average in strength. These correspond to correlations of roughly about .30, give or take several points. Larger effect sizes are considered strong, and effect sizes well below .4 (correlations near about .1) are generally considered to be weak.

Statistical significance, relationship strength, and *substantive significance* should not be confused with one another. Statistically significant relationships are not necessarily strong or substantively meaningful. Strong relationships are not necessarily substantively significant, and some seemingly weak relationships can have great substantive significance. The substantive significance of a finding pertains to its practical or theoretical value or meaningfulness; it cannot be assessed without making value judgments about the importance of the variables or problem studied, what the finding adds to what is already known or not known about alleviating a problem, whether the benefits of implementing the study's implications are worth the costs of that implementation, and so on.

REVIEW QUESTIONS

1. In trying to understand why many clients prematurely terminate services in your agency, you find that 51% of males terminate, compared to 49% of females. Which of the following statements is true about the process of inferential data analysis regarding this finding?

    a. You should ascertain the probability that chance, or sampling error, accounts for the difference between the men and women.
    b. You should infer that men are more likely to prematurely terminate than are women.
    c. You should infer that a relationship exists between gender and premature termination.
    d. Both b and c, only, are true.

2. Which of the following statements is true about testing for statistical significance?

    a. Even weak relationships can be statistically significant.
    b. It involves assessing the probability that chance explains our findings.
    c. It will yield a probability between 0 and 1.0 that the observed relationship was obtained simply due to chance.
    d. All of the above.
    e. None of the above.

3. Which of the following statements is true about theoretical sampling distributions?

    a. They show what proportion of random distributions of data would produce relationships at least as strong as the one observed in our findings.
    b. They show the probability that observing the relationship we observed was due to the luck of the draw when and if no such relationship really exists in a population or in a theoretical sense.
    c. The critical region of the distribution is pre-selected.
    d. All of the above.
    e. None of the above.

4. The .05 level of significance is commonly chosen because:

    a. Mathematics dictates it as the only correct level.
    b. It means there is at least a .05 correlation between the independent and dependent variables.
    c. Two groups would have to show a .05 difference in order to be significant.
    d. All of the above.
    e. None of the above.

5. Refuting the null hypothesis means:

   a. Rejecting the research hypothesis
   b. Refuting chance as a plausible explanation for the findings
   c. Not having statistically significant results
   d. Proving that the research hypothesis is true

6. One-tailed tests of significance can be used when:

   a. We test hypotheses that do not specify whether the predicted relationship will be positive or negative.
   b. We test nondirectional hypotheses.
   c. We test directional hypotheses.
   d. We split the critical region of significant values at both ends of the theoretical sampling distribution.

7. Which of the following statements is true about Type I and Type II errors?

   a. Every time we make a decision about the statistical significance of a tested relationship, we risk making either a Type I or a Type II error.
   b. Type I errors are always more serious than Type II errors.
   c. Type I errors occur when we accept a false null hypothesis.
   d. Type II errors occur when we reject a true null hypothesis.
   e. All of the above.

8. Larger samples:

   a. Have less sampling error
   b. Have less risk of a Type II error
   c. Are more likely to find that weak relationships are statistically significant
   d. All of the above

9. Which of the following statements is true about significance levels?

   a. They indicate how strong the relationship is.
   b. A relationship significant at the .001 level is stronger than one significant at the .05 level.
   c. A weak relationship can be significant at the .001 level if the sample size is very large.
   d. A strong relationship will always be significant at the .05 level, regardless of sample size.

10. Which of the following statements is true about measures of association?

    a. They assess how strong a relationship is.
    b. Which measure of association to use depends primarily on the level of measurement of your variables.
    c. Some measures of association range between 0 and 1.
    d. Many measure-of-association statistics can be squared to indicate the proportion of variation in the dependent variable that is explained by the independent variables.
    e. All of the above.

11. In an evaluation of the effectiveness of an intervention to reduce depression, the experimental group's posttest mean is 20, which indicates less depression than the control group's posttest mean of 30. The standard deviation is 5. The effect size is:

    a. + 2
    b. + 10
    c. - 2
    d. - 10

12. Which of the following statements is true about effect size statistics?

    a. They show whether the finding is statistically significant.
    b. They show whether the finding is substantively significant.
    c. They enable us to compare the effects of different interventions across studies using different types of outcome measures.
    d. If they fall below .30, they are not significant.
    e. All of the above.
    f. Only a and d are true.

13. Which of the following statements is true about substantive significance?

    a. Strong relationships will be substantively significant.
    b. It is possible for a weak relationship to be substantively significant.
    c. Assessing the substantive significance of a finding requires that we avoid making value judgments.
    d. All of the above.

14. Suppose you evaluate the effectiveness of your agency's program and find that program recipients had better outcomes than non-recipients, but the results are not statistically significant. This means that:

    a. The program was not effective.
    b. The program was effective, but not at a significant level.
    c. Sampling error cannot be ruled out as an explanation for the difference in outcomes.
    d. None of the above.

EXERCISE 21.1

A program evaluation study with an extremely rigorous experimental design assesses the effectiveness of a program to prevent child abuse among high-risk families by providing them with intensive, comprehensive social work services. Using a valid measurement of actual abuse, it finds that the experimental group families had a mean of .1 incidents of abuse, compared to a control group mean of .3. The standard deviation was .4. The significance level was .05, and the probability of committing a Type I error was less than .05.

1. Were the results statistically significant? Specify the basis for your answer.

2. What type of error would you be choosing to risk, given your answer to the previous questions?

3. Should a one- or two-tailed test of significance have been used? Why?

4. What was the effect size? Was it positive or negative, and why? Would you consider it to be strong, medium, or weak, and why?

5. Discuss whether you would find these results substantively significant, and why.

EXERCISE 21.2

Another program evaluation study with a moderately rigorous quasi-experimental design assesses the effectiveness of a parent education program to improve knowledge of child rearing among parents at high risk for child abuse by providing them with ten sessions of parent education classes. Using a self-report scale that the program evaluators constructed for the purpose of this evaluation, the study finds that the parents who participated in the classes had a mean score of 50, which was better than the comparison group's mean score of 30, indicating that the program recipients provided more correct answers about child-rearing. The standard deviation was 10. The significance level was .05, and the probability of committing a Type I error was less than .001.

1. Were the results statistically significant? Specify the basis for your answer.

2. What type of error would you be choosing to risk, given your answer to the previous question?

3. Should a one- or two-tailed test of significance have been used? Why?

4. What was the effect size? Was it positive or negative, and why? Would you consider it to be strong, medium, or weak, and why?

5. Discuss whether you would find these results substantively significant, and why.

EXERCISE 21.3

A third program evaluation study with a moderately rigorous quasi-experimental design assesses the effectiveness of a family preservation program whose aim is to prevent the out-of-home placement of children of parents who have been referred by the courts for child abuse or neglect. The program measures its outcome not in terms of actual child abuse, but simply according to whether or not children are placed out of the home. It finds that only 10% of the children in the families receiving family preservation services were placed out of the home, compared to 40% of children in a comparison group receiving routine child welfare services. The strength of this relationship, measured by the phi statistic, was .30, which becomes .09 when squared. The significance level was .05, and the probability of committing a Type I error was less than .01.

1. Were the results statistically significant? Specify the basis for your answer.

2. What type of error would you be choosing to risk, given your answer to the previous question?

3. Would you consider the phi statistic of .30 to indicate a strong, medium, or weak relationship, and why?

4. What does the phi-squared of .09 mean?

5. Discuss whether you would find these results substantively significant, and why.

EXERCISE 21.4

1. Reexamine each of the above three program evaluation vignettes in Exercises 21.1 to 21.3. Considering the findings as well as design issues and the nature of the outcome variables measured, which of the three outcomes would you consider most and least substantively significant? Why?

2. Suppose you had relatively meager funding to develop a program either for preventing child abuse or for intervening with parents referred for child abuse. Suppose that the target population for your program was very large, and that the parent education approach would reach ten times as many high-risk families as would either of the other two approaches (in Exercises 21.1 and 21.3). In light of this consideration, as well as your answer to question 1 above, which of the three program approaches would you develop in your program (assuming that you could afford to choose only one, that you decided to be guided by research in your decision, and that these three studies represented the research)? Discuss the reasons for your selection.

DISCUSSION QUESTIONS

1. Suppose an evaluation of a program to prevent teen pregnancy is conducted with a very small sample. It finds that none of the ten teens in the experimental group became pregnant, while two of the ten teens in the control group became pregnant. However, the results are not statistically significant. Discuss how you would interpret these results, keeping in mind issues of Type II errors and the influence of sample size. What would you recommend be done by the field in light of these results?

2. Discuss the purpose of the null hypothesis. Why do we need one? In your answer, discuss why/how both the null hypothesis and the research hypothesis can be false.

3. Suppose you conducted an evaluation of a spouse abuse treatment program with a ridiculously small sample size of only two men in the experimental group and two men in the control group. Construct a theoretical sampling distribution, as follows. Give each man a fake name, and then divide the names into all possible dichotomous outcome arrangements of names (that is, all four commit further abuse, none do, three do and one doesn't, and so on). After you exhaust all possible outcomes, you should have 16 different arrangements of names. The probability of each possible arrangement (or outcome) is 1/16, or .0625. Would it be possible for this study to come up with statistically significant findings with a .05 significance level? Why or why not? Discuss what this illustrates about the influence of sample size on statistical significance and the risk of Type II errors.

4. When they learn that judging the substantive significance of a finding involves making value judgments, some students conclude that the whole business of inferential statistics is irrelevant that in the end everything is completely subjective. Do you agree with them? Why or why not? If you disagree with them, indicate the ways science and objectivity play a big role in the process, despite the inescapable involvement of some value judgments.

CROSSWORD PUZZLE

ACROSS

1 A RIVAL HYPOTHESIS REFUTED BY STATISTICAL SIGNIFICANCE
6 TYPE ONE ERRORS OCCUR WHEN WE REJECT A ______ NULL HYPOTHESIS
9 Queen Isabella's answer to Columbus
11 ______ ______ the score (win in a landslide)
12 Not open
13 WWII American soldiers
14 Abbreviation for airports where SSTs land
15 ______ FOR STATISTICAL SIGNIFICANCE SHOWS THE PROBABILITY THAT A RELATIONSHIP CAN BE ATTRIBUTED TO SAMPLING ERROR
16 IF YOU SPLIT YOUR .05 INTO .025 AT BOTH ENDS OF THE THEORETICAL SAMPLING DISTRIBUTION, YOU ARE USING A TWO-______ TEST
18 Suffix for sugars
19 Organization in New York City where ambassadors interact (abbrev.)
20 Common abbreviation for large businesses
21 TYPE I AND TYPE II ______
24 You're ______! (playground exclamation)
26 Robert E. ______
27 Pound sounds
28 MEASURES OF ______ DEPICT THE STRENGTH OF RELATIONSHIPS
33 Abbreviation meaning for example
34 Fat
35 Lady ______
36 Bible not found in synagogues (abbrev.)
37 TYPE OF HYPOTHESIS PERMITTING A ONE-TAILED TEST
41 Mexican dollar
43 Graduate student position for a professor's research grant (abbrev.)
44 HOW MANY TAILS DO YOU HAVE WHEN YOUR ENTIRE CRITICAL REGION IS AT ONE END OF THE THEORETICAL SAMPLING DISTRIBUTION
45 An American holiday in January honors his birthday (initials)
46 Opposite of SW
48 What to watch for NBC, CBS, or ABC
49 Very wide shoe size
50 After do, re, mi
53 Where to find a monument depicting the faces of GW, TJ, AL, and TR
55 TYPE OF STATISTICS USED IN SIGNIFICANCE TESTING
59 Where llamas roam
60 Odors
61 Forearm bone
63 Phi Beta ______
64 EFFECT SIZES DEPICT THE ______ OF RELATIONSHIPS
65 ACRONYM FOR THE TERM REGARDING THE NUMBER OF ERRORS WE REDUCE WHEN WE USE MEASURES OF ASSOCIATION TO PREDICT DEPENDENT VARIABLE VALUES
66 Forced to submit to sexual intercourse
71 Type size
74 An important early presidential primary occurs in this state every four years
75 Neighbor of 74 across
77 First lady
79 SUBSTANTIVE SIGNIFICANCE MIGHT BE CALLED ______ SIGNIFICANCE
81 SQUARING R TELLS US THE PROPORTION OF ______ EXPLAINED IN THE DEPENDENT VARIABLE
82 Pointed tool for making small holes

DOWN

1 ______ REGION (ZONE WHERE STATISTICALLY SIGNIFICANT FINDINGS ARE FOUND)
2 Province in China
3 Clownish act
4 ______ HYPOTHESIS (REJECTED WHEN WE HAVE STATISTICAL SIGNIFICANCE)
5 Rank between private and sgt.
6 TYPE OF SAMPLING DISTRIBUTION USED IN INFERENTIAL STATISTICS
7 Movie actress Rene ______
8 Say
9 IF THE POSSIBILITY OF A TYPE I ERROR IS .0001, THE FINDING IS PROBABLY STATISTICALLY ______
10 "War ______ hell"
12 Main ______, USA
13 Large antelope
17 Where to buy a pastrami sandwich
22 Textbook studier
23 ______ Domingo
25 Poet's initials
29 THE LARGER THE ______, THE GREATER THE LIKELIHOOD THAT A RELATIONSHIP WILL BE STATISTICALLY SIGNIFICANT
30 Jr. next yr.
31 SIGNIFICANCE LEVELS DEPICT THE ______ THAT A FINDING WAS DUE TO CHANCE
32 Vegetable that can bring tears to your eyes
38 Electrically charged atom
39 Just say ______
40 .10, .05, AND .01 MIGHT BE USED AS SIGNIFICANCE ______
42 Barely get by
45 AN EFFECT SIZE OF ABOUT .5 TO .7 MIGHT BE CONSIDERED ______
47 THE DIFFERENCE BETWEEN TWO MEANS, DIVIDED BY THE STANDARD DEVIATION TELLS US THE ______ SIZE
51 DDE's opponent in 1952 and 1956
52 AN EFFECT SIZE OF .10 DEPICTS A ______ RELATIONSHIP THAN AN EFFECT SIZE OF .5
53 ______ in the name of love
54 Cheek indentation
55 Silly
56 Fargo, ______
57 Gun lobby acronym
58 Ideal bond rating or drivers' organization
59 Madder
62 ______ top computer
67 First name of two wives of Henry VIII
68 ONE MEASURE OF ASSOCIATION STATISTIC FOR NOMINAL DATA
69 Game that ends in a tie
70 Gun a motor
71 Pod veggie
72 2.0 grade average report card
73 Ginger ______
76 Sick
78 ______ hospital for former soldiers
80 Most populous state in the USA

CHAPTER 22

Inferential Data Analysis: Part 2

OBJECTIVES

1. Define statistical power.
2. Incorporate statistical power considerations in utilizing research with null findings to guide practice.
3. Explain the role of statistical power analysis in planning research studies or in interpreting the implications of the results of these studies for practice.
4. Identify the risks inherent in neglecting statistical power considerations in planning or utilizing research.
5. Utilize meta-analyses as a basis for selecting a priori effect sizes in statistical power analysis in planning research.
6. Utilize meta-analyses as a guide to practice.
7. Identify the pitfalls inherent in meta-analysis methods.
8. Select tests of statistical significance that fit the relevant methodological characteristics of a study.
9. Identify the criteria for using parametric versus nonparametric tests of statistical significance and the differences between them.
10. Understand and apply to practice the results of studies reporting multivariate analyses.
11. Identify and discuss common misuses and misinterpretations of inferential statistics.
12. Identify and discuss common controversies in the use of inferential statistics.

PRACTICE-RELEVANT SUMMARY

The summary of Chapter 21 began by asserting that there is no way to escape inferential statistics in utilizing hypothesis testing research to guide your practice. Chapter 22 continues the discussion of inferential data analysis begun in Chapter 21, but in connection to some statistical concepts that you will probably experience as more advanced and more challenging than most of the material in the previous chapter.

The first concept to be considered, statistical power analysis, actually is extremely relevant to social work practice. It is terribly important that practitioners be able to understand and apply statistical power analysis, even if they only utilize research to guide their practice, and never do research. The basis for this assertion is that many practice evaluation studies report findings that fall short of statistical significance and therefore fail to confirm hypotheses about practice effectiveness. Thus, they risk making Type II errors.

Statistical power analysis enables us to calculate the risk of making a Type II error when we fail to support hypotheses about the effectiveness of a particular intervention or program. Thus, even if we are only utilizing the research of others about practice or program effectiveness and not conducting the research ourselves, it is essential that we perform a statistical power analysis on the study we are utilizing, so we will know the likelihood that the study has made a Type II error in failing to support the effectiveness of the intervention or program we are considering for our own use. If we find that that likelihood is high, we might want to still consider utilizing the tested intervention or program, despite the study's failure to reject the null hypothesis. If, on the other hand, we find that the likelihood of a Type I error is tiny, we might put much more stock in the lack of statistical significance in the findings and be persuaded not to adopt the tested intervention or program for our own use.

We can conduct statistical power analyses, and thus estimate the probability of committing Type II errors, simply by examining statistical power tables like Table 22-1, which displays the power of testing the significance of correlation coefficients at the .05 and .10 levels of significance for small, medium, and large effect sizes. In using Table 22-1 to plan a research study, the first step is to choose a significance level. The next step is to estimate the strength of the correlation between your independent and dependent variables that you expect exists in the population. The columns in the table pertain to small, medium, and large effect sizes. The figures in the columns indicate the probability of correctly rejecting the null hypothesis at different levels of sample size. Therefore, the probability of incorrectly accepting the null hypothesis -- which is the probability of committing a Type II error -- is 1.00 minus the figure in the column. The figure in the column is the statistical power, and subtracting the power from 1.00 gives you the probability of committing a Type II error.

By using Table 22-1, you can select a sample size that will provide you with the level of risk of a Type II error that you desire. You can also use Table 22-1 to calculate the probability that studies you are reading have committed a Type II error. To do this, you follow the same steps as above, but simply use the correlation and sample size already reported in the study to locate the study's power.
Another advanced statistical concept connected to statistical power analysis and highly relevant to social work practice is *meta-analysis*. Meta-analyses help us select an appropriate a priori correlation when conducting a statistical power analysis in the planning of a research study. Meta-analyses also help us in attempting to develop practice guidelines from studies with diverse findings about the same research questions about practice. Meta-analysis involves calculating the mean effect size across previously completed research studies on a particular topic.

In addition, more complex meta-analytic procedures can be used to calculate the statistical significance of an overall set of results aggregated across various studies. The results of meta-analyses give us benchmarks for considering the relative effectiveness of various interventions. A related benefit of meta-analysis is its ability to ascertain how the mean effect size varies depending on various clinical or methodological factors.

Despite its benefits, meta-analysis has limitations and is controversial. Poorly conducted meta-analyses might lump together studies that are methodologically strong with those that have serious methodological limitations and treat their results equally in the analysis. The results of meta-analyses done this way can be misleading because the findings of methodologically strong studies should outweigh dubious findings produced by methodologically weak studies. Some meta-analysts have rated the methodological quality of studies and then used that rating as a factor in their meta-analyses. The reliability and validity of those ratings, however, is open to question. Some meta-analysts simply exclude studies with poor methodologies. However, there is no guarantee that their methodological judgment will be adequate in this regard. Another potential pitfall in meta-analysis involves sampling bias, which can result when the meta-analyst misses some important studies or when research with null outcomes is not published.

One topic in Chapter 22 that is harder to relate to practice involves the criteria for selecting the proper test of statistical significance. Nevertheless, it is important that practitioners be familiar with these criteria, so they are not entirely mystified when interacting with researchers or program evaluators or when reading their reports. The prime criteria influencing the selection of a statistical significance test are: (1) the level of measurement of the variables, (2) the number of variables included in the analysis (bivariate or multivariate) and the number of categories in the nominal variables, (3) the type of sampling methods used in data collection, and (4) the way the variables are distributed in the population to which the study seeks to generalize. Depending on a study's attributes regarding these criteria, a selection will be made between two broad types of significance tests: parametric tests and nonparametric tests. *Parametric tests* assume that at least one of the variables being studied has an interval or ratio level of measurement, that the sampling distribution of the relevant parameters of those variables is normal, and that the different groups being compared have been randomly selected and are independent of one another. Commonly used parametric tests include the t-test, analysis of variance, and Pearson product-moment correlation. *Nonparametric tests*, on the other hand, have been created for use when not all of the assumptions of parametric statistics can be met. Most can be used with nominal- or ordinal-level data that are not distributed normally. Some do not require independently selected samples.

The most commonly used nonparametric test is *chi-square*, which is used when we are treating both our independent and dependent variables as nominal-level. The chi-square test assesses the extent to which the frequencies you observe in your table of results differ from what you would expect to observe if the distribution was created by chance.

Commonly used parametric tests include the *t*-test, analysis of variance (ANOVA), and Pearson product-moment correlation (*r*). The *t-test* is appropriate for use with a dichotomous nominal independent variable and an interval- or ratio-level dependent variable. *ANOVA* can be used to test for the significance of bivariate and multivariate relationships. Like *t-tests*, the dependent variable must be interval- or ratio-level. When testing bivariate relationships, the only difference between ANOVA and the *t*-test is that the *t-test* can be applied only when the independent variable is dichotomous. ANOVA, on the other hand, can be used when the independent variable has more than two categories. The *Pearson product-moment correlation (r)* is used when both the independent and dependent variables are at the interval or ratio level of measurement. It can be used both as a measure of association and to test for statistical significance.

Inferential statistical tests can be used at the bivariate or multivariate level of data analysis. Partial correlation coefficients, for example, have the same meaning and uses as do bivariate correlations except that they measure the association between two variables after other, extraneous variables have been controlled. A commonly used extension of correlational analysis for multivariate inferences is multiple regression analysis. *Multiple regression analysis* shows the overall correlation between each of a set of independent variables and an interval- or ratio-level dependent variable. A multivariate statistic analogous to multiple regression analysis, but designed for use when the dependent variable is dichotomous, is called *discriminant function analysis*. Also based on regression analysis is *path analysis*, which is a causal model that provides a graphic picture for interpreting causal chains and networks of variables.

Inferential statistics are commonly misused and misinterpreted by the producers and consumers of social research. These errors are common across social science disciplines, not just in social work research. Common mistakes include the failure to consider statistical power, the belief that failure to reject the null hypothesis means the same thing as verifying it, interpreting a rejection of the null hypothesis as a confirmation of the research hypothesis, failing to distinguish between statistical significance and relationship strength, failing to distinguish substantive significance from either statistical significance or relationship strength, and conducting multiple bivariate tests of significance without adjusting for the inflated probability of committing a Type I error.

There are some basic issues in the use of inferential statistics about which even the foremost authorities on statistics disagree. One point of disagreement concerns whether statistical significance is irrelevant and misleading unless all of the assumptions of the chosen significance test have been met. Some statisticians prefer parametric tests of significance over nonparametric tests even when the characteristics of the variables being tested call for the use of nonparametric tests. Statisticians also disagree as to whether tests of significance can be applied to data gathered from an entire population rather than a sample. The best statistical options are often debatable. When analyzing your own data you should use whatever procedure you judge to be best in light of what you have learned and not to let these controversies immobilize you. Also, when you encounter research done by others that seems to be methodologically rigorous, you should not disregard it just because its inferential statistics violate some assumptions. The replication process ultimately should be used to verify the generalizations made in any particular study.

REVIEW QUESTIONS

1. When we conduct a statistical power analysis, we:

   a. Calculate the probability of avoiding a Type II error.
   b. Subtract from one the probability of making a Type II error.
   c. Calculate the odds that our results were due to chance.
   d. All of the above.
   e. None of the above.
   f. Only a and b are correct.

2. Conducting a statistical power analysis in planning a study will help us:

   a. Identify a desired sample size
   b. Pick an appropriate significance level
   c. Know the likelihood of obtaining findings that would support a true hypothesis
   d. All of the above
   e. None of the above
   f. Only a and b are correct

3. We can increase statistical power by:

   a. Increasing sample size
   b. Using a lower (more stringent) significance level
   c. Assuming a weaker relationship in the population
   d. All of the above
   e. None of the above
   f. Only b and c are correct

4. Which of the following statements is true about considering the statistical power of a completed study?

   a. Statistical power is no longer relevant, since the study has already been completed.
   b. The study's reported findings can be used for the correlation column in a statistical power table.
   c. Subtract the significance level from 1.0 to find the probability of a Type II error.
   d. Subtract the significance level from 1.0 to find the statistical power.

5. Which of the following statements is/are true about meta-analysis?

   a. Meta-analyses can be used as a basis for selecting a correlation in an a priori power analysis.
   b. Meta-analyses can help us develop practice guidelines from studies with diverse findings.
   c. Meta-analysis involves calculating the mean effect size across previously completed research studies on a particular topic.
   d. All of the above.
   e. None of the above.

6. Which of the following statements is/are true about meta-analysis?

   a. There is very little controversy about it.
   b. Because it is based on many studies it avoids coming up with misleading conclusions.
   c. The findings of studies with poor methodologies may be averaged in with findings from methodologically strong studies.
   d. It guarantees the avoidance of sampling bias.
   e. All of the above.

7. In selecting a test of statistical significance, we should consider:

   a. The level of measurement of the variables
   b. The number of variables included in the analysis
   c. The type of sampling methods used in data collection
   d. The way the variables are distributed in the population
   e. All of the above

8. Which of the following is *not* an assumption of parametric tests of significance?

    a. None of the variables has an interval or ratio level of measurement.
    b. The sampling distribution of the relevant parameters of the variables is normal.
    c. The different groups being compared have been randomly selected and are independent of one another.
    d. None of the above; they all are assumptions of parametric tests.

9. Which of the following is *not* a parametric test of significance?

    a. t-test
    b. Analysis of variance
    c. Chi-square
    d. Pearson's product-moment correlation

10. Which statistical test of significance should be used in a study of nominal data in a frequency distribution of ethnicity by whether or not the person is a school dropout?

    a. t-test
    b. Analysis of variance
    c. Chi-square
    d. Pearson's product-moment correlation

11. Which statistical test of significance should be used in a study of the relationship between number of children and years on welfare?

    a. t-test
    b. Analysis of variance
    c. Chi-square
    d. Pearson's product-moment correlation

12. Which of the following statements is *not* true about multivariate statistical analyses?

    a. If each of two variables, on a bivariate basis, separately accounts for 10% of the variation in a third variable, we can be certain that together they will account for 20% of the variation in the third variable.
    b. If two variables are correlated with each other, the amount of variation they both account for in a third variable will be less than the sum of their separate bivariate correlations with the third variable.
    c. Partial correlation coefficients measure the association between two variables after other, extraneous variables have been controlled.
    d. Multiple regression analysis shows the overall correlation between each of a set of independent variables and an interval- or ratio-level dependent variable.

13. Which of the following statements is/are true about inferential statistics?

a. Failure to reject the null hypothesis means the same thing as verifying it.
b. Rejecting the null hypothesis is a confirmation of the research hypothesis.
c. When conducting multiple bivariate tests of significance we must adjust for the inflated probability of committing a Type I error.
d. All of the above.

14. Which of the following statements is/are true about inferential statistics?

a. All expert statisticians agree that statistical significance is irrelevant and misleading unless all of the assumptions of the chosen significance test have been met.
b. Some statisticians prefer parametric tests of significance over nonparametric tests even when the characteristics of the variables being tested call for the use of nonparametric tests.
c. There is very high agreement among statisticians that tests of significance can be applied to data gathered from an entire population rather than a sample.
d. All of the above.

15. Which of the following statements is/are true about path analysis?

a. Path analysis by itself finds the causal order of the variables.
b. The researcher decides the structure of relationships among the variables and uses computer analysis to calculate the path coefficients that apply to such a structure.
c. The computer, by itself, decides the structure of relationships among the variables.
d. All of the above.
e. None of the above.
f. Both a and c, only, are true.

EXERCISE 22.1

Using Table 22.1 in the text, answer the following questions.

1. What sample size is needed to have statistical power exceeding .80:

   a. Assuming a .05 significance level and a small effect size?

   b. Assuming a .05 significance level and a medium effect size?

   c. Assuming a .05 significance level and a large effect size?

   d. Assuming a .10 significance level and a small effect size?

   e. Assuming a .10 significance level and a medium effect size?

   f. Assuming a .10 significance level and a large effect size?

2. What will your statistical power and probability of committing a Type II error be if your study:

   a. Assumes a medium effect size, has a .05 significance level, and has a sample size of 30?

   b. Assumes a medium effect size, has a .10 significance level, and has a sample size of 20?

   c. Assumes a small effect size, has a .05 significance level, and has a sample size of 100?

   d. Assumes a large effect size, has a .10 significance level, and has a sample size of 20

EXERCISE 22.2

Suppose you wanted to conduct an experimental evaluation of an intervention to help parents of children with AIDS. Suppose further you are doing this in a small city, there is no way to find more than 40 sets of parents to participate in your study, and no other intervention with this target population is known to be effective. Discuss the adequacy of your statistical power. Would you use a .05 level of significance? Justify your answer in light of your use of Table 22.1 in the text. Explain why you would or would not choose to do the study, in light of your statistical power. Would your answer change if a previous pilot study had tentatively suggested that your intervention has very strong effects? Why or why not (in light of Table 21.1 in the text)?

EXERCISE 22.3

Suppose you are reviewing research to help you decide whether to use Intervention Approach A or Intervention Approach B to prevent high school dropout. You find only two studies. Study 1 found that in a community using Intervention Approach A, the dropout rate among the 5000 high-risk youths studied was 40%, while the rate in a comparable community that had no dropout prevention program was 45%. The difference was statistically significant. Study 2 randomly assigned 10 high-risk youths to Intervention Approach A and 10 high-risk youths to Intervention Approach B. The dropout rates were 40% for Approach A and 20% for Approach B, but the difference was not statistically significant. Which approach would you be inclined to use and to evaluate in your program, in light of the above data and the figures in Table 18.1 of the text? Why? (Include the concept of Type II errors in your answer.)

EXERCISE 22.4

Suppose you review a meta-analysis on the effectiveness of social work interventions in preventing high school dropout. It finds a mean effect size of .6 for intervention A, based on ten randomized experiments and five studies in which the group receiving the intervention was initially at higher risk of dropping out than the comparison group. The meta-analysis also finds a mean effect size of 1.5 for intervention B, based on a much larger number of studies, none of which were randomized experiments, and all of which used comparison groups that initially seemed to be at lower risk than the group receiving intervention B. Which of the two interventions would you be more inclined to use in light of this information? Why?

EXERCISE 22.5

Which test of statistical significance would you use for each of the following hypotheses? Why?

1. Students receiving intervention A are less likely to drop out of school than students receiving intervention B.

2. Students receiving intervention A will have fewer absences than students receiving intervention B.

3. Students receiving case management intervention will have fewer absences than students receiving a behavioral intervention, and students receiving the behavioral intervention will have fewer absences than students receiving supportive counseling.

4. The younger the student's mother, the more absences the student will have.

DISCUSSION QUESTIONS

1. Discuss the criteria that determine what test of statistical significance is most appropriate.

2. Suppose in bivariate correlations variable A accounts for 10% of the variance in a dependent variable, and variable B accounts for 10% of the variance in the same dependent variable, but variable A and variable B combined, in a multiple correlation, account for less than 20% of the variance in that dependent variable. Explain how this could be and illustrate it with overlapping circles.

3. Identify six common misuses or misinterpretations of inferential statistics and explain why each is a mistake.

4. Discuss both sides of the debate over whether it is appropriate to test the statistical significance of relationships found in data gathered from an entire population. Which side of the debate do you find more persuasive? Why?

CROSSWORD PUZZLE

1	2	3	4	■	5	■	6	7	8	9	10	11	
12				■	13	14							■
15				16			■	17				■	18
	■	■	19				■	■	■	■	20	21	
■	22	23		■		■	24	25	26	27	■	28	
29			■	■	■	30							■
31			32	33	■	34					■	■	■
35		■	36						■	37	38	39	■
40		41			■	■	■	42	43				■
44					■	■	■	45					■
■	■	■	■		■	■	■	■	■	■	■	■	■

ACROSS

1 Beer ingredient
6 Medical school course
12 Give off
13 Study of cancer
15 ERROR RISKED WITH LOW STATISTICAL POWER
17 Stadium section
19 Norse name
20 Santa's helper
22 Drunkard
24 Bright, gaseous light
28 Dinner _____ eight
29 Half of a Parisian dance
30 Maxwell House and Taster's Choice
31 Don't make _____ _____ while we're gone
34 Teamster boss who disappeared
35 AWOL hunters
36 English answer to "Como esta usted?"
37 There are four of these in monopoly
40 Julie or Audrey in My Fair Lady
42 Poker moves
44 THE _____ OF SIGNIFICANCE AFFECTS POWER
45 Secret meeting

DOWN

1 TYPE OF ANALYSIS IN WHICH THE SAMPLE CONSISTS OF MANY STUDIES
2 Daughter of Jimmy and Rosalyn
3 Type of service
4 COMMON PARAMETRIC SIGNIFICANCE TEST
5 BEFORE YOU START YOUR STUDY IT IS PRUDENT TO ANALYZE THIS
6 Good feature to have in your car if you live in Texas or Florida
7 To have and have _____
8 Formerly Clay
9 _____ the line
10 Fairy tale villain
11 The way Sinatra did it
14 WHEN ALL YOUR VARIABLES ARE AT THE NOMINAL LEVEL OF MEASUREMENT, USE A _____-PARAMETRIC TEST
16 Where to see Seinfeld reruns
18 Fore's opposite
21 _____ Vegas
22 WITH 32 DOWN: THE LARGER THIS IS, THE MORE STATISTICAL POWER YOU'LL HAVE
23 THIS MINUS POWER EQUALS TYPE II ERROR PROBABILITY
24 "High ____" (Gary Cooper classic)
25 META-ANALYSES CALCULATE MEAN _____ SIZES
26 Buzz _____!
27 Almost
29 Horse created by a committee
30 _____-SQUARE TEST
32 SEE 22 DOWN
33 A DESIRABLE ATTRIBUTE OF TYPE II ERROR RISKS
38 19th century literary monogram best remembered on Friday
39 Supersonic transport initials
41 You might get this in an E.R. if you've suffered dehydration
43 PARAMETRIC CORRELATION LETTER

CHAPTER 23

Writing Research Proposals and Reports

OBJECTIVES

1. Describe how to identify appropriate potential funding sources for different kinds of research proposals and how the type of funding source will vary depending on the scope and purpose of the proposal.

2. Differentiate research contracts and research grants, particularly in terms of the process of seeking funding and the researcher's leeway in how to conduct the research.

3. Describe what steps to take before writing a research proposal – steps that will improve the chances that the proposal will be funded.

4. Identify and describe the main components of research proposals and the main attributes that distinguish between weak and strong proposals.

5. Describe the similarities and differences between qualitative and quantitative research proposals.

6. Describe how the nature of a research report will be influenced by its purpose and its intended audience.

7. Describe the ways to avoid plagiarism when reporting the work of others.

8. Identify the common components of research reports and the order in which they usually appear.

9. Describe some of the common ways in which qualitative research reports often differ from quantitative ones.

PRACTICE-RELEVANT SUMMARY

Earlier in the text, Chapter 13 described how program evaluation has become ubiquitous in the planning and administration of social welfare programs. Because of that, many social work practitioners eventually are confronted with the need to seek funding for evaluation research projects. The chances may be greater than you think that you will be confronted with the need to seek such funding rather early in your career. You might even someday want to earn a Ph.D. in social work and pursue more ambitious research projects for which you will seek relatively large amounts of funding. In either case, what you learn in Chapter 23 will be relevant to your practice.

The nature of the research proposals you will write will depend on the scope and purpose of the research you seek to conduct. The more ambitious the study, the lengthier and more rigorous your proposal will have to be. One of the choices you will confront is whether to become committed to a specific study and then seek funding for it, or to remain flexible so that you can formulate a research problem after you learn the priorities of a potential funding source. Regardless, you should learn about the expectations of the funding source before you prepare your proposal, and then develop your proposal according to those expectations.

Finding a funding source for a research grant will be facilitated if you follow several guidelines. One is to stay current in reading various publications and announcements from a wide range of funding sources, looking for a *Request for Proposals (RFP)* relevant to what you want to do. An RFP will identify the research questions and types of designs and dollar amounts the funding source has in mind, along with other information about the source's expectations and funding process. Another guideline is to use the Internet to learn about new RFPs and other funding opportunities. Particularly helpful sites include the Institute for the Advancement of Social Work Research Web site at http://www.cosw.sc.edu/iaswr/links.html and the Society for Social Work and Research Web site at www.SSWR.org, Chapter 23 mentions many other sources and sites for identifying potential funding opportunities, including going to search engines like www.google.com or www.yahoo.com an entering search terms such as *research grants* and your problem area.

The process of finding a funding source for *research contracts* may differ from the process for *research grants*. The funding source for a research contract might seek out a specific researcher or research center and work closely with them in preparing the proposal. Research grants will typically give researchers considerable leeway regarding the specifics of the purpose and methods of the investigation. In contrast, research contracts typically provide much greater specificity regarding what the funding source wants to have researched and how the research is to be conducted. The research proposal for a research contract probably will have to conform rather precisely to those specifications.

Whether applying for a contract or a grant, your chances of being funded might be improved if you previously established a relationship with key staff at the funding source. With some funding sources, however, it might be necessary to write a brief, preliminary letter summarizing your research idea before you can begin to relate to any of their staff. In either case, you'd also be well advised to learn about the expectations of the funding source before you prepare your proposal, and then develop your proposal according to those expectations. Another potentially helpful preliminary step is to examine some proposals that have previously been funded by the source you are considering. Doing so might provide some further insights as to the funding source's expectations.

Early in your career, when you are writing your first research proposal, you should remember that without an established track record in funded research, your prospects for being funded might be enhanced significantly if the funding source sees that someone with a good "track record" is collaborating on your project. You should realize that the process of getting your proposal funded might be a long one. You should not get too discouraged if your first proposal is not funded. Learn from the process. If the funding source provides feedback as to the reasons your proposal was not funded, revise the proposal and resubmit it (perhaps several times!), perhaps to the same funding source.

The components of your proposal will vary depending on the purpose of your research and the expectations of your funding source. Common components of quantitative research proposals include: *cover letter; executive summary statement; problem and specific aims; literature review; conceptual framework; measurement procedures; sampling; design and data collection methods; data analysis plans, schedule,* and *budget.* Appendices also may be required displaying such things as IRB approval, your resume, letters of support from administrators of agencies where data will be collected, and plans for disseminating results.

Your specific aims should be in the form of a brief list and should be specified in precise terms. They need to be answerable by observable evidence and feasible to investigate and answer. Most importantly, you need to explain how their answers have significance for practice and policy. Your literature review should show how the prior work influenced your proposed study and how your study will relate to, yet go beyond, the previous studies. Do not cite monotonous, minute details about every relevant study that has ever been done. If the body of existing literature is extensive, concentrate on the most recent findings, while also including "classic" studies. Be extensive enough to show reviewers that you are on top of the field and will build on the prior research, yet brief enough not to become tedious. Other things to avoid include bias in selecting what studies to cite and ritualistically listing details about each study in a perfunctory manner that doesn't flow well.

Your *conceptual framework* should clearly specify and provide rationales for your research questions, hypotheses, variables and operational definitions. You should justify why and how you chose to study each. Your explanation should flow in part from your literature review. It also should show the logic of your own thinking about the inquiry, as well as how your study goes beyond and builds upon the prior literature. Your *measurement* section should flow smoothly from your operational definitions and should elaborate on the specific measures you will use and their reliability and validity (if relevant and known). Your *sampling* section should identify who or what you will study to collect data, any inclusion or exclusion criteria, and your sampling procedures. If you use non-probability sampling procedures, you will need to justify that, including attention to the chances that your sample will be biased and unrepresentative of your target population. Describe the efforts you will make to try to offset or avoid those potential biases. Regardless of whether you use probability or non-probability sampling procedures, address issues associated with sample attrition and refusal to participate and the special efforts you will make to enhance recruitment and retention. You will also need to justify the projected size of your sample and tell reviewers why you think it will be feasible to obtain the needed sample size. Your section on *design and data collection methods* should indicate the type of design you will employ (survey? experiment? etc.) and address methodological issues connected to design logic, avoiding bias, the specifics of data collection procedures, and so on.

If you are proposing to conduct a qualitative inquiry, your proposal will share some of the above features, but it will differ in some important ways. As with quantitative proposals, you will need to begin with a statement of the problem or objective and follow that with a literature review, and description of your research methods. Likewise, you will have to make a persuasive case as to the importance of the research question and the value of the study. Other similarities include the nature of the literature review, the need for a schedule with a realistic time line, a section covering human subjects review approval, a reasonable budget that anticipates all of the various costs you will encounter, and a neat professional appearance that reflects clear and interesting writing and laser printing.

Qualitative proposals, however, may be more difficult to write than quantitative proposals, mainly because of the greater degree of structure and preplanning involved in designing quantitative research. The relatively unstructured, unpredictable nature of qualitative research complicates the process of writing a proposal that promises exciting results or is even specific about the types of alternative conclusions the study is likely to generate. Qualitative research designs tend have open-ended starting points from which methods and truth will emerge through encountering subjects in their natural environment. Thus, it is more difficult than with quantitative research to spell out in detail in advance such things as research methods and specific alternative findings that can be anticipated. The dilemma for the qualitative researcher, then, is figuring out how to put enough detail about the plan in the proposal to enable potential funders to evaluate the proposal's merits, while remaining true to the unstructured, flexible, inductive qualitative approach. This task is even more challenging to the extent that the merits of the proposal will be judged by reviewers who are likely to be more oriented to quantitative research and who expect the precise planning that goes into proposals for quantitative research studies.

One suggestion for preparing qualitative proposals is to indicate that the methodological plan is only a tentative and initial direction that is open to change as the study proceeds and new insights emerge. Also, the proposal can specify the type of qualitative approach being employed and then describe the general ideas underlying that approach. The literature review in qualitative proposals may need to be more extensive than in quantitative proposals to demonstrate the investigator's expertise, because it may appear as though the funders are being told "Trust me" in qualitative studies more than in quantitative ones. It might also be helpful to conduct a pilot study on the topic addressed in your proposal and then describe that pilot study in your proposal and submit it as an appendix to the proposal. This will show your commitment and competence. It can also demonstrate how you might go about analyzing the data that might emerge in the proposed study.

Like guidelines for writing research proposals, guidelines for writing *research reports* will vary depending on the intended audience, the scope and purpose of the study, and the nature of the study design. One universal guideline, however, is to avoid *plagiarism*. To avoid plagiarism, you must *not* present someone else's words and thoughts as though they were your own. If you use someone else's exact words, be sure to use quotation marks or some other indication that you are quoting. If you paraphrase someone else's ideas, be sure to cite them, providing a full bibliographic citation.
Quantitative research reports commonly begin with a title page, followed by an abstract, an introduction and literature review, a methods section, a results section, a discussion and conclusions section, and then a references list and any needed appendices. The sections preceding the results section should be written much the same as with research proposals (but not in the future tense, of course).

The results section should provide a maximum of detail without being cluttered. Describe all aspects of the data analysis in sufficient detail to permit a secondary analyst to replicate the analysis from the same body of data. The discussion section develops explicit conclusions, draws practical implications based on those conclusions, discusses the methodological limitations of the study, and draws implications for future research.

Reports of qualitative studies will share some of the above features, but several differences typically make qualitative reports lengthier than quantitative ones. Their data are harder to condense than the statistics in quantitative studies. Also, a deep, empathic understanding of a phenomenon cannot be conveyed adequately with some summary statistics. It also may take longer to explain the development of new concepts or theory, describe less structured, less standardized data collection methods, and supply lengthy quotes or other types of qualitative evidence. Qualitative reports are also more likely than quantitative ones to use a creative and literary writing style in order to convey to readers a deeper and more empathic understanding of what it is like to walk in the shoes of the people being portrayed in the report.

REVIEW QUESTIONS

1. When seeking a funding source for a research proposal, you should:

   a. avoid using the Internet
   b. learn about the expectations of the funding source before you prepare your proposal
   c. begin by sending a thorough proposal to the source to ascertain their potential interest
   d. All of the above
   e. None of the above

2. Your chances of being funded might improve if you:

   a. stay current in reading various publications and announcements from a wide range of funding sources, looking for a relevant Request for Proposals.
   b. examine some proposals that have previously been funded by the source you are considering.
   c. establish a relationship with key staff at the funding source.
   d. All of the above.
   e. None of the above.

3. Which of the following is/are true about comparing research grants and research proposals?

   a. The researcher has more leeway as to how to design and implement a grant.
   b. With grants, researchers have no leeway as to how to design and implement the study
   c. The process of finding funding for grants and contracts typically are virtually identical
   d. The proposal for a research contract rarely needs to conform closely with any specifications of the funding source.
   e. Both b and d, only, are true.

4. Your prospects for getting your research proposal funded will be enhanced if you:

   a. are a new investigator without a track record in funded research.
   b. avoid having a collaborator with an established track record.
   c. revise and resubmit your proposal based on the feedback you receive when it is rejected.
   d. All of the above.
   e. None of the above.
   f. Both a and b, only, are true.

5. Which of the following is a recommended guideline for writing a quantitative research proposal?

   a. Specify a long list of broad, ambitious aims.
   b. Do *NOT* try to anticipate potentially useful implications of possible findings; wait until you get your results for that.
   c. Make a list describing all previous studies in minute detail.
   d. All of the above.
   e. None of the above.

6. Which of the following is a recommended guideline for writing a quantitative research proposal?

    a. Explain how your proposed research will build on previous studies.
    b. Avoid providing rationales for your hypotheses, variables or operational definitions.
    c. Make sure your measures are quite unlike your operational definitions.
    d. All of the above.
    e. None of the above.

7. The sampling section of a research proposal should:

    a. describe the reliability and validity of measurement instruments.
    b. indicate why it will be feasible to obtain the needed sample size.
    c. promise that no subjects will drop out or refuse to participate.
    d. All of the above.
    e. None of the above.

8. The measurement section of a research proposal should:

    a. address the sensitivity of any scales to be used.
    b. avoid proposing any triangulation procedures.
    c. include a statistical power analysis.
    d. justify the projected size of the sample.
    e. All of the above.
    e. None of the above.

9. The design and data collection section of a research proposal should:

    a. indicate the type of design you will employ.
    b. address methodological issues connected to design logic.
    c. specify data collection procedures.
    d. describe how bias will be avoided.
    e. All of the above.
    e. None of the above.

10. Which of the following statements is true about qualitative research proposals?

    a. Unlike quantitative proposals, they do *NOT* have to address the importance of the research question and the value of the study.
    b. It is easier than with quantitative proposals to spell out methodological detail in advance.
    c. They are easier to write than quantitative proposals, because of their greater degree of structure and preplanning.
    d. A dilemma is figuring out how to put enough detail about the plan in the proposal to enable potential funders to evaluate the proposal's merits, while remaining true to the unstructured, flexible, inductive qualitative approach.
    e. None of the above.

11. When writing a qualitative proposal you should consider:

    a. indicating that the methodological plan is only a tentative direction that is open to change as the study proceeds.
    b. conducting a pilot study on the topic addressed in your proposal and then describing that pilot study in an appendix to your proposal.
    c. writing a literature review that is more extensive than in most quantitative proposals.
    d. All of the above.
    e. None of the above.

12. Which of the following is/are true about writing a quantitative research report?

    a. You should place the abstract near the end of the report.
    b. It is acceptable to paraphrase another's words and present them as your own as long as you don't use their exact words.
    c. The discussion section develops explicit conclusions, draws practical implications based on those conclusions, discusses the methodological limitations of the study, and draws implications for future research.
    d. All of the above.
    e. None of the above.

13. Which of the following is/are true about qualitative research reports?

    a. They tend to be lengthier than quantitative reports.
    b. Their data are harder to condense than the statistics in quantitative studies.
    c. They are more likely than quantitative reports to use a creative and literary writing style.
    d. All of the above.
    e. None of the above.

EXERCISE 23.1

Obtain a copy of one quantitative research proposal and one qualitative research proposal. Describe the similarities and differences between them regarding generic proposal writing guidelines. (You may need to seek the assistance of some instructors in helping you locate these proposals. If your school has a center for social work research, you might ask there. Also, individual faculty members may have written proposals that they can show you. There might also be a university-wide research center that can help you. Local or state social service agencies might also have some funded grants or contracts they can share.)

EXERCISE 23.2

Try to obtain interviews with authors of the proposals you found for Exercise 23.1. Ask them to describe their experiences in seeking funding for those proposals. Using notes from your interviews, discuss the ways in which their experiences were similar and different.

EXERCISE 23.3

Using the Internet sites identified in the Internet Exercises at the end of Chapter 23 of the text, and/or using your library, obtain a copy of one published quantitative research report that piques your interest and one published qualitative research report that piques your interest. Describe the similarities and differences between them regarding generic guidelines for writing research reports.

EXERCISE 23.4

Imagine a social work research question or hypothesis that you think would be important to investigate. Develop an executive summary statement for a research proposal on that question or hypothesis. Emphasize in the summary the specific aims of the research and why the study has value in guiding practice or policy. Then briefly summarize the design and methodology you would employ.

EXERCISE 23.5

Share the executive summary you developed above with one or more of your classmates. Ask them to imagine that they serve as proposal reviewers for a funding source and to give you feedback as to how successful your summary is in stimulating their interest in potentially funding your study and how it could be improved. If they have prepared a summary, you can give them feedback on theirs, too.

EXERCISE 23.6

Using the Internet sites identified in the Internet Exercises at the end of Chapter 23 of the text, search for an RFP or a funding source that appears relevant to the project you've summarized in Exercise 23.4. Summarize what you find in your search and why you think it might be relevant to the project you've summarized. If you cannot find a relevant RFP or funding source, discuss what you would do next if you were really committed to obtaining research funding.

EXERCISE 23.7

Imagine that you received funding and completed the research study you summarized in Exercise 23.4. Making up your own findings for the study, write a brief research report for that mock study. To make this exercise more feasible, keep the literature review section very brief, and make up imaginary studies you want to review if that will help.

DISCUSSION QUESTIONS

1. Imagine that you are a research proposal reviewer for a funding source whose main priority is to discover more effective ways to prevent domestic violence and to alleviate its emotional effects on its victims. In light of the ways in which quantitative and qualitative research proposals are likely to differ, would you be equally predisposed to recommending funding for sound qualitative and sound quantitative research proposals, or would you be more predisposed to recommend funding for one of these two types of proposals than the other? Explain your reasons.

2. Describe how the nature of a research report will be influenced by its purpose and its intended audience.

3. The following is an excerpted paragraph from Chapter 1 of the Rubin and Babbie textbook's 5th edition:

   Unlike "authority-based practice" Gambrill (1999), **evidence-based practice** "is the conscientious, explicit, and judicious use of current best evidence in making decisions about the care of individual" clients (Sackett et al., 1997). Practitioners engaged in evidence-based practice will be critical thinkers. Rather than automatically accept everything others with more experience or authority tell them about practice, they will question things. They will recognize unfounded beliefs and assumptions and think for themselves as to the logic and evidence supporting what others may convey as practice wisdom. Rather than just conform blindly to tradition or authority, they will use the best scientific evidence available in deciding how to intervene with individuals, families, groups, or communities.

Discuss why or why not you think that each of the following excerpts later written by another author who read Rubin and Babbie would be plagiarism. Neither excerpt has any footnotes or citations.

Excerpt 1:

Unlike authority-based practitioners, evidence-based practitioners will diligently, explicitly, and judiciously use current best evidence in making decisions about serving individual clients.

Excerpt 2:

Evidence-based practitioners will think critically. They won't accept automatically everything they hear from authorities who have more experience. Instead, they will question things and think for themselves regarding the supporting evidence.

CROSSWORD PUZZLE

ACROSS

1 Left
5 Commandment word
10 LEARN ABOUT THE _____ OF FUNDING SOURES BEFORE PREPARING A RESEARCH PROPOSAL TO IT
14 Where to find stools and brawls
15 Bullets
16 South of NC
17 NBC comedy show since 1975
18 Swat
19 Just do _____
20 Summer in France
21 Glide on high
23 Type of energy or bomb
24 THIS IS MORE FLEXIBLE THAN A CONTRACT
26 Egotist's obsession
27 New Deal program that remains a priority of the AARP
29 Hammock
31 Good _____ tries to communicate well rather than impress
34 GM car nickname
38 Florida county site of 2000 voting controversy
39 Onset
41 THE LITERATURE REVIEW SHOULD BE BOTH THOROUGH AND _____
43 QUALITATIVE RESEARCH REPORTS OFTEN HAVE MORE _____ AS TO ORGANIZATION AND STYLE
44 "_____ I Love You" (Beatles hit)
45 Jackie's second
46 "_____ the Sheriff" (old rock song)
49 Espy
50 SECTION NEAR THE END OF A RESEARCH PROPOSAL
53 _____ Beta Kappa
54 SECTION BETWEEN METHODS AND DISCUSSION

DOWN

1 EFFICIENT PLACES TO FIND POTENTIAL FUNDING SOURCES
2 BE SURE TO USE QUOTATION MARKS IF YOU USE SOMEONE ELSE'S _____ WORDS
3 Radio counterpart to PBS
4 THE TITLE OF YOUR RESEARCH REPORT SHOULD BE AS _____ AS POSSIBLE (Pardon the repetition!)
5 Robbed
6 Overact
7 _____ a loss for words
8 SOMEONE WITH WHOM YOU SHOULD DEVELOP A RELATIONSHIP BEFORE WRITING YOUR PROPOSAL
9 Hand drum
11 THIS IS MORE RESTRICTIVE THAN A GRANT
12 Abbreviation for state where you can find White Sands and the site where the first A-bomb was built
13 GEAR YOUR PROPOSAL TO THE EXPECTATIONS OF THE FUNDING _____
22 Goal
23 Envelope abbrev.
24 Avant _____
25 Din
28 Attempts to kill flies
30 TYPE OF PAGE OR LETTER THAT OFTEN PREFACES A RESEARCH PROPOSAL
32 Comparative word ending
33 For me and my _____
35 Jerry, Shari, or Richard
36 Genetic initials
37 READ AND REREAD STRUNK AND WHITE TO IMPROVE YOUR WRITING _____
40 Fatalities
42 Pig abodes
44 Where to get a brewsky
47 1950's TV comedy series star _____ Erwin
48 Choose
51 Ph.D. or MD
52 American corp. that makes many appliances

ANSWERS TO REVIEW QUESTIONS

Ch. 1
1.e 2.f 3.e 4.c 5.e 6.c 7.a 8.e 9.a 10.e 11.d 12.d

Ch. 2
1.b 2.e 3.c 4.d 5.d 6.b 7.d 8.a 9.c 10.c 11.d

Ch. 3
1.a 2.c 3.b 4.c 5.a 6.b 7.c 8.d 9.d 10.c 11.a 12.b 13.d 14.b 15.a 16.b 17.a

Ch. 4
1.d 2.f 3.d 4.c 5.b 6.d 7.c 8.c 9.e 10.b

Ch. 5
1.d 2.c 3.e 4.e 5.c 6.a 7.b 8.e 9.a 10.a 11.d 12.d 13.a

Ch. 6
1.e 2.e 3.d 4.b 5.c 6.a 7.b 8.d 9.b 10.a

Ch. 7
1.b 2.c 3.b 4.a 5.c 6.a 7.b 8.c 9.a 10.d 11.f 12.c

Ch. 8
1.d 2.a 3.c 4.b 5.d 6.f 7.d 8.e

Ch. 9
1.d 2.a 3.d 4.c 5.c 6.b 7.g 8.d 9.a 10.f 11.c

Ch. 10
1.f 2.d 3.e 4.d 5.e 6.e 7.a 8.c

Ch. 11
1.e 2.b 3.e 4.c 5.e 6.e 7.e 8.e 9.a 10.d 11.d 12.a 13.d 14.b 15.e 16.e

Ch. 12
1.b 2.c 3.e 4.a 5.b 6.b 7.c 8.c 9.e 10.e 11.e 12.e 13.d

Ch. 13
1.c 2.c 3.c 4.c 5.e 6.a 7.d 8.a 9.d 10.d 11.b 12.c 13.c 14.d

Ch. 14

1.b 2.d 3.a 4.b 5.b 6.e 7.d 8.d 9.f 10.b 11.c

Ch. 15

1.e 2.a 3.c 4.e 5.b 6.d 7.e 8.d 9.a 10.e

Ch. 16

1.e 2.a 3.b 4.a 5.c 6.d 7.b 8.f 9.c 10.a

Ch. 17

1.d 2.b 3.d 4.e 5.a 6.f 7.d 8.b 9.d

Ch. 18

1.a 2.c 3.c 4.d 5.d 6.d 7.d 8.d 9.a 10.b

Ch. 19

1.e 2.a 3.d 4.d 5.d 6.d 7.a 8.d 9.f 10.b 11.c 12.d

Ch. 20

1.d 2.c 3.b 4.a 5.e 6.d 7.b 8.a 9.d 10.d 11.a 12.b 13.c 14.d 15.a

Ch. 21

1.a 2.d 3.d 4.e 5.b 6.c 7.a 8.d 9.c 10.e 11.a 12.c 13.b 14.c

Ch. 22

1.f 2.d 3.a 4.b 5.d 6.c 7.e 8.a 9.c 10.c 11.d 12.a 13.c 14.b 15.b

Ch. 23

1.b 2.d 3.a 4.c 5.e 6.a 7.b 8.a 9.e 10.d 11.d 12.c 13.d

ANSWERS TO CROSSWORD PUZZLES

CHAPTER 1

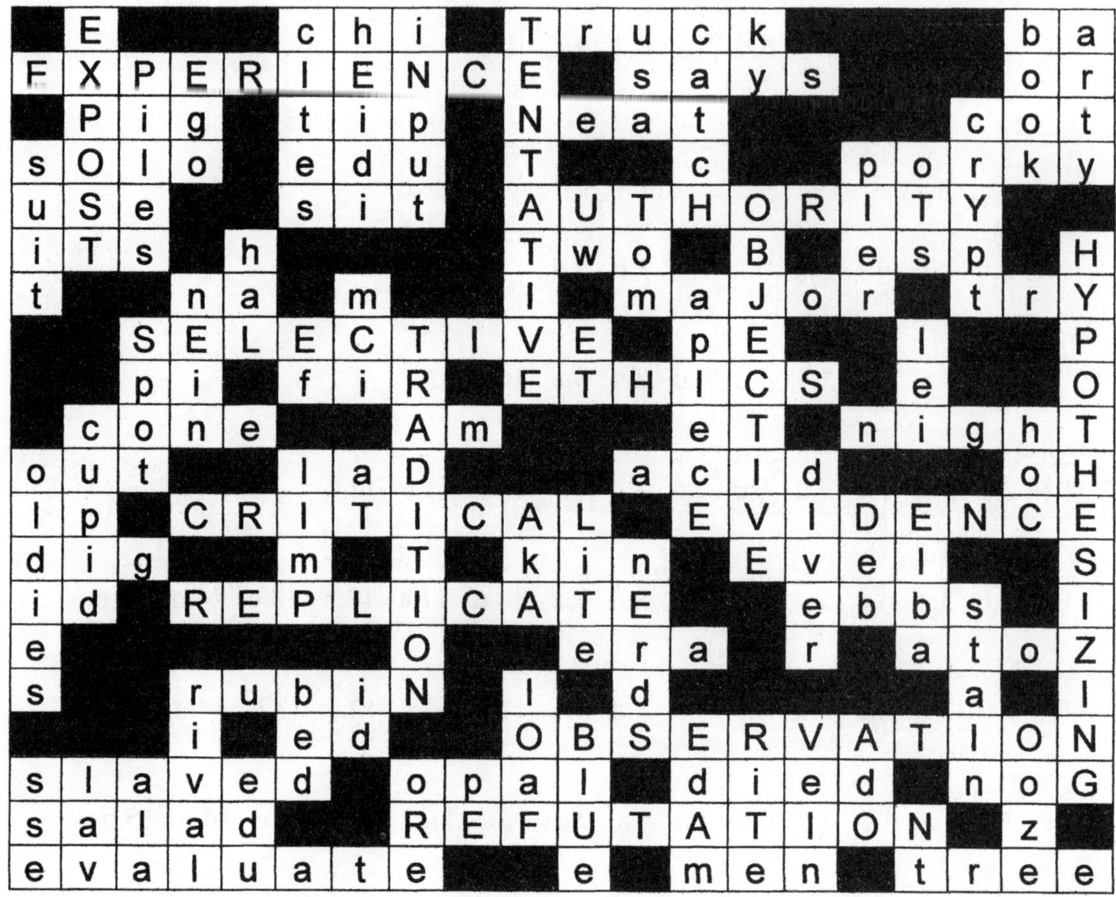

CHAPTER 2

B	E	S	T		C	O	C	H	R	A	N	E
O	l	E	o		o	n	O		y	s	e	r
T	v	A		a	m	e	L	l	e	s		r
T	I	R	e	s		r	L	s		u	f	o
O	s	C	a	r	s		A		a	m	o	r
M		H	u	e	s		B	o	n	e	r	s
	s			d	e	c	O		d	d	e	
A	t	r	I	a		u	R	s	a		v	a
P	a	l	N	s		d	A	p	p	l	e	s
P	l	n	T			s	T	a	r	e	r	s
R	n		E	B	M		I	m	a	n		
A			R	I	n	g	O		y	o	u	r
I	c	I	N	g			N	e	e		s	a
S	I	T	E		g	m		d	r	e	a	m
E	t		T	R	I	A	L	S		l	f	s

CHAPTER 3

P	O	S	I	T	I	V	I	S	M					a	m		s	o	S
A	n		N	o		A		t	o	m	b		P	r	i	n	t		U
R	e	a	D	y		R	E	A	L			c	O	i	n		o	r	B
A			E			I		r	a	h			S		t	a	n		J
D	e	e	P			A	T	T	R	I	B	U	T	E	S		e	v	E
I			E			B			s		u		M			Q			C
G	a	i	N			L		I			t	o	O	I		U	P		T
M			D	E	P	E	N	D	E	N	T		D		p	A	R		I
S	a	l	E		o			E			e	v	E	n		L	O		V
			N		T	H	E	O	R	Y			R				B		I
D	o	n	T		e		I	L					N		s	h	A	I	T
E					N	O	M	O	T	H	E	T	I	C		e	B	a	Y
D	u	c	k		t			G		e			S			r	I	d	
U		h				b		Y	e	a	r		M	O	D	E	L	S	
C	R	I	T	I	C	A	L			r							I		
T		I				I		D	E	T	E	R	M	I	N	I	S	M	
I	N	D	U	C	T	I	V	E				o			o		T	a	x
V					u			a		d		a		a	s	t	I	r	
E					n		I	D	I	O	G	R	A	P	H	I	C		
			Q	U	A	N	T			g				e		m			

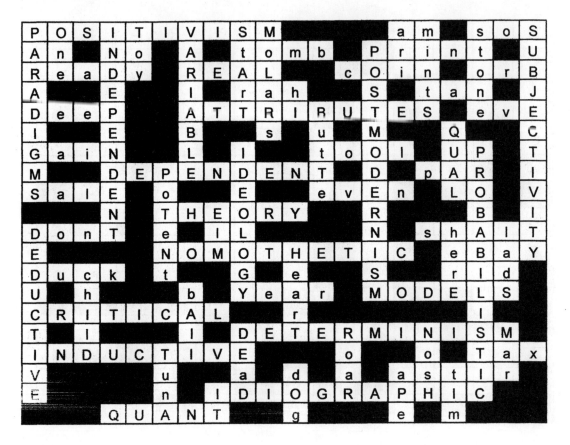

CHAPTER 4

T	U	S	K	E	G	E	E		u	S		A	N	A	L	Y	S	I	S
e		l	i	m	e		D	E	C	E	I	V	I	N	G		E	R	a
a		u	t	i	l	e		x		X		e	g	O			R	B	i
R	I	G	H	T			C		h				E	N	D		V		l
o	n			s		V	O	L	U	N	T	A	R	Y		p	I		o
o	d	d					N	O	H	A	R	M		M	a	r	C		r
m	y		I		N	A	S	W		p	i	e		I		o	E	R	
			N		a	p	E		h		a	r	u	T			S	A	m
C	O	N	F	I	D	E	N	T	I	A	L	I	T	Y		s		C	a
o	B		O	d	e		T					c			a	c	t	E	d
	E	r	R	o	r				d		N	A	Z	I		h	e		e
e	D	a	M			P		d	o	N		N	O		C	O	D	E	
	I	D	E	O	L	O	G	I	C	A	L		o		C	O	S	T	S
h	E	i	D	i		L	o	c	k	S		r		t		l		h	e
u	N	o		l	e	l		i		W	E	I	G	H			h	i	t
r	C		B	e	a	T	i	n	g			c	E	e		B	a	c	h
R	E	P	O	R	T	I	N	G			B	E	N	E	F	I	T	S	
y			G			C			f	i	o	r	D		r	A			a
	J	O	U	R	N	A	L		l		a		E	r	o	S	i	o	n
a	r	m	S		a	L		C	U	L	T	U	R	E			t	h	y

CHAPTER 5

t	r	i	B	a	l		A	N	C	H	O	R
a	n	d	l					n	O	a	h	
M	A	I	L		F	L	U	E	N	T		S
			I		I	I			C	e	I	T
T	h	i	N	k	i	N	g		E		o	R
R	i	n	G	i	n	G		s	P	a	c	E
A	C	C	U	L	T	U	R	A	T	I	O	N
C			A	t		I		n	U	t		G
K	i	l	L	S		S	a	g	A		a	T
I	f	i				T			L	A	s	H
N		M	E	T	R	I	C			G		S
G	a	p		R		C		a	p	E	r	
	g		b	A				d	e	N	y	
	E	Q	U	I	V	A	L	E	N	C	E	
g	n	u		N		b	e	n	n	Y		
o	t	i	s			b	s					
	S	T	I	G	M	A	T	I	Z	E	D	
		s	t	o	p			m	o	l	d	
			s	o	s			p	o	k	e	

CHAPTER 6

P	l	e	A	s	e		D	o			S	i	R	
A	g	e	N	t	s		E	X	P	L	O	R	E	
N			A	I			S		u		W	a	V	e
E	C	O	L	O	G	I	C	A	L		H		I	t
L		N	Y				R	e	p	l	A	c	E	
	I	E	S	s		F	I	r			T	o	W	
	i		I	s		A	B	o	U	t		m		
F	E	A	S	I	B	L	E		N		G	m		
I	n					L		h	I		R	o	d	
S		E	X	P	L	A	N	A	T	I	O	N		
C		V			a	C	e	r	S		U			
A	h	A		C	r	Y		m		s	P	y		
L	i	L		O	k		a		m	u	S	e		
	m	U	c	H			t	w	i	n				
f		A	d	O			t	a	m		C	b	s	
L	I	T	E	R	A	T	U	R	E		R	a	t	
a	m	I		T	R	E	N	D		c	O	k	e	
b		O	d			p	e		l	o	S	e	r	s
	I	N	D	I	V	I	D	U	A	L	S		n	o
o	f		e		a	d		h	s	t				n

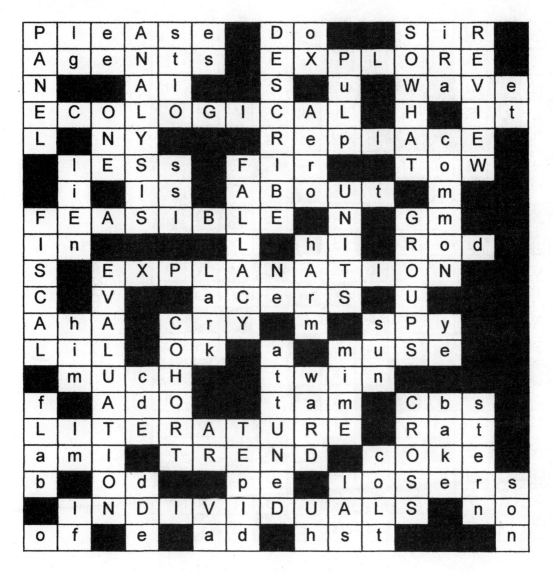

CHAPTER 7

C	O	N	T	R	O	L		f	R	O	m
O	n	e		e	f		s	l	E	P	t
N		a						e	L	E	m
C	U	R	V	I	L	I	N	E	A	R	
E					o	N	e	s	T	A	r
P	O	S	I	T	I	V	E		E	T	
T	n	t		E	r	E		p	S	I	
		O	B	S	E	R	V	E		O	
	s	p	i	T		S		t	o	N	e
B		S	C	A	L	E	S		v	A	n
I				B	e			S	a	L	t
A	V	A	I	L	A	B	L	E			r
S	A	T		E	n	e		L	i	m	y
	L	T			s	t	a	F	f		
p	U	R	r			o			f	a	d
r	E	I	n	v	e	n	t		y	o	u
o		B		e	m		r			r	e
	C	U	L	T	U	R	A	L		t	
c	u	T	e				d	e	l	a	y
	M	E	A	S	U	R	E		o		o

CHAPTER 8

F	A	C	E		n	o	t	e				C	O	N	T	E	N	T	
	c	O	n	g	o		h		Z	E	R	O		a	h		i		D
R	A	N	D	O	M		r					N	o	m	e		l		I
E	d	S			a		o		a			C		e	n	t	e	r	S
L		T		K	N	O	W	N	G	R	O	U	P	S		y			C
I		R							i		m	R			u	p	P	e	R
A	I	U	m					I	N	T	E	R	R	A	T	E	R		I
B		C		C		r			g	o	n	E				s	E	e	M
I	N	T	E	R	N	A	L					N	o	v	a		D		I
L				I		t		d		C	a	T			a	v	I	a	N
I	n	e	r	T		I		a		O	h			S			C	i	A
T				E		o	r	d	I	N	a	l		T			T		N
Y		F		R				d		S		o		A	r	t	I	s	T
	V	A	L	I	D	I	T	Y		I		o		B	r	a	V	e	
		C		O						S		s		L		r	E	n	t
s	e	T		N			T	E	S	T	R	E	T	E	S	T		t	
a		O			B			a		E			i					r	
n	o	R	m		I			S	E	N	S	I	T	I	V	I	T	Y	
D	E	S	I	R	A	B	L	E		C			I		i		R		
s	r		d		S				S	Y	S	T	E	M	A	T	I	C	

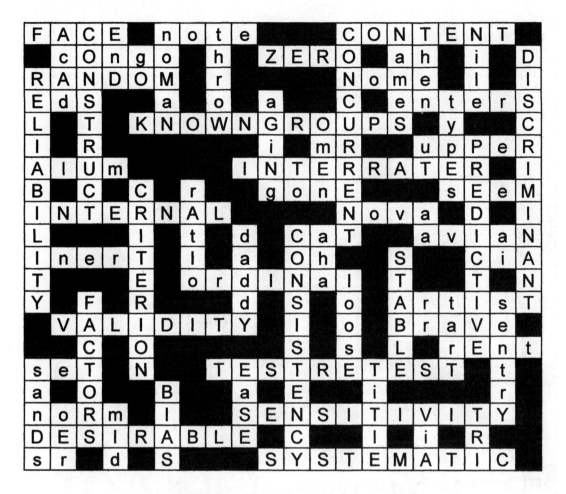

CHAPTER 9

e	v	e	■	l	a	m	b	■	f	a	t	■	t	r
n	■	q	t	■	B	I	A	S	■	r	a	V	e	l
D	O	U	B	L	E	■	a	C	c	r	u	A	l	s
e	P	a	■	l	t	e	■	A	h	■	■	L	e	■
d	E	l	■	K	s	■	S	L	a	p	■	l	v	y
■	N	■	s	E	■	B	E	E	p	■	■	D	i	e
■	■	s	t	R	e	A	M	■	■	n	■	A	s	s
■	C	U	L	T	U	R	A	L	L	Y	■	T	e	t
t	O	r	o	■	■	R	N	■	■	e	N	E	■	e
e	N	e	■	P	R	E	T	E	S	T	E	D	■	r
a	T	r	i	a	■	L	I	■	o	■	G	■	a	d
r	I	■	■	m	u	L	C	h	■	M	A	n	i	a
i	N	r	e	■	■	E	■	■	e	A	T	e	r	y
e	G	g	■	l	s	D	■	e	n	T	I	t	y	■
r	E	■	a	a	h	■	f	■	■	R	V	■	■	■
■	N	■	P	R	O	B	E	S	■	I	E	■	■	■
■	C	L	E	A	R	■	a	p	e	X	■	■	■	■
d	Y	a	d	■	t	i	t	a	n	■	■	■	■	■

CHAPTER 10

P	R	E	T	E	S	T		V	A	L	I	D	I	T	Y		C	R	O	S	S
O			e		t	i	m	i	d			I	s	E	e		A	I	e	P	h
S	a	k	e		r	e	o	s		a	l	S		S	a	g	S		r	U	e
T		I	N	T	E	R	N	A	L		i	T		T	H	R	E	E		R	e
T	E	t		r	a		k				k	O		I		o		X		I	n
E	X	T	R	E	M	E	S	C	O	R	E	R		N		o		P	r	O	s
S	T	e	A	k				u	c			T		G	i	m	m	E		U	
T	E	n	N		s	e	l	e	c	t	e	E	s					R	g	s	
	R		D						u			R	I	s			I	I	I		m
u	N	t	O		a		a		l		d		o		a	l	a	M	o		e
n	A		M	A	T	U	R	A	T	I	O	N		P	L	A	C	E	B	O	s
a	L				t		t			d	w	i			c		e	N	e		s
b		R	E	G	R	E	S	S	I	O	N				o			T			l
l	o	a			l			p		l				C	A	U	S	A	L		n
e		H	I	S	T	O	R	Y			r	o	t	h		p		L		l	e
					l				s		a		B	I	A	S			p	c	s
		u		L	O	N	G	I	T	U	D	I	N	A	L			k	o	l	s
D	E	S	I	G	N				l		a			m	e	l	a	n	g	e	
c	r	e	a	m			C	O	N	T	R	O	L			o	l	e	o	s	
	a	r	m			p	o	n	g			d	e	f	e	n	s	e		t	

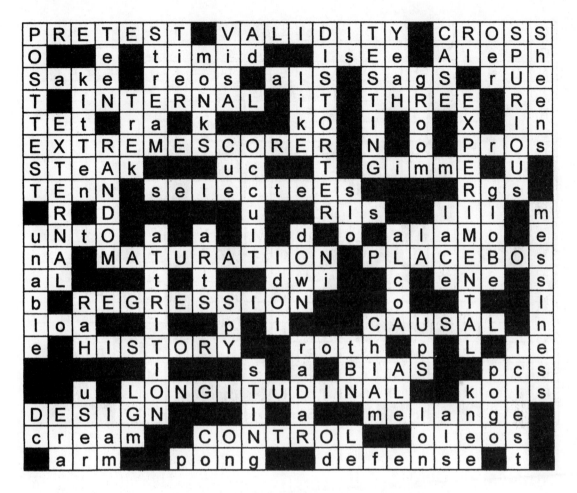

CHAPTER 11

C	A	S	E	S		p	i	l	o	t			g	a	s		a	R	k
O	l	a	V		M	o	n	e	y		E	V	A	L	U	A	T	E	
N	O	N	E	Q	U	I	V	A	L	E	N	T		I	i	I		P	
T	e	e	N		L		o	k			G		P	I	T	F	A	L	L
R			T		I		i		F	r	A	n	c	e				I	
O			S	W	I	T	C	H	I	N	G			d	R	e	n	C	h
L	S	d			P		e		D		E		R		E	t	n	A	
	L	e	a		L				E				E		S		e	T	e
v	O	l	l	i	E	r		f	L	a	u	n	T		I			I	
	P	a	t				s		I				E	m	S		C	O	w
	E	y	e	s		C	O	N	T	A	M	I	N	A	T	I	O	N	
			r	e	f		y		Y	o	o		T	r	A		M	S	w
		a		p		s				l	t		I		N	a	P		r
		Q	U	A	S	I			I		h		O		C	h	A	s	e
	Q	U	A	L	I	T	A	T	I	V	E		N		E	a	R		s
	u	a						h	a	i	r						A	n	t
b	i		T	I	M	E	S	E	R	I	E	S		I		a	B	e	
o	v	a		c	a	f	e	s			d		S	I	M	P	L	E	
R	E	C	R	U	I	T	M	E	N	T				R	I	S	E		
E	r	E			n		i		S	E	P	A	R	A	T	E			

CHAPTER 12

S	T	A	B	L	E		j		T	R	I	A	N	G	U	L	A	T	E
i		n	A	g		A	a			E		M	e	a	n		G	o	V
d	a		S		I	B	i	d		P		B	e	r	i	N	G		A
E	X	T	E	R	N	A	L			L		I		p	o	O	R		L
	i		L		T	B		T	h	I	n	G	s		n	N	E		U
e	n	T	I	c	E			H		C		U		U			G		A
	G	E	N	E	R	A	L	I	Z	A	T	I	O	N		d	A	R	T
p		N	E	o	N		o	R		T		T		L	i		T	E	E
e			S		A	B	C	D		I	v	Y		I		P	E	T	
a	b	C		a	L		a		b	O	a			K		A		R	
	e	A	r	l		a	t	e		N			b	E		S	a	O	
H	e	R		i	s	e	e		O		S	t	y	L	i	S	t	S	
I	R	R	E	V	E	R	S	I	B	I	L	I	T	Y		A	m	P	s
S		Y		e	c	o		r	T		O	l	e		M	G		E	
T	r	O	d				a	b	R	u	P	t		T	O	E		C	
O		V	I	S	U	A	L		U	s	E		w	I	N		a	T	I
R	e	E	v	e		B	I	A	S					M	I	n	n	I	e
Y		R	e	v		a		r	I	f	e		g	E	T		o	V	a
			R	E	A	C	T	I	V	I	T	Y			O	R	D	E	R
			t	r	e	k		d	E	t	e	r		f	R	e	e		y

CHAPTER 13

N	E	E	D	S		D	I	R	E	C	T	
o	f	F			t	e	n		G	O	A	L
r		F	a	r	i	n	g		g	o	R	e
U	T	I	L	I	T	Y		e		l	G	
S	O	C	I	A	L		a	l	B	e	E	
h	o	l	s	t	e	d		b	E	r	T	
		E	t	a			m	a	N			
		N			o	D	e		E	s	P	
F	O	C	U	S		E		I	F		R	
O		Y	a	p		M	O	N	I	T	O	R
R			r	r		A		F	T		C	o
U	p	I		i	n	N		O		K	E	Y
M	A	N	A	G	E	D		R		i	S	
		H			x			M	o	m	S	
	P	O	L	I	T	I	C	A	L			
b	r	U	i	n		g	a	N	d	e	r	
C	O	S	T		p	a	r	T		v	a	
	m	E	e	t		V	E	S	T	E	D	
	p		R	A	T	E	S		a	l	i	
	t	a	s	t	e		s	e	x		o	

CHAPTER 14

J	U	D	G	M	E	N	T	A	L					S	u	P	p	e	r
o			E		d	u	e				s			Y		U		n	o
h		S	N	O	W	B	A	L	L		l	p		S	t	R	i	c	t
n			D		a					k	i	a		T		P	u	r	e
	o	D	E		r				S	I	M	P	L	E		O		y	
p	a	I	R		d	P	s		a	s		a	i	M		S		p	
i	f	S				O		a	s	s			s	A	d	I	s	t	
e		P		R	E	P	R	E	S	E	N	T	A	T	I	V	E		
c	u	R	s	e		U		s		r		r		I	d	E	a		
e		O		m		L			e		S	o		C					
		P	R	O	B	A	B	I	L	I	T	Y			c	a	t	C	h
		O		v	e	T			I		R							L	
m		R		i	d	I			a	r	A	f	a	t			t	U	b
i		T	E	N		O		E			T	e						S	
n		I		G	E	N	E	R	A	L	I	Z	A	B	I	L	I	T	Y
o		O			I			R			F			a		i		E	
R	A	N	D	O	M			O			I			b		n		R	e
i		A			e		F	R	A	M	E			b	u	d			r
t	o	T	t	e	r	s					D	o		i	r	e			g
y		E												e	l	n	i	n	o

CHAPTER 15

R	E	S	P	O	N	D	E	N	T		M	i	s	F	i	t		b	y
E	v	E	r		O	r	c	a		g	O	d		E	d	u		a	d
T	E	L	E		T		O	N	L	I	N	E		W	o	r	S	t	
U	n	F	a	i	R				E		I	s		E		b	A	h	
R			c		E		G	e	T	i	T		G	R	O	O	M	E	D
N	a	c	h	o	S		O		T		O	i	l		x		P		E
	t	b			P	R	O	B	E		R		a			s	L	a	M
		s	E	c	O	n	D	a	R	y		d	n	A			E	y	E
S	t		M	a	N			k		e	F		D	R	E	S	S		A
T	u	n	A		D		g	e			A	m		T	v	a		o	N
A	b	o	I	I		P	a		I	m	M	e	d	I	a	t	e		O
M	A	I	L			U		i	N		I		o	F		e		m	R
P		s			o	S	s		T	a	L	k		I	d		p		
	T	E	L	E	P	H	O	N	E		I		E	C	O	N	O	M	Y
o	R		a	X	e				R	c	A		H	I	G	H	E	R	
I	A	s		A	n		C	O	V	E	R			A		I		s	I
d	I	p		C	e	d	e		I	e		m		L	i				T
	N	E	U	T	R	A	L		E		D	I	G	I	T		t	s	E
p	E	n	a	L		s	l	o	W		a		e	T	a		r	e	M
o	D	d	I	Y		h			S	U	R	V	E	Y		B	I	A	S

CHAPTER 16

t	i	M	e	s		L	E	S	S		t	v		
	P	A	S	T		E	t	r	E		i	o	U	
C	O	N	T	E	N	T			C	O	D	I	N	G
a	s	I	a			T	i	V	O		e	d	I	t
m		F		F	E	E	L	I	N	G	S		T	o
I	D	E	A	L		R		E	D			a	S	
l	e	S		a		S	e	W	A	r	D	s		
L	A	T	E	N	T			S	R		A	h	a	
e	d			k	i	w	i		Y	e	T	i	s	
					p	e	s	t			A	e	s	
												r		

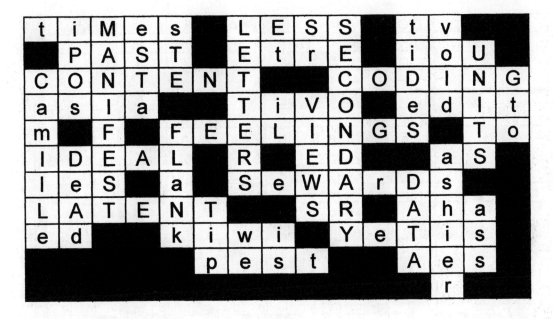

CHAPTER 17

c	r	a	t	E		G	e	n	t	s			a	l	i	e	n			J	
h	e		a	T		R	a		D	E	P	T	H		c	a	n	t	d	O	
a	a		T	H	E	O	R	Y		m	R		a		e	t	e		a	U	k
T	R	I	A	N	G	U	L	A	T	I	O	N		N					t	R	y
		I		O		N	y				L		C	A	S	E		S	u	N	
s	t	i	n	G		D		I	t	t	O		s	T	u	d		U	m	A	
o	r		t	R	u	E		N	e	o	N		a	U	n	t		B		L	
b	a	D	h	A	n	D		F	a	n	G			R			i	J	k		
e	v	E		P	t		f	O	r		E	N	G	A	G	E	M	E	N	T	
r	e	V		H	o	p		R	o	a	D		a	L	i		a	C	e		
s	l	I	m	Y		l	e	M	o	n			l	l	f	e		T	e	e	
		A				e	x	A	m			p	a	S	t		m	I	l	d	
	S	N	O	W	B	A	L	L		a	d	o		T			i	V		g	a
i	o	T	a		e		a		a		R	E	L	I	A	B	L	E		y	d
n	h		r	e	l	a	x	e	d		a		a	C	l	u	e		w		o
d	o	e	s	n	o	t		c	a	r	t	e	d		m	d		y	e	a	r
y				a	w	e	s	o	m	e			s	l	s				d	d	e

CHAPTER 18

E	M	I	C		O	B	S	E	R	V	E	R
T	a	m	a	r	a		o	g	e	E		
I	c	a	m	e			m	o	o	R		G
C	O	M	P	L	E	T	E			B	t	U
	n		e	y	e	s			m	A	h	I
		d	r		r	a		h	a	T	e	D
	H	I	S	T	O	R	Y		L	I	F	E
P	b	s		v			u	s		M	a	
F	O	C	U	S		O	P	E	N		t	

CHAPTER 19

C	O	D	E	S	■	u	s	e	d	■	g	p	■	■	■
O	r	e	■	t	■	■	P	R	O	G	R	A	M	S	■
N	e	a	■	e	■	■	e	■	m	R	i	■	A	t	e
C	O	N	V	E	R	S	A	T	I	O	N	■	P	e	a
E	■	■	i	l	o	o	k	■	n	U	■	s	P	a	t
P	A	T	T	E	R	N	S	■	i	N	■	l	I	l	■
T	H	E	O	R	Y	■	■	■	o	D	■	o	N	t	■
■	a	m	■	■	■	a	S	O	n	E	■	u	G	h	■
s	■	p	o	l	k	■	E	P	■	D	s	c	■	■	■
p	o	o	h	■	a	c	M	E	■	■	t	h	o	u	■
y	r	■	M	E	M	O	I	N	G	■	a	■	a	n	■
■	d	c	■	■	p	l	O	■	■	L	I	N	K	S	■
D	e	a	n	■	f	e	T	e	d	■	n	U	■	u	■
A	R	T	■	■	■	■	I	g	o	r	■	D	o	n	■
T	i	n	■	D	I	S	C	O	V	E	R	I	N	G	■
A	N	A	L	Y	S	I	S	■	e	x	i	S	t	■	■
■	g	p	a	s	■	■	■	■	■	■	o	T	o	e	■

CHAPTER 20

M	E	A	N		h	i	t	c	h
O	d	e		D	A	T	A		u
D	I	S	P	E	R	S	I	O	N
E	t			V	e	a	l		t
	h		p	I				G	e
		S	T	A	N	D	A	R	D
		t		T		O	n	O	
	M	E	D	I	A	N		U	p
b	u	r	r	O		T	a	P	e
C	L	E	A	N				E	l
	l	o	g			C	O	D	E
E	s	s	o			r	b		
a			N	O	M	I	N	A	L
s	o	s		R	o	b	o	t	
t	h	e	o	D	d		x	l	
e		e	d	I	e		l	a	n
r	a	m	o	N	s		o	s	u
l	l		r	A	t	o	u	t	
y	d		s	L	y		s		

CHAPTER 21

C	H	A	N	C	E		T	R	U	E		S	i
R	u	n	U	p		s	H	u	t		g	I	s
I	n	t	L			T	E	S	T	I	N	G	
T	A	I	L	E	D		O	s	e		u	N	
I	n	c			E	R	R	O	R	S		I	t
C					l	e	E			a	r	F	s
A	S	S	O	C	I	A	T	I	O	N		I	e
L	A	r	D			d	I		n	t		C	
	M		D	I	R	E	C	T	I	O	N	A	L
	P	e	S	o		r	A		o		O	N	E
M	L	k		n	E		L		n			T	V
E	E	e			F	a		w		s	d		E
D			I	N	F	E	R	E	N	T	I	A	L
I		a	n	d	E	s		a	r	o	m	a	S
U	I	n	a		C			k	a	p	p	a	
M	A	G	N	I	T	U	D	E			I		
	P	R	E					r	a	P	e	d	
r		i		p	i	c	a		n	H		r	i
e	v	e		e		C	L	I	N	I	C	A	L
V	A	R	I	A	N	C	E		e		a	w	l

CHAPTER 22

M	a	l	T		P		a	n	a	t	o	m	y
E	m	i	T		O	N	c	o	l	o	g	y	
T	Y	P	E	T	W	O		t	i	e	r		a
A			S	v	E	N					e	l	f
	S	O	T		R		n	E	o	n		a	t
c	A	N				C	o	F	f	e	e	s	
a	M	E	S	S		H	o	F	f	a			
m	P		I	M	f	I	n	E		r	r	s	
e	L	i	Z	A				C	a	l	l	s	
L	E	V	E	L				T	r	y	s	t	
				L									

CHAPTER 23

W	E	n	T		s	h	a	L	t			
E	X	P	E	C	T	A	T	I	O	N	S	
B	A	r	R	O	o	m		A	m	m	O	
S	C		S	N	I		h	I	t		U	
I	T		E	T	e			S	o	a	R	
T				R		a	t	O	m	i	C	
E		G	R	A	N	T		N		m	E	
S	s	a		C	o	t			C			
	w	r	i	T	i	n	g		O	l	d	S
d	a	d	e		s		a	d	V	e	n	T
	T	E	R	S	E		L	E	E	W	A	Y
p	s			t				a	R	i		L
u				i	s	h	o	t		s	e	E
B	U	D	G	E	T		p	h	i			
		R	E	S	U	L	T	S				

To the owner of this book

I hope that you have enjoyed Practice-Oriented Study Guide for Research Methods for Social Work, Sixth Edition, as much as I enjoyed writing it. I would like to know as much about your experience as you would care to offer. Only through your comments and those of others can I learn how to make this a better text for future readers.

School ____________________ Your Instructor's name ____________________

1. What did you like the most about Practice-Oriented Study Guide for Research Methods for Social Work, Sixth Edition?

____

____

____

2. Do you have any recommendations for ways to improve the next edition of this text?

____

____

____

3. In the space below or in a separate letter, please write any other comments you have about the book. (For example, were any chapters or concepts particularly difficult?) I'd be delighted to hear from you!

____

____

____

____

Optional:

Your name ____________________ Date ____________________

May the publisher quote you, either in promotion for Practice-Oriented Study Guide for Research Methods for Social Work, Sixth Edition, or in future publishing ventures? Yes ❑ No ❑

Sincerely,

Allen Rubin